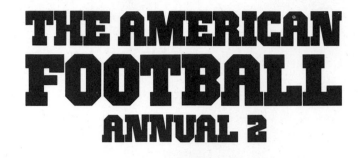

THE AMERICAN
FOOTBALL
ANNUAL 2

THE AMERICAN FOOTBALL ANNUAL 2

KEN THOMAS

ORBIS · LONDON

In association with Channel Four Television Company Limited

ACKNOWLEDGEMENTS

It hardly seems possible that a whole year has gone by since last I sat down to express my thanks to all those people without whose help, in its many forms, I could not possibly have achieved a personal ambition, namely to write books about NFL Football. Once again then, I am most grateful to the National Football League for permission to reproduce both the 1984 Schedule and all the photographs contained herein. The photographs were kindly supplied by Phil Grace and Mike Niblock, the publishers of *Touchdown* magazine, at no little inconvenience to themselves: 'Thank you gentlemen'. The imperturbable Peter Arnold has once more (hopefully) modified my jargon into something approaching intelligibility. Mick Hodson has been no less tolerant of me in arriving at a design and Mrs Susanna Yager, the Publishing and Merchandising Manager of Channel Four Television, has been a constant source of reassurance and sound advice. My two good friends, Roger Smith and Nick Wridgway, have been of enormous assistance, not only in the laborious business of proof reading but also by contributing an expertise which, in some areas, exceeds my own. They were particularly helpful in the analyses of teams under the headings of NFC and AFC respectively. Finally, to my wife Janie, who has managed to put up with me for yet another football season: 'Thanks, love'.

First published in Great Britain by Orbis Publishing Limited, London 1984.
© 1984 by Ken Thomas

ISBN 0-85613-685-9

The American Football Annual is associated with Channel Four Television's coverage of the sport produced by Cheerleader Productions Limited.

Typeset in Great Britain by Letterspace Ltd.
Printed in Spain by Grijelmo S.A.

PHOTOGRAPHS
All photographs have been supplied courtesy of the NFL. In addition, the following photographers took the pictures on the pages indicated: Allen's Studio 84; A.N. Anderson 18, 59; J. Biever 11, 54, 152/3; Vernon Biever 12, 38; Dave Boss 23, 68, 70T; Clifton Boutelle 58; Bruce Dierdorff 14B; Malcolm Emmons 9L, 55, 81, 111; G. Gojkorich 109; Pete Groh 10/11, 40; Paul Jasienski 147; R. Mackson 49; Al Messerschmidt 36, 42, 51, 52, 98/9, 124, 126; P.R. Miller 19, 46/7, 63B, 87; Darryl Norenberg 32, 43, 45, 90; Dick Raphael 53; George Rose 77; Ron Ross 97; Manny Rubio 44, 60, 105, 137; R.H. Stagg 57; Bill Smith 70B; Robert L. Smith 22, 95; Tony Tomsic 21, 56, 63T, 73R, 80; Herb Weitman 26; Lou Witt 17; Michael Zasano 157.

CONTENTS

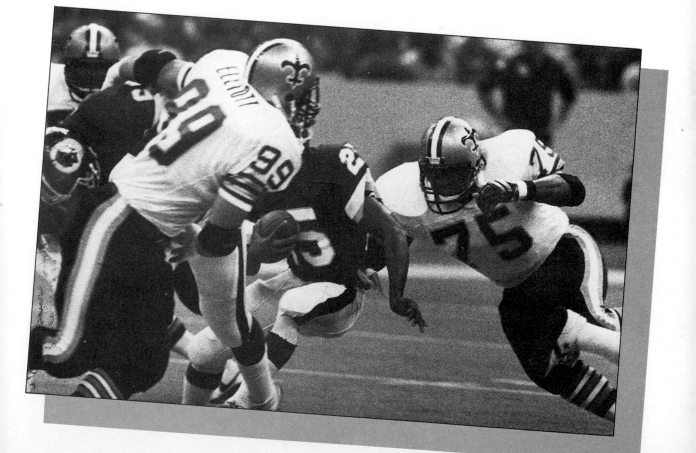

INTRODUCTION

I well remember spending Christmas, 1982, opening up the letters sent in by viewers of Channel Four, requesting the introductory leaflet on American Football and enclosing their predictions of the teams which would contest Super Bowl XVII. Many fans opted for two teams from the same division, and it was not unusual to read combinations such as 'Los Angeles Steelers v the Bengal Tigers'. At that time then, only few people understood even the basic structure of the National Football League, to say nothing about the complexities of the game. And yet, the spectacle and potential excitement were sufficient to keep over four million fans riveted to their sets until the early hours, to see John Riggins carry the Washington Redskins to victory over the Miami Dolphins. Twelve months later, some six million viewers were watching the second quarter of Super Bowl XVIII, when the mighty Raiders established a game-winning lead. Furthermore, by then, there was a body of knowledge to which an American commentary no longer represented a terminological minefield and, equally, one which could readily appreciate the tactical options available to both the offense and defense.

Not surprisingly, this explosion of interest has stimulated the formation of some sixty groups of 'Brits' itching to have a go, and certainly two serious attempts to establish leagues. Over 100,000 people read the monthly magazine, *Touchdown*. It is also significant that a British press which, until recently, saw the game as an exercise in robotics involving armour-clad be-hemoths, now adopts a more serious attitude. The whole thing has been 'not without a struggle' and I do not hestitate once more to thank John Bromley and his lads of 'World of Sport', for their pioneering efforts and subsequently, Adrian Metcalfe, Channel Four's Head of Sport, for his vision and commitment. Whatever did we do on Sunday evenings before Miles Aiken, Nicky Horne and NFL Football?

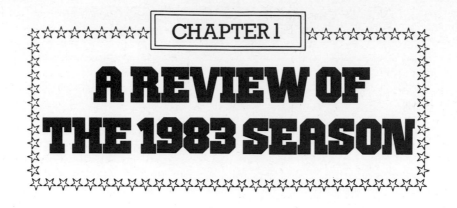

CHAPTER 1

A REVIEW OF THE 1983 SEASON

Prologue

Having endured the frustrations of 1982's fifty-seven-day players' strike, it was with more than usual anticipation that one could settle down to ponder the prospects for the NFL's sixty-fourth season. Eight teams would have new, though not necessarily rookie, head coaches. Dan Henning (Atlanta), Kay Stephenson (Buffalo), John Mackovic (Kansas City), Bill Parcells (New York Giants), Joe Walton (New York Jets) and John Robinson (Los Angeles Rams) were in the hot seat for the first time. Chuck Knox joined Seattle after having spent successful terms with first the Rams and then Buffalo, whilst Philadelphia's Marion Campbell had been in charge of the Atlanta Falcons for twenty-five games, spanning the 1975 season. At the other end of the scale, Tom Landry (Dallas) was entering his twenty-fourth season with 222 victories (including postseason) to his credit.

There was also an exciting crop of rookie players. In the annual collegiate draft (it was held on 26 and 27 April), the Baltimore Colts had bestowed the honour of overall number one selection upon Stanford University's John Elway, who was considered to be the best of the nation's college quarterbacks (he was subsequently traded to Denver). Dan Marino, selected in twenty-seventh position by the Miami Dolphins, was the last of six quarterbacks taken in the first round. For devotees of the rushing game, it was refreshing to see running backs Eric Dickerson (Los Angeles Rams) and Curt Warner (Seattle Seahawks), selected second and third respectively. The only pure wide receiver chosen in round one, Willie Gault (eighteenth), had his eye on the 1984 Olympic Games (he is one of the world's best 110-metres hurdlers) and, tantalizingly, agonized over relinquishing his amateur status, before signing for the Chicago Bears in mid-August. Ten of the twenty-eight first-round draftees were defensive players and of these, six were defensive backs (cornerbacks and

safeties). Having selected cornerback Darrell Green (twenty-eighth), the Washington Redskins now had, arguably, the fastest man in the NFL.

Several veteran players entered the season within sight of NFL career records. The most glittering prize of all, Jim Brown's career rushing total of 12,312 yards, was not likely to fall, but Pittsburgh's Franco Harris (10,943 yards) and Chicago's Walter Payton (10,204 yards) were expected to establish the platform for a final assault in 1984. Cincinnati's Ken Anderson (28,057 yards), Pittsburgh's Terry Bradshaw (27,912 yards) and San Diego's Dan Fouts (27,139 yards), were poised to join the elite group of seven NFL quarterbacks who had passed for a career total of over 30,000 yards. Anderson had the additional goal of seeking to become the first man ever to lead all NFL quarterbacks in passing (as measured by his passer rating) for the third consecutive season. Similarly, cornerback Everson Walls (Dallas), who had been the NFL's leading interceptor in both 1981 and 1982, was going for the hat-trick. Jan Stenerud of the Green Bay Packers, embarking on

Tom Landry

his seventeenth season in the NFL, needed only nineteen field goals to surpass George Blanda's career record of 335. On the less glamorous, yet equally valuable side of football, Mike Fuller (Cincinnati) and Rick Upchurch (Denver) could expect to register the punt returns (they needed seven and fifteen respectively) which would take them past Emlen Tunnell's career record of 258.

Of the fourteen NFC teams, the Washington Redskins and the Dallas Cowboys were strongly

Terry Bradshaw

fancied to contest the Conference Championship Game, but first they would have to settle their domestic rivalry in the Eastern division. Despite having placed four of its members in the eight-team 1982 NFC postseason tournament, the Central division was not expected to produce a serious Super Bowl contender. The Western division race was anybody's guess. The 49ers and the Rams would surely bounce back after disappointing 1982 seasons, but they would have to face the challenge from both an improving New Orleans Saints and the enigmatic Atlanta Falcons, the latter having the best balanced offense in the division.

In the AFC Eastern division, the New York Jets looked set to take over from the Miami Dolphins, though Don Shula's Miami team would never be far behind; indeed the Dolphins had beaten the Jets three times in 1982. The Pittsburgh Steelers and the Cincinnati Bengals appeared to have the Central division to themselves. Over in the Western division, a great deal depended on the San Diego Chargers constructing a dependable defense; the 'Air Force' (this is one of the nicknames for San Diego's formidable passing offense) would see to the rest. But the Los Angeles Raiders are always confident of seeing to anybody, and the Seattle Seahawks, for the first time, promised to have a *bona fide* rushing offense.

Entering the regular season then, the Redskins and the Cowboys shared favouritism in the NFC, and whilst the AFC race was more open, the probability was that one of four teams, namely the Chargers, the Dolphins, the Jets and the Raiders, would catch the plane for Tampa to play in Super Bowl XVIII.

John Elway

WEEK ONE

American Football Conference
Baltimore 29 at New England 23 (OT)
Denver 14 at Pittsburgh 10
Los Angeles Raiders 20 at Cincinnati 10
Miami 12 at Buffalo 0
New York Jets 41 at San Diego 29
Seattle 13 at Kansas City 17

National Football Conference
Atlanta 20 at Chicago 17
Detroit 11 at Tampa Bay 0
Los Angeles Rams 16 at New York Giants 6
Philadelphia 22 at San Francisco 17
St Louis 17 at New Orleans 28
Dallas 31 at Washington 30

Interconference Games
Green Bay 41 at Houston 38 (OT)
Minnesota 27 at Cleveland 21

Interconference Play
NFC 2, AFC 0

Tony Dorsett

George Rogers

In addition to broadening the mind, travel is also apparently good preparation for a football game — on the opening weekend, twelve teams won away from home. There were no real shocks but amongst the surprises was Denver's 14-10 victory over the Pittsburgh Steelers, who faced the prospect of a season without their injured quarterback, Terry Bradshaw. Denver's rookie quarterback, John Elway, made a poor start. Successful with only one of eight passing attempts, he had been intercepted once and sacked four times before being withdrawn from the game at half-time. His replacement, seventh-year veteran Steve DeBerg, fired a 2-yard touchdown pass to tight end Ron Egloff for the winning score, with less than three minutes to play.

The Green Bay Packers and the Houston Oilers did their best to blow the fuses on the electronic scoreboard in the Astrodome, where the two teams combined to amass 977 yards total offense (the NFL record is 1,133 yards) and 79 points, in a game decided by Jan Stenerud's 42-yard field goal in overtime. In response to the expected aerial bombardment by the San Diego Chargers, for whom quarterback Dan Fouts extended his own NFL record for 300-yard passing games to 31, the New York Jets used their more balanced offense to good effect. They took a 13-7 lead in the second quarter and always stayed one jump ahead of the Chargers, before a late 1-yard touchdown run by Mike Augustyniak made the game safe.

In front of a capacity crowd gathered in Washington's RFK Stadium for the NFC's first major confrontation, the Cowboys were caught napping.

A field goal by Rafael Septien was their only reply to a scoring blitz which culminated with a 41-yard touchdown pass from Joe Theismann to Charlie Brown, taking the Redskins into half-time with a 23-3 lead. After the break, however, it was the home team which had seemingly forgotten to set the alarm. Dallas quarterback Danny White combined with wide receiver Tony Hill on touchdown plays covering 75 and 51 yards. White then rushed for a touchdown before passing to tight end Doug Cosbie for another, to give the Cowboys a 31-23 lead with less than two minutes remaining. A late touchdown pass, from Theismann to Don Warren, salvaged a little Redskins pride but, by the score of 31-30, it was first blood to the Cowboys.

Outstanding Individual Performances

George Rogers (New Orleans) rushed for 206 yards and scored two touchdowns, one of which covered 76 yards.

Tony Dorsett (Dallas) rushed for 151 yards on only fourteen attempts and had a longest gain of 77 yards.

Tim Smith (Houston) caught eight passes for 197 yards, having previously caught only four passes in his three-year career.

James Lofton (Green Bay) caught eight passes for 154 yards, including one of 74 yards for a touchdown.

Lynn Dickey (Green Bay) completed 27 of 31 passes for 333 yards and five touchdowns. By completing 18 consecutive passes, he fell short of the NFL record (held by Cincinnati's Ken Anderson) by only two.

William Gay (Detroit) registered 5·5 quarterback sacks.

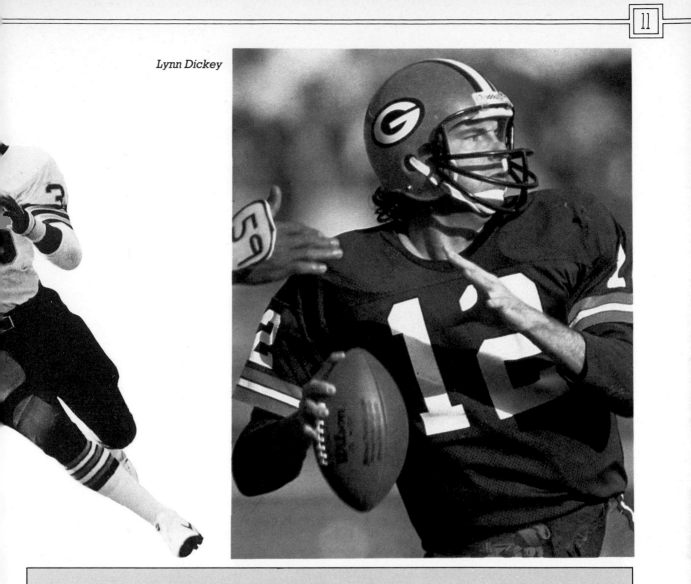

Lynn Dickey

STANDINGS

AFC East	W	L	T	PF	PA	NFC East	W	L	T	PF	PA
Baltimore	1	0	0	29	23	Dallas	1	0	0	31	30
Miami	1	0	0	12	0	Philadelphia	1	0	0	22	17
N.Y. Jets	1	0	0	41	29	N.Y. Giants	0	1	0	6	16
Buffalo	0	1	0	0	12	St Louis	0	1	0	17	28
New England	0	1	0	23	29	Washington	0	1	0	30	31
AFC Central						**NFC Central**					
Cincinnati	0	1	0	10	20	Detroit	1	0	0	11	0
Cleveland	0	1	0	21	27	Green Bay	1	0	0	41	38
Houston	0	1	0	38	41	Minnesota	1	0	0	27	21
Pittsburgh	0	1	0	10	14	Chicago	0	1	0	17	20
AFC West						Tampa Bay	0	1	0	0	11
Denver	1	0	0	14	10	**NFC West**					
Kansas City	1	0	0	17	13	Atlanta	1	0	0	20	17
L.A. Raiders	1	0	0	20	10	L.A. Rams	1	0	0	16	6
San Diego	0	1	0	29	41	New Orleans	1	0	0	28	17
Seattle	0	1	0	13	17	San Francisco	0	1	0	17	22

WEEK TWO

American Football Conference
Buffalo 10 at Cincinnati 6
Denver 17 at Baltimore 10
Houston 6 at Los Angeles Raiders 20
New England 24 at Miami 34
Seattle 17 at New York Jets 10
San Diego 17 at Kansas City 14

National Football Conference
San Francisco 48 at Minnesota 14
Dallas 34 at St Louis 17
New Orleans 27 at Los Angeles Rams 30
New York Giants 16 at Atlanta 13 (OT)
Tampa Bay 10 at Chicago 17
Washington 23 at Philadelphia 13

Interconference Games
Cleveland 31 at Detroit 26
Pittsburgh 25 at Green Bay 21

Interconference Play
AFC 2, NFC 2

Once again, there was little evidence of travel sickness as ten teams won away from home. The Seattle Seahawks, for whom rookie running back Curt Warner notched up his first 'century' (he rushed for 128 yards and two touchdowns), raised a few eyebrows by beating the New York Jets. Yet it was of little surprise to those who believe in trends — after seven games between the two, the Jets have still to register their first win. Pittsburgh's Franco Harris was another running back to break into three figures as he 'crept' 118 yards closer to Jim Brown's record. With a useful contribution of 90 yards from Frank Pollard, the Steelers used their rushing offense to outlast the Packers, despite the staggering exploits of James Lofton, who caught touchdown passes covering 71, 73 and 12 yards. Quarterback Joe Montana slipped into top gear with four touchdown passes as the 49ers ran up the week's highest score against the Minnesota Vikings. But for Denver's John Elway, who again made little impact before leaving the game with a bruised shoulder, it was another day of disappointment. Repeating his performance of week one, Steve DeBerg stepped in to pass for a touchdown and rush for another, bringing the Broncos from behind to beat the Colts. Against St Louis, the Cowboys came back from a 10-0 deficit and just kept on going, scoring 31 points before relaxing late in the game. By contrast, the Redskins, for whom John Riggins gained an even 100 yards, took more than three quarters of the game to subdue the Eagles in the 100-degree temperature of Philadelphia Veterans Stadium.

Freeman McNeil

Outstanding Individual Performances

Leonard Thompson (Detroit) caught eight passes for 179 yards including one for an 80-yard touchdown.

James Lofton (Green Bay) caught five passes for 169 yards and scored three touchdowns, covering 71, 73 and 12 yards.

Steve Watson (Denver) caught six passes for 161 yards and scored one touchdown.

Freeman McNeil (New York Jets) rushed for 140 yards on 22 carries.

Mike Pruitt (Cleveland) rushed for 137 yards on 24 carries.

STANDINGS

AFC East	W	L	T	PF	PA	NFC East	W	L	T	PF	PA
Miami	2	0	0	46	24	Dallas	2	0	0	65	47
Baltimore	1	1	0	39	40	N.Y. Giants	1	1	0	22	29
Buffalo	1	1	0	10	18	Philadelphia	1	1	0	35	40
N.Y. Jets	1	1	0	51	46	Washington	1	1	0	53	44
New England	0	2	0	47	63	St Louis	0	2	0	34	62
AFC Central						**NFC Central**					
Cleveland	1	1	0	52	53	Chicago	1	1	0	34	30
Pittsburgh	1	1	0	35	35	Detroit	1	1	0	37	31
Cincinnati	0	2	0	16	30	Green Bay	1	1	0	62	63
Houston	0	2	0	44	61	Minnesota	1	1	0	44	69
AFC West						Tampa Bay	0	2	0	10	28
Denver	2	0	0	31	20	**NFC West**					
L.A. Raiders	2	0	0	40	16	L.A. Rams	2	0	0	46	33
Kansas City	1	1	0	31	30	Atlanta	1	1	0	33	33
San Diego	1	1	0	46	55	New Orleans	1	1	0	55	47
Seattle	1	1	0	30	27	San Francisco	1	1	0	65	39

James Lofton

Leonard Thompson

WEEK THREE

American Football Conference
Cincinnati 7 at Cleveland 17
Baltimore 23 at Buffalo 28
New York Jets 13 at New England 23
Pittsburgh 40 at Houston 28
San Diego 31 at Seattle 34
Miami 14 at Los Angeles Raiders 27

National Football Conference
Atlanta 30 at Detroit 14
Chicago 31 at New Orleans 34 (OT)
Los Angeles Rams 24 at Green Bay 27
Minnesota 19 at Tampa Bay 16 (OT)
New York Giants 13 at Dallas 28
San Francisco 42 at St Louis 27

Interconference Games
Kansas City 12 at Washington 27
Philadelphia 13 at Denver 10

Interconference Play
NFC 4, AFC 2

Steve Bartkowski

Walter Payton

After having eased into the season with two comfortable wins, the Raiders rolled up their sleeves and proceeded to make a point with the Miami Dolphins. Marcus Allen rushed for 105 yards, but it was an overall team performance which produced 27 points, unanswered well into the final quarter. With the game out of reach, Miami head coach Don Shula gave his rookie quarterback, Dan Marino, the opportunity to display his talents. He responded with two touchdown passes to stake a claim for the starting role. Up the coast in Seattle, the Seahawks confirmed their improved status with a controlled victory over the San Diego Chargers. Based on a sound rushing offense, to which Curt Warner and David Hughes contributed 109 and 90 yards respectively, they built up a 34-17 lead and their defense kept its nerve in the face of an onslaught from Dan Fouts, three of whose four touchdown passes came in the final quarter.

In the NFC, the Redskins continued to stutter, at least until half-time in their interconference game against Kansas City, who led 12-0 on four Nick

Lowery field goals. But the reigning Super Bowl Champions gave notice of a return to form with 17 points in the third quarter and a further 10 in the fourth, none of which brought a reply from the Chiefs. The Cowboys had surprising difficulty with the New York Giants. As was becoming usual, they conceded the first score and, indeed, led by only one point entering the final quarter. But strong safety Dextor Clinkscale returned an interception 68 yards for a touchdown and, from the ensuing kickoff, free safety Michael Downs did likewise with a fumble which he recovered on the Giants' 10-yard line. Once again, the 49ers chalked up the week's biggest score but, despite their victory, they remained in a four-way tie in the NFC Western division. The weekend's football ended on a sad note when it was learned that the Vikings' quarterback, Tommy Kramer, had suffered an injury which would keep him out for the season and possibly beyond.

Outstanding Individual Performances

Tony Collins (New England) rushed for a season's best 212 yards and scored three touchdowns.

Walter Payton (Chicago) rushed for 161 yards on 28 carries, scored one touchdown, and *threw* touchdown passes of 56 and 21 yards to Willie Gault.

Mike Quick (Philadelphia) caught six passes for 152 yards and scored one touchdown.

Steve Bartkowski (Atlanta) completed 24 of 34 passes for 366 yards and three touchdowns.

Joe Montana (San Francisco) completed 20 of 32 passes for 341 yards and three touchdowns.

Tony Collins

STANDINGS

AFC East	W	L	T	PF	PA	NFC East	W	L	T	PF	PA
Buffalo	2	1	0	38	41	Dallas	3	0	0	93	60
Miami	2	1	0	60	51	Philadelphia	2	1	0	48	50
Baltimore	1	2	0	62	68	Washington	2	1	0	80	56
New England	1	2	0	70	76	N.Y. Giants	1	2	0	35	57
N.Y. Jets	1	2	0	64	69	St Louis	0	3	0	61	104
AFC Central						**NFC Central**					
Cleveland	2	1	0	69	60	Green Bay	2	1	0	89	87
Pittsburgh	2	1	0	75	63	Minnesota	2	1	0	63	85
Cincinnati	0	3	0	23	47	Chicago	1	2	0	65	64
Houston	0	3	0	72	101	Detroit	1	2	0	51	61
AFC West						Tampa Bay	0	3	0	28	47
L.A. Raiders	3	0	0	67	30	**NFC West**					
Denver	2	1	0	41	33	Atlanta	2	1	0	63	47
Seattle	2	1	0	64	58	L.A. Rams	2	1	0	70	60
Kansas City	1	2	0	43	57	New Orleans	2	1	0	89	78
San Diego	1	2	0	77	89	San Francisco	2	1	0	107	66

WEEK FOUR

American Football Conference
Cleveland 30 at San Diego 24 (OT)
Houston 13 at Buffalo 30
Kansas City 6 at Miami 14
Los Angeles Raiders 22 at Denver 7
New England 28 at Pittsburgh 23

National Football Conference
Atlanta 20 at San Francisco 24
Detroit 17 at Minnesota 20
New Orleans 20 at Dallas 21
St Louis 14 at Philadelphia 11
Green Bay 3 at New York Giants 27

Interconference Games
Chicago 19 at Baltimore 22 (OT)
Cincinnati 23 at Tampa Bay 17
Los Angeles Rams 24 at New York Jets 27 (OT)
Washington 27 at Seattle 17

Interconference Play
AFC 5, NFC 5

In Seattle's Kingdome, the Seahawks were brought down to earth by the Redskins, who confirmed their approach to 1982's form. If not yet rolling, their rushing offense was relentless and Joe Theismann exercised his big-play wide receivers, Charlie Brown and Alvin Garrett, with two of his three touchdown passes. Just for a change, the Cowboys scored first but then had no end of bother with the New Orleans Saints before scrambling home, thanks to a late 2-point safety when Anthony Dickerson sacked Ken Stabler in the end zone. A 76-yard touchdown reception by rookie wide receiver Stephen Starring brought the Patriots from behind to beat the Steelers but, with 106 yards rushing, Franco Harris swept past O.J. Simpson's 11,236-yard career total to end the game with 11,309 yards, now in second place in the list of all time leading rushers. Trailing Jim Brown by only 1,003 yards and still with twelve games to play, Harris needed to average some 83 yards per game to crack the record. His close rival, Walter Payton, gained only four yards on three carries in Chicago's overtime loss to the Colts.

Minnesota won a typically close game against Detroit, to go top of the NFC's 'Black and Blue' division. (This is a reference to the old days when the rules governing physical contact were some-what less strict.) In a pulsating interconference game at Shea Stadium, the Jets beat the Rams with a Pat Leahy field goal in overtime but their playoff hopes were dealt a severe blow when Pro Bowler Freeman McNeil suffered a dislocated shoulder. A comfortable Raiders victory over Denver was

Richard Todd

similarly marred by an injury to Marcus Allen, though this turned out to be less serious.

Outstanding Individual Performances

Eric Dickerson (Los Angeles Rams) rushed for 192 yards and scored two touchdowns, one of which was for 85 yards. In addition, he caught five passes for 45 yards.

Earl Campbell (Houston) rushed for 142 yards and scored one touchdown.

Richard Todd (New York Jets) completed 37 of 50 passes for 446 yards and two touchdowns.

Wesley Walker (New York Jets) caught eight passes for 135 yards and scored two touchdowns.

Wes Chandler (San Diego) caught six passes for 134 yards and scored two touchdowns.

Mike Quick (Philadelphia) caught six passes for 133 yards.

Joe Cribbs (Buffalo) had only 22 carries in gaining 166 yards and scoring one touchdown.

Ron Fellows (Dallas) returned a blocked field goal attempt 62 yards for a touchdown.

STANDINGS

AFC East	W	L	T	PF	PA	NFC East	W	L	T	PF	PA
Buffalo	3	1	0	68	54	Dallas	4	0	0	114	80
Miami	3	1	0	74	57	Washington	3	1	0	107	73
Baltimore	2	2	0	84	87	N.Y. Giants	2	2	0	62	60
New England	2	2	0	98	99	Philadelphia	2	2	0	59	64
N.Y. Jets	2	2	0	91	93	St Louis	1	3	0	75	115
AFC Central						**NFC Central**					
Cleveland	3	1	0	99	84	Minnesota	3	1	0	83	102
Pittsburgh	2	2	0	98	91	Green Bay	2	2	0	92	114
Cincinnati	1	3	0	46	64	Chicago	1	3	0	84	86
Houston	0	4	0	85	131	Detroit	1	3	0	68	81
AFC West						Tampa Bay	0	4	0	43	70
L.A. Raiders	4	0	0	89	37	**NFC West**					
Denver	2	2	0	48	55	San Francisco	3	1	0	131	86
Seattle	2	2	0	81	85	Atlanta	2	2	0	83	71
Kansas City	1	3	0	49	71	L.A. Rams	2	2	0	94	87
San Diego	1	3	0	101	119	New Orleans	2	2	0	109	99

Earl Campbell

WEEK FIVE

American Football Conference
Baltimore 34 at Cincinnati 31
Houston 10 at Pittsburgh 17
New York Jets 34 at Buffalo 10
Seattle 24 at Cleveland 9

National Football Conference
Dallas 37 at Minnesota 24
Detroit 10 at Los Angeles Rams 21
Philadelphia 28 at Atlanta 24
Tampa Bay 14 at Green Bay 55

Interceference Games
Denver 14 at Chicago 31
Los Angeles Raiders 35 at Washington 37
Miami 7 at New Orleans 17
St Louis 14 at Kansas City 38
San Diego 41 at New York Giants 34
San Francisco 33 at New England 13

Interceference Play
NFC 9, AFC 7

In a game which had more than its share of verbal exchanges, the Washington Redskins came back from being 15 points down in the fourth quarter, to hand the Raiders their first defeat of the season. Capitalising on the Raiders' philanthropy (they turned the ball over on their first four possessions), the Redskins had a 20-7 lead in the third quarter.

Cliff Branch

One bright spot for the Raiders had been Cliff Branch's 99-yard touchdown reception (it equals the NFL record). But a 13-point Raider deficit was transformed into an apparent game-winning 35-20 lead by four unanswered touchdowns, which included two spectacular receptions by Calvin Muhammad and a 97-yard punt return by Greg Pruitt. Then came the reply, culminating with Joe Washington's 6-yard touchdown reception, leaving the Raiders with just 33 seconds and a long flight home to reflect on what might have been. Anticipation began to stir down in New Orleans, where the old master, Ken 'The Snake' Stabler, engineered the Saints' first ever victory over Miami.

The Seahawks returned to their winning ways against Cleveland and, with a victory over Cincinnati, the Baltimore Colts (they didn't win a game in 1982) found themselves (at least alphabetically) on top of the AFC Eastern division. The Cowboys were up to their old tricks against Minnesota, whom they trailed 0-7, 3-17 and 10-24, before unleashing a 27-point shower to which the Vikings had no answer. Whilst the Houston Oilers could not quite hold on to a fourth-quarter 10-7 lead against the Steelers, their cellar mates, the Buccaneers, took a real pasting from the Packers, whose 49-point first half set an NFL record in that category. After five weeks of the regular season then, the Cowboys remained as the NFL's only unbeaten team and for both the Oilers and the Buccaneers, the cupboard was still bare.

Outstanding Individual Performances

Eric Dickerson (Los Angeles Rams) rushed for 199 yards and scored three touchdowns.

Wayne Wilson (New Orleans) rushed for 160 yards on 34 carries.

William Andrews (Atlanta) rushed for 150 yards on 25 carries.

Cris Collinsworth (Cincinnati) caught eight passes for 206 yards including a 63-yard touchdown.

Mike Quick (Philadelphia) caught four passes for 122 yards including a 53-yard touchdown.

Phil Epps (Green Bay) returned a punt 90 yards for a touchdown.

Kendall Williams (Baltimore) returned a kickoff 90 yards.

Mark Gastineau (New York Jets) had three sacks (and three war dances) and recovered a fumble in the end zone for a touchdown (and another war dance).

STANDINGS

AFC East	W	L	T	PF	PA	NFC East	W	L	T	PF	PA
Baltimore	3	2	0	118	118	Dallas	5	0	0	151	104
Buffalo	3	2	0	78	88	Washington	4	1	0	144	108
Miami	3	2	0	81	74	Philadelphia	3	2	0	87	88
N.Y. Jets	3	2	0	125	103	N.Y. Giants	2	3	0	96	101
New England	2	3	0	111	132	St Louis	1	4	0	89	153
AFC Central						**NFC Central**					
Cleveland	3	2	0	108	108	Green Bay	3	2	0	147	128
Pittsburgh	3	2	0	115	101	Minnesota	3	2	0	107	139
Cincinnati	1	4	0	77	98	Chicago	2	3	0	115	100
Houston	0	5	0	95	148	Detroit	1	4	0	78	102
AFC West						Tampa Bay	0	5	0	57	125
L.A. Raiders	4	1	0	124	74	**NFC West**					
Seattle	3	2	0	105	94	San Francisco	4	1	0	164	99
Denver	2	3	0	62	86	L.A. Rams	3	2	0	115	97
Kansas City	2	3	0	87	85	New Orleans	3	2	0	126	106
San Diego	2	3	0	142	153	Atlanta	2	3	0	107	99

Eric Dickerson

WEEK SIX

American Football Conference
Buffalo 38 at Miami 35 (OT)
Denver 26 at Houston 14
Kansas City 20 at Los Angeles Raiders 21
New England 7 at Baltimore 12
New York Jets 7 at Cleveland 10
Pittsburgh 24 at Cincinnati 14
Seattle 21 at San Diego 28

National Football Conference
Green Bay 14 at Detroit 38
Los Angeles Rams 10 at San Francisco 7
Minnesota 23 at Chicago 14
New Orleans 19 at Atlanta 17
Philadelphia 17 at New York Giants 13
Tampa Bay 24 at Dallas 27(OT)
Washington 38 at St Louis 14

Week six in the NFL was very much a matter of 'For old times' sake' — at least nine games could be identified as rivalries of some tradition. The Steelers could thank an alert defense which scored all three touchdowns in their victory over the Bengals. Rick Woods returned a fumble 38 yards for a touchdown and Ron Johnson did likewise, after intercepting on the Cincinnati 34-yard line. Then, with the Bengals still threatening, rookie corner-back Harvey Clayton rambled 70 yards with yet another interception to deliver the knockout blow. But the Browns kept pace, keeping the 'Sack Exchange' at bay, in a close win over the Jets. Not since 1966 had the Bills beaten the Dolphins in the Miami Orange Bowl but they put an end to that sequence with a Joe Danelo overtime field goal, after the two teams had shared 70 points. But there was no shaking off the Colts, who completed the double over the Patriots.

The NFC West was an all domestic affair, at the end of which there was still no clue to the identity of the division winner. The Cowboys who, as usual, gave up the first score, made heavy weather of beating the luckless Buccaneers and only 47 seconds of normal time remained when Timmy Newsome tied the scores with a 52-yard touchdown reception. Rafael Septien's overtime field goal brought sighs of relief. The week's prize for escapology surely goes to the Chargers who, at one time, trailed Seattle by the score of 21-0. But Dan Fouts came off the bench to ignite a recovery which was completed when Andre Young scored with a 40-yard interception return, late in the game. Still in the AFC Western division, a one-point Raider lead was preserved when the NFL's premier kick blocker, Ted Hendricks, batted down a 48-yard Nick Lowery field goal attempt, with only nine

Mark Duper

seconds remaining. In the wake of Houston's 26-14 loss to Denver, their head coach, Ed Biles, resigned and was replaced by defensive coordinator Chuck Studley.

Outstanding Individual Performances

Joe Ferguson (Buffalo) completed 38 of 55 passes for 419 yards and five touchdowns.

Dan Marino (Miami) completed 19 of 29 passes for 322 yards and three touchdowns.

Mark Duper (Miami) caught seven passes for 202 yards and scored two touchdowns, including one covering 63 yards.

Sammy Winder (Denver) rushed for 165 yards on 29 carries.

John Riggins (Washington) rushed for 115 yards on 22 carries and scored three touchdowns.

Morten Andersen (New Orleans) kicked four field goals, the last with no time remaining, to win the game.

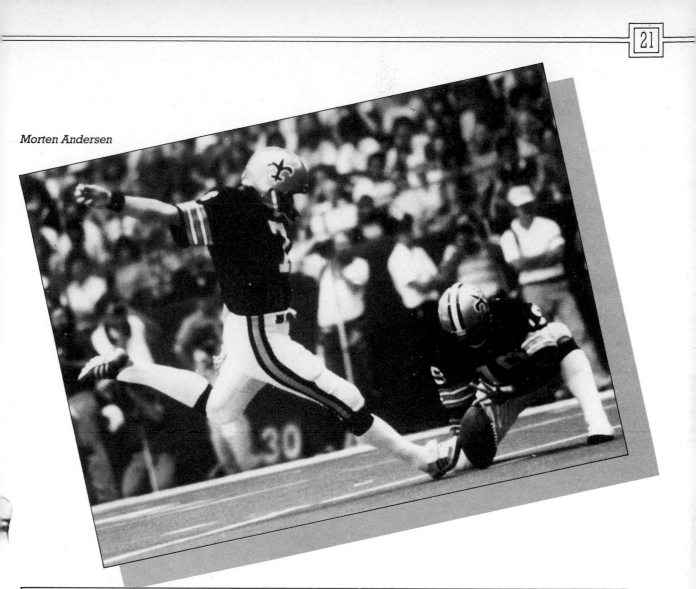

Morten Andersen

STANDINGS

AFC East	W	L	T	PF	PA	NFC East	W	L	T	PF	PA
Baltimore	4	2	0	130	125	Dallas	6	0	0	178	128
Buffalo	4	2	0	116	123	Washington	5	1	0	182	122
Miami	3	3	0	116	112	Philadelphia	4	2	0	104	101
N.Y. Jets	3	3	0	132	113	N.Y. Giants	2	4	0	109	118
New England	2	4	0	118	144	St Louis	1	5	0	103	191
AFC Central						**NFC Central**					
Cleveland	4	2	0	118	115	Minnesota	4	2	0	130	153
Pittsburgh	4	2	0	139	115	Green Bay	3	3	0	161	166
Cincinnati	1	5	0	91	122	Chicago	2	4	0	129	123
Houston	0	6	0	109	174	Detroit	2	4	0	116	116
AFC West						Tampa Bay	0	6	0	81	152
L.A. Raiders	5	1	0	145	94	**NFC West**					
Denver	3	3	0	88	100	L.A. Rams	4	2	0	125	104
San Diego	3	3	0	170	174	New Orleans	4	2	0	145	123
Seattle	3	3	0	126	122	San Francisco	4	2	0	171	109
Kansas City	2	4	0	107	106	Atlanta	2	4	0	124	118

WEEK SEVEN

American Football Conference
Buffalo 30 at Baltimore 7
Cincinnati 17 at Denver 24
Cleveland 17 at Pittsburgh 44
Los Angeles Raiders 36 at Seattle 38
Miami 32 at New York Jets 14
San Diego 21 at New England 37

National Football Conference
Atlanta 21 at Los Angeles Rams 27
Chicago 17 at Detroit 31
Philadelphia 7 at Dallas 37
St Louis 34 at Tampa Bay 27
San Francisco 32 at New Orleans 13
Washington 47 at Green Bay 48

Interconference Games
Houston 14 at Minnesota 34
New York Giants 17 at Kansas City 38

Interconference Play
NFC 10, AFC 8

On an evening when the defenses might just as well have stayed at home, the Packers and the Redskins combined to amass 1,025 yards of total offense and score 95 points. It was only after having scored seven times to Green Bay's five that the Redskins went ahead, 33-31, and the lead was to be

Joe Cribbs

exchanged a further four times before Jan Stenerud's 20-yard field goal gave Green Bay the upper hand, 48-47, with 54 seconds to go. Still the Redskins would not yield and they drove to the Green Bay 22-yard line, only to see Mark Moseley's field goal attempt drift wide of the uprights on the final play of the game. The Cowboys opened up a two-game lead in the NFC Eastern division by rolling over the Philadelphia Eagles, who were restricted to just 44 yards rushing.

In the battle for the lead in the AFC Eastern division, the Baltimore Colts scored first, on a 52-yard touchdown reception by Ray Butler. However, that was their lot for the day as the Bills, led by running back Joe Cribbs, piled on the agony. Against Cleveland, the Steelers were out-rushed and outpassed but not outscored as they took over the leadership of the AFC Central division. The Bengals, meanwhile, dropped further out of contention with a loss to Denver, for whom Steve DeBerg had replaced John Elway as the starting quarterback. The Vikings retained their lead in the NFC Central division at the expense of the Houston Oilers, whose loss was their fourteenth in an unbroken sequence stretching back to 22 November 1982.

Over on the West coast, the Raiders had their lead trimmed to one game, falling prey to the surprising Seahawks, for whom the defense reco-vered three fumbles, snared three interceptions and sacked quarterbacks Jim Plunkett and Marc Wilson a combined total of eight times. In the NFC Western division's neighbourhood squabble, both the 49ers and the Rams came from behind for victories which left them tied for the division lead. For the Falcons, who led 21-7 in the third quarter, it was a loss that they could ill afford and it left them with an uphill struggle.

Outstanding Individual Performances

Boyce Green (Cleveland) rushed for 137 yards on 28 carries and scored two touchdowns.

Earl Campbell (Houston) rushed for 130 yards on 29 carries and scored one touchdown.

Joe Cribbs (Buffalo) rushed for 105 yards on 19 carries, and caught four passes for 50 yards and scored one touchdown.

Bill Kenney (Kansas City) completed 25 of 36 passes for 342 yards and four touchdowns.

Todd Christensen (Los Angeles Raiders) caught 11 passes for 152 yards and scored three touchdowns.

Stacey Bailey (Atlanta) caught 6 passes for 106 yards and scored one touchdown.

Stacey Bailey

STANDINGS

AFC East	W	L	T	PF	PA	NFC East	W	L	T	PF	PA
Buffalo	5	2	0	146	130	Dallas	7	0	0	215	135
Baltimore	4	3	0	137	155	Washington	5	2	0	229	170
Miami	4	3	0	148	126	Philadelphia	4	3	0	111	138
New England	3	4	0	155	165	N.Y. Giants	2	5	0	126	156
N.Y. Jets	3	4	0	146	145	St Louis	2	5	0	137	218
AFC Central						**NFC Central**					
Pittsburgh	5	2	0	183	132	Minnesota	5	2	0	164	167
Cleveland	4	3	0	135	159	Green Bay	4	3	0	209	213
Cincinnati	1	6	0	108	146	Detroit	3	4	0	147	133
Houston	0	7	0	123	208	Chicago	2	5	0	146	154
AFC West						Tampa Bay	0	7	0	108	186
L.A. Raiders	5	2	0	181	132	**NFC West**					
Denver	4	3	0	112	117	L.A. Rams	5	2	0	152	125
Seattle	4	3	0	164	158	San Francisco	5	2	0	203	122
Kansas City	3	4	0	145	123	New Orleans	4	3	0	158	155
San Diego	3	4	0	191	211	Atlanta	2	5	0	145	145

WEEK EIGHT

American Football Conference
Cleveland 21 at Cincinnati 28
Kansas City 13 at Houston 10 (OT)
Miami 21 at Baltimore 7
New England 31 at Buffalo 0
Pittsburgh 27 at Seattle 21
San Diego 6 at Denver 14

National Football Conference
Chicago 7 at Philadelphia 6
Detroit 17 at Washington 38
Minnesota 20 at Green Bay 17 (OT)
New Orleans 24 at Tampa Bay 21
New York Giants 20 at St Louis 20 (OT)
San Francisco 45 at Los Angeles Rams 35

Intercoference Games
Atlanta 27 at New York Jets 21
Los Angeles Raiders 40 at Dallas 38

Interconference Play
NFC 11, AFC 9

At Riverfront Stadium the scores were tied, 21-21, when veteran Bengals cornerback Ken Riley celebrated his 60th career interception with a 42-yard touchdown return to deal Cleveland its second consecutive loss. Victory for the Steelers, who established a 24-point lead and then rode the storm of a three-touchdown Seahawk recovery, gave them a two-game cushion on top of the AFC Central division. The Vikings, too, opened up a little daylight with victory over the Packers. Green Bay drew level on a Mike Meade touchdown reception, with only two seconds of normal time remaining, to take the game into overtime. But they were subsequently forced to punt on their first series of downs and the Vikings drove to the Packers' 13-yard line, from where Benny Ricardo did the rest with his third game-winning field goal of the season.

On his previous visit to Rich Stadium, New England running back Tony Collins gained only five yards on four carries and fumbled twice. but on week eight he cut loose, rushing for 147 yards as

Billy 'White Shoes' Johnson

STANDINGS

AFC East	W	L	T	PF	PA	NFC East	W	L	T	PF	PA
Buffalo	5	3	0	146	161	Dallas	7	1	0	253	175
Miami	5	3	0	169	133	Washington	6	2	0	267	187
Baltimore	4	4	0	144	176	Philadelphia	4	4	0	117	145
New England	4	4	0	186	165	N.Y. Giants	2	5	1	146	176
N.Y. Jets	3	5	0	167	172	St Louis	2	5	1	157	238
AFC Central						**NFC Central**					
Pittsburgh	6	2	0	210	153	Minnesota	6	2	0	184	184
Cleveland	4	4	0	156	187	Green Bay	4	4	0	226	233
Cincinnati	2	6	0	136	167	Chicago	3	5	0	153	160
Houston	0	8	0	133	221	Detroit	3	5	0	164	171
AFC West						Tampa Bay	0	8	0	129	210
L.A. Raiders	6	2	0	221	170	**NFC West**					
Denver	5	3	0	126	123	San Francisco	6	2	0	248	157
Kansas City	4	4	0	158	133	L.A. Rams	5	3	0	187	170
Seattle	4	4	0	185	185	New Orleans	5	3	0	182	176
San Diego	3	5	0	197	225	Atlanta	3	5	0	172	166

the Patriots hammered the Bills with 31 unanswered points, 24 of which came in the final quarter. The Dolphins mastered the elements (it poured down) to beat the error-prone Colts and move into a tie for first place in the AFC Eastern division. In the NFC Western division, the 49ers won the battle at the top, outscoring the Rams 28-7 in the fourth quarter. However, the Saints remained in contention, though they trailed the Buccaneers

Ted Brown

for 37 minutes before Bobby Johnson intercepted and raced 70 yards for the winning touchdown.

Late on Sunday evening in a packed Texas Stadium and watched by a nationwide television audience, two truly great football organizations came face to face for the day's finale. Raiders quarterback Marc Wilson, who had replaced the out-of-form Jim Plunkett, threw three touchdown passes and, with the Cowboys closing down on Marcus Allen, Frank Hawkins rushed for 118 yards. Nonetheless, after a furious exchange of points, the Raiders still trailed, 37-38, before Chris Bahr kicked the winning field goal with only 20 seconds remaining. The Cowboys' first defeat was all the more significant for, earlier in the day and even without John Riggins, the Redskins had blasted the Detroit Lions.

Outstanding Individual Performances

Vince Ferragamo (Los Angeles Rams) completed 26 of 35 passes for 327 yards and five touchdowns.

Ted Brown (Minnesota) rushed for 179 yards on 29 carries and scored one touchdown.

Joe Washington (Washington) rushed for 147 yards on 22 carries.

Franco Harris (Pittsburgh) rushed for 132 yards on 31 carries and scored one touchdown.

Doug Martin (Minnesota) had five quarterback sacks.

Roland James (New England) intercepted three passes.

Billy 'White Shoes' Johnson (Atlanta) scored touchdowns with a 15-yard reception and a 71-yard punt return, and set up further scores with a 41-yard punt return and a 36-yard run.

WEEK NINE

American Football Conference
Houston 19 at Cleveland 25 (OT)
Kansas City 24 at Denver 27
Seattle 34 at Los Angeles Raiders 21

National Football Conference
Dallas 38 at New York Giants 20
Detroit 38 at Chicago 17
Minnesota 31 at St Louis 41

Intercontinental Games
Baltimore 22 at Philadelphia 21
Green Bay 14 at Cincinnati 34
Los Angeles Rams 14 at Miami 30
New England 13 at Atlanta 24
New Orleans 21 at Buffalo 27
New York Jets 27 at San Francisco 13
Tampa Bay 12 at Pittsburgh 17
Washington 27 at San Diego 24

Interconference Play
AFC 15, NFC 13

With their second victory over the Raiders in three weeks, the Seahawks could no longer be considered as 'surprising'. Raiders quarterback Marc Wilson was sacked five times and threw four interceptions in a loss for which there could be few excuses. The Broncos seized their opportunity to move into a tie for first place in the AFC Western division, by beating the Chiefs on a sparkling performance by quarterback Steve DeBerg against the NFL's top-rated pass defense. For the NFC Western division, three of whose teams, the 49ers, the Rams and the Saints, lost to their AFC Eastern division opponents, it was a bad day. However, the Atlanta Falcons avoided a whitewash by beating New England, who were strangely indecisive after having thrashed the Bills, and contributed to their own demise with turnovers inside the Atlanta ten-yard line on four separate occasions. Their loss enabled the Colts, for whom Raul Allegre kicked five field goals, to squeeze into third place.

The Packers felt the full weight of running back Pete Johnson (270 lb), who bulldozed for 112 yards in a victory which gave the Bengals a faint glimmer

Ottis Anderson

of hope. Despite a 21-point fourth-quarter scoring burst, the Vikings could not overhaul the St Louis Cardinals and would now have to keep an eye on Detroit, who underlined their mastery over the Chicago Bears. In the AFC Central division, the luckless Houston Oilers lost their second overtime decision in consecutive weeks and their third of the season, to extend the misery to sixteen games. Their NFC equivalent, the Tampa Bay Buccaneers, seemed bound for victory against Pittsburgh when, on four Bill Capece field goals, they entered the final quarter with a 12-0 lead. But the Steelers clawed back to retain their two-game lead in the AFC Eastern division and establish the AFC's best current won-lost record. Whereas the Cowboys had pounded the Giants, the Redskins needed a late field goal from Mark Moseley to break a 24-24 tie with the San Diego Chargers. Nonetheless, the big two were beginning to ease away from their nearest challengers in the NFC Eastern division.

Outstanding Individual Performances

Danny White (Dallas) completed 15 of 33 passes for 304 yards and five touchdowns.

Steve DeBerg (Denver) completed 21 of 41 passes for 350 yards and one touchdown.

Ottis Anderson (St Louis) rushed for 136 yards on 24 carries and scored one touchdown.

James Wilder (Tampa Bay) set an NFL record for number of carries, 42, in gaining 126 yards.

Raul Allegre (Baltimore) kicked five field goals.

Steve DeBerg

STANDINGS

AFC East	W	L	T	PF	PA	NFC East	W	L	T	PF	PA
Buffalo	6	3	0	173	182	Dallas	8	1	0	291	195
Miami	6	3	0	199	147	Washington	7	2	0	292	211
Baltimore	5	4	0	166	197	Philadelphia	4	5	0	138	167
New England	4	5	0	199	189	St Louis	3	5	1	198	269
N.Y. Jets	4	5	0	194	185	N.Y. Giants	2	6	1	166	214
AFC Central						**NFC Central**					
Pittsburgh	7	2	0	227	165	Minnesota	6	3	0	215	225
Cleveland	5	4	0	181	206	Detroit	4	5	0	202	188
Cincinnati	3	6	0	170	181	Green Bay	4	5	0	240	267
Houston	0	9	0	152	246	Chicago	3	6	0	170	198
AFC West						Tampa Bay	0	9	0	141	227
Denver	6	3	0	153	147	**NFC West**					
L.A. Raiders	6	3	0	242	204	San Francisco	6	3	0	261	184
Seattle	5	4	0	219	206	L.A. Rams	5	4	0	201	200
Kansas City	4	5	0	182	160	New Orleans	5	4	0	203	203
San Diego	3	6	0	221	252	Atlanta	4	5	0	196	179

WEEK TEN

American Football Conference
Baltimore 17 at New York Jets 14
Buffalo 7 at New England 21
Cincinnati 55 at Houston 14
Denver 19 at Seattle 27
Los Angeles Raiders 28 at Kansas City 20
San Diego 3 at Pittsburgh 26

National Football Conference
Atlanta 10 at New Orleans 27
Chicago 14 at Los Angeles Rams 21
Dallas 27 at Philadelphia 20
New York Giants 9 at Detroit 15
St Louis 7 at Washington 45
:Tampa Bay 17 at Minnesota 12

Interconference Games
Cleveland 21 at Green Bay 35 (played in Milwaukee)
Miami 20 at San Francisco 17

Interconference Play
AFC 16, NFC 14

Over the last six weeks, the Raiders had alternated wins with losses and on week ten they continued the sequence though, when Kansas City's Nick Lowery stepped up for a field goal attempt, with just under two minutes remaining and the Chiefs trailing by only one point, things were looking bad. But poor Lowery shanked the kick and, with a

James Wilder

subsequent Rod Martin insurance touchdown following his pass interception, the Raiders came away with a slightly flattering victory over their old rivals. Nonetheless, by the end of the day's play, they were back in sole ownership of the AFC Western division lead, following Seattle's win over Denver. With a significant return to form, the Patriots gained maximum points from Buffalo and, but for conceding a late touchdown, would have held the Bills scoreless in two full games. Surprisingly however, the emerging pressure on the Dolphins was coming from the Baltimore Colts, who capitalized on four Jets turnovers and a deflected pass which came to rest in the arms of Curtis Dickey, standing free in the end zone.

Not for the first time in the NFL's history, the bottom team beat the top team as, at last, the Tampa Bay Buccaneers made it into the win column at the expense of the Vikings. The Bengals showed just how good they could be with a 55-14 mauling of the Oilers, who lost their seventeenth consecutive game. For Cincinnati, at least, there was still a chance but their best hope was for a wild card spot since, with a three-game lead, the Steelers were all but out of reach. In the NFC Eastern division, the Cowboys were up to their old tricks, falling behind, 0-10, early in the game, and having to withstand a spirited Philadelphia comeback to win a close one. The Redskins, on the other hand, were beginning to look frighteningly good, pouring it onto the Cardinals. After ten weeks of football, the NFC Western division was still a puzzle and even the Falcons, two games adrift of the three co-leaders, were not out of the race.

Outstanding Individual Performances

James Wilder (Tampa Bay) rushed for 219 yards on 31 carries and scored a touchdown on a 75-yard run.

Eric Dickerson (Los Angeles Rams) rushed for 127 yards on 34 carries and scored two touchdowns.

George Rogers (New Orleans) rushed for 137 yards on 20 carries.

Curt Warner (Seattle) rushed for 134 yards on 25 carries.

Mike Quick (Philadelphia) caught seven passes for 120 yards and scored one touchdown.

John Jefferson (Green Bay) caught seven passes for 102 yards and scored one touchdown.

Tony Galbreath (Minnesota) caught eleven passes for 110 yards.

Clarence Weathers (New England) caught only two passes but they were both for touchdowns, covering 58 and 40 yards respectively.

John Jefferson

STANDINGS

AFC East	W	L	T	PF	PA	NFC East	W	L	T	PF	PA
Miami	7	3	0	219	164	Dallas	9	1	0	318	215
Baltimore	6	4	0	183	211	Washington	8	2	0	339	218
Buffalo	6	4	0	180	203	Philadelphia	4	6	0	158	194
New England	5	5	0	220	196	St Louis	3	6	1	205	314
N.Y. Jets	4	6	0	208	202	N.Y. Giants	2	7	1	175	229
AFC Central						**NFC Central**					
Pittsburgh	8	2	0	253	168	Minnesota	6	4	0	227	242
Cleveland	5	5	0	202	241	Detroit	5	5	0	217	197
Cincinnati	4	6	0	225	195	Green Bay	5	5	0	275	288
Houston	0	10	0	166	301	Chicago	3	7	0	184	219
AFC West						Tampa Bay	1	9	0	158	239
L.A. Raiders	7	3	0	270	224	**NFC West**					
Denver	6	4	0	172	174	L.A. Rams	6	4	0	222	214
Seattle	6	4	0	246	225	New Orleans	6	4	0	230	213
Kansas City	4	6	0	202	188	San Francisco	6	4	0	278	204
San Diego	3	7	0	224	278	Atlanta	4	6	0	206	206

WEEK ELEVEN

American Football Conference
Buffalo 24 at New York Jets 17
Cincinnati 15 at Kansas City 20
Denver 20 at Los Angeles Raiders 22
Miami 6 at New England 17
Pittsburgh 24 at Baltimore 13

National Football Conference
Green Bay 29 at Minnesota 21
Los Angeles Rams 36 at Atlanta 13
New Orleans 0 at San Francisco 27
Philadelphia 14 at Chicago 17
Washington 33 at New York Giants 17

Interconference Games
Dallas 23 at San Diego 24
Detroit 17 at Houston 27
Seattle 28 at St Louis 33
Tampa Bay 0 at Cleveland 20

Interconference Play
AFC 19, NFC 15

Neil Lomax

Miami's home loss to New England and Buffalo's victory over the Jets, thanks to a Joe Cribbs touchdown reception with only 22 seconds to go, brought about a reshuffle in the AFC Eastern division. Even so, and despite losing to the Pittsburgh Steelers, the Colts remained as one of four teams which could take the division title, whereas the Jets needed a miracle of some proportions just to reach the playoffs. The Cleveland Browns, after having lost their way somewhat over the last few weeks, re-established consistent offensive momentum and, on defense, did what they had to, namely stop James Wilder, in a tidy win over the Buccaneers. Sadly for Wilder, two broken ribs brought a premature end to the season.

The Houston Oilers finally did it, ending a sequence of seventeen consecutive losses with victory over the Lions, who had been mounting a challenge in the NFC Central division. Nonetheless, following Green Bay's win over the Vikings, for whom running back Darrin Nelson had his best ever NFL day, here too, four teams were still in the playoff race. There were signs of a sort-out in the NFC Western division, where both the Rams and the 49ers scored comprehensive wins over their domestic opponents, but there would be much more melting in the pot before this one was settled. The Raiders had to dig deeply into their traditions for victory over the Broncos, after having fallen behind, 20-19, with only 58 seconds remaining. But Jim Plunkett, who had stepped back in following an injury to Marc Wilson, completed four passes to Todd Christensen, gaining 48 yards in 43 seconds, to set up Chris Bahr's 39-yard winning field goal. With Seattle falling to the volatile St Louis Cardinals, the Raiders broke free of the pack in the AFC Western division. The Cowboys suffered a minor setback against the Chargers, who held on in the face of a typical Dallas rally. Rafael Septien's missed extra point attempt (he caught his studs in the mud of Jack Murphy Stadium) proved to be the difference. They were joined on top of the NFC Eastern division by the Redskins, who established a comfortable 33-3 lead before allowing the Giants the consolation of two late touchdowns.

Outstanding Individual Performances

Darrin Nelson (Minnesota) rushed for 119 yards on sixteen carries and caught seven passes for 137 yards.

Walter Payton (Chicago) rushed for 131 yards on 23 carries.

Ottis Anderson (St Louis) rushed for 130 yards on 29 carries.

Roy Green (St Louis) caught six passes for 130 yards and scored four touchdowns, including a longest of 63 yards.

Neil Lomax (St Louis) completed 21 of 27 passes for 253 yards and four touchdowns.

Fred Dean (San Francisco) had six quarterbacks sacks against New Orleans.

STANDINGS

AFC East	W	L	T	PF	PA	NFC East	W	L	T	PF	PA
Buffalo	7	4	0	204	220	Dallas	9	2	0	341	239
Miami	7	4	0	225	181	Washington	9	2	0	372	235
Baltimore	6	5	0	196	235	St Louis	4	6	1	238	342
New England	6	5	0	237	202	Philadelphia	4	7	0	172	211
N.Y. Jets	4	7	0	225	226	N.Y. Giants	2	8	1	192	262
AFC Central						**NFC Central**					
Pittsburgh	9	2	0	277	181	Green Bay	6	5	0	304	309
Cleveland	6	5	0	222	241	Minnesota	6	5	0	248	271
Cincinnati	4	7	0	240	215	Detroit	5	6	0	234	224
Houston	1	10	0	193	318	Chicago	4	7	0	201	233
AFC West						Tampa Bay	1	10	0	158	259
L.A. Raiders	8	3	0	292	244	**NFC West**					
Denver	6	5	0	192	196	L.A. Rams	7	4	0	258	227
Seattle	6	5	0	274	258	San Francisco	7	4	0	305	204
Kansas City	5	6	0	222	203	New Orleans	6	5	0	230	240
San Diego	4	7	0	248	301	Atlanta	4	7	0	219	242

Darrin Nelson

WEEK TWELVE

American Football Conference
Baltimore 0 at Miami 37
Cleveland 30 at New England 0
Houston 10 at Cincinnati 38
Los Angeles Raiders 27 at Buffalo 24
Seattle 27 at Denver 38

National Football Conference
Chicago 27 at Tampa Bay 0
Detroit 23 at Green Bay 20 (OT)
New York Giants 23 at Philadelphia 0
San Francisco 24 at Atlanta 28
Washington 42 at Los Angeles Rams 20

Interconference Games
Kansas City 21 at Dallas 41
Minnesota 17 at Pittsburgh 14
New York Jets 31 at New Orleans 28
San Diego 14 at St Louis 44

Interconference Play
AFC 20, NFC 18

With both New England and Buffalo losing, the Miami Dolphins took the opportunity to open up a lead in the AFC Eastern division and gave their best offensive display in a 37-0 thrashing of Baltimore. The game was adequately summed up by Miami defensive end Doug Betters, who remarked: 'We came into this game intending to kick someone's rear end' (or words to that effect). Buffalo's loss to the Raiders was a real heartbreaker. At one time losing 24-3, they fought back to tie the scores at 24-24, with under five minutes remaining, only to lose on Chris Bahr's field goal with the last kick of the game. The Broncos did both themselves and the Raiders a lot of good by stopping the error-prone Seahawks, whose eight turnovers (four fumbles and four interceptions) led directly to 30 of the Broncos' points. The Steelers

Charlie Brown

could afford their mildy surprising lapse against the Vikings and, even after Cleveland's 30-0 blowout over New England, remained two games clear in the AFC Central division. With their victory, Minnesota stayed on top of the NFC Central division but Detroit kept pace with an overtime win over Green Bay. The Packers had appeared set for a comfortable win and were rolling, 20-3, at half-time, when quarterback Lynn Dickey left the game with concussion. With him departed the Packers' offense and, yielding to running back Billy Sims' career best performance, they were forced into overtime, eventually losing to Ed Murray's field goal.

There was high drama over in the NFC Western division, where the Falcons gave evidence that they were still alive and kicking. On the game's final play, with Atlanta trailing 21-24, quarterback Steve Bartkowski dropped back and heaved a rather hopeful 50-yarder, somewhere in the direction of three receivers flooding the deep left corner area. (It is known as a 'Hail Mary' pass in football terminology.) After bouncing off three players, the ball was caught, knee-high, by Billy 'White Shoes' Johnson, who scrambled the last five yards to (just) break the plane of the end zone. The Rams had been humbled by Washington and later, on Monday evening, the Saints threw away a 28-14 lead against the Jets, whose 17-point fourth quarter culminated with Kirk Springs' 76-yard punt return for a touchdown.

Outstanding Individual Performances

Billy Sims (Detroit) rushed for 189 yards on 36 carries.

Butch Woolfolk (N.Y. Giants) rushed for 159 yards on 43 carries (a new NFL record) and scored one touchdown.

Pete Johnson (Cincinnati) rushed for 137 yards on 30 carries and scored two touchdowns.

Mike Pruitt (Cleveland) rushed for 136 yards on 24 carries and scored one touchdown.

Walter Payton (Chicago) rushed for 106 yards to move into third place in the list of all time leading rushers.

Charlie Brown (Washington) caught eight passes for 140 yards and scored one touchdown.

Carlos Carson (Kansas City) caught seven passes for 135 yards and scored two touchdowns.

Mark Duper (Miami) caught five passes for 121 yards including an 85-yard touchdown.

Steve Watson (Denver) caught four passes for 119 yards including a 78-yard touchdown.

Dave Krieg (Seattle) completed 31 of 42 passes for 420 yards and three touchdowns.

STANDINGS

AFC East	W	L	T	PF	PA
Miami	8	4	0	262	181
Buffalo	7	5	0	228	247
Baltimore	6	6	0	196	272
New England	6	6	0	237	232
N.Y. Jets	5	7	0	256	254
AFC Central					
Pittsburgh	9	3	0	291	198
Cleveland	7	5	0	252	241
Cincinnati	5	7	0	278	225
Houston	1	11	0	203	356
AFC West					
L.A. Raiders	9	3	0	319	268
Denver	7	5	0	230	223
Seattle	6	6	0	301	296
Kansas City	5	7	0	243	244
San Diego	4	8	0	262	345

NFC East	W	L	T	PF	PA
Dallas	10	2	0	382	260
Washington	10	2	0	414	255
St Louis	5	6	1	282	356
Philadelphia	4	8	0	172	234
N.Y. Giants	3	8	1	215	262
NFC Central					
Minnesota	7	5	0	265	285
Detroit	6	6	0	257	244
Green Bay	6	6	0	324	332
Chicago	5	7	0	228	233
Tampa Bay	1	11	0	158	286
NFC West					
L.A. Rams	7	5	0	278	269
San Francisco	7	5	0	329	232
New Orleans	6	6	0	258	271
Atlanta	5	7	0	247	266

Steve Watson

WEEK THIRTEEN

American Football Conference
Baltimore 23 at Cleveland 41
Cincinnati 14 at Miami 38
Denver 7 at San Diego 31
Kansas City 48 at Seattle 51 (OT)
New England 3 at New York Jets 26

National Football Conference
Green Bay 41 at Atlanta 47 (OT)
Minnesota 16 at New Orleans 17
Philadelphia 24 at Washington 28
St Louis 17 at Dallas 35
San Francisco 3 at Chicago 13

Interconference Games
Buffalo 17 at Los Angeles Rams 41
Houston 24 at Tampa Bay 33
New York Giants 12 at Los Angeles Raiders 27
Pittsburgh 3 at Detroit 45

Interconference Play
AFC 21, NFC 21

Curt Warner

Such had been the dominance of Dallas and Washington, not only in their division but also in the National Football Conference as a whole, that with victories over St Louis and Philadelphia respectively, both teams made sure of entering the playoffs. One of them was certain to win the division title whilst the other would gain a wild card entry. After suffering the initial shock of a Roy Green 71-yard touchdown reception, the Cowboys buckled down to it and sacked St Louis quarterback Neil Lomax seven times whilst cruising to an impressive win. For the second time in the season, the Redskins had to work hard to beat Philadelphia. Washington's big-play wide receiver, Charlie Brown, caught a 75-yard touchdown pass and John Riggins rushed for two touchdowns (his 20th and 21st), with the first of which he established a new NFL single-season record in this category.

Cleveland's handsome victory over Baltimore brought them to within one game of, by now, a nervous Pittsburgh team which had been savaged by the Detroit Lions who, in turn, moved into a first-place tie with Minnesota in the NFC Central division. Bullets were flying and coincidences abounded in the Kingdome and at Atlanta, where both teams overcame 21-7 deficits to win in overtime. The Falcons could thank cornerback Kenny Johnson, who returned two interceptions for touchdowns, the first with less than two minutes of regular time remaining and the second after just

over two minutes of overtime. The Seattle-Kansas City shootout produced the NFL's third biggest ever points total in a regular season game (Washington's 72-41 win over the Giants in 1966 stands as the record). The Seahawks too could be grateful to one of the NFL's twenty-one Johnsons. It was their kicker, Norm Johnson, who tied the scores on a 42-yard field goal with two seconds of normal time remaining, and won the game with another 42-yarder in overtime. Following Denver's loss to San Diego, the Seahawks joined the race for a wild card spot.

Outstanding Individual Performances

Curt Warner (Seattle) rushed for 207 yards on 32 carries and scored three touchdowns.

Eric Dickerson (Los Angeles Rams) rushed for 125 yards on 32 carries and scored one touchdown.

William Andrews (Atlanta) rushed for 129 yards on 20 carries and scored two touchdowns.

Bill Kenney (Kansas City) completed 21 of 38 passes for 311 yards and four touchdowns.

Jack Thompson (Tampa Bay) completed 17 of 29 passes for 224 yards and four touchdowns.

James Lofton (Green Bay) caught seven passes for 161 yards and scored one touchdown.

Carlos Carson (Kansas City) caught seven passes for 149 yards and scored one touchdown.

Earnest Gray (New York Giants) caught five passes for 134 yards.

Ozzie Newsome (Cleveland) caught eight passes for 108 yards including a 66-yard touchdown reception.

Ozzie Newsome

STANDINGS

AFC East	W	L	T	PF	PA	NFC East	W	L	T	PF	PA
Miami	9	4	0	300	195	*Dallas	11	2	0	417	277
Buffalo	7	6	0	245	288	*Washington	11	2	0	442	279
Baltimore	6	7	0	219	313	St Louis	5	7	1	299	391
New England	6	7	0	240	258	Philadelphia	4	9	0	196	262
N.Y. Jets	6	7	0	282	257	N.Y. Giants	3	9	1	227	289
AFC Central						**NFC Central**					
Pittsburgh	9	4	0	294	243	Detroit	7	6	0	302	247
Cleveland	8	5	0	293	264	Minnesota	7	6	0	281	302
Cincinnati	5	8	0	292	263	Chicago	6	7	0	241	236
Houston	1	12	0	227	389	Green Bay	6	7	0	365	379
AFC West						Tampa Bay	2	11	0	191	310
L.A. Raiders	10	3	0	346	280	**NFC West**					
Denver	7	6	0	237	254	L.A. Rams	8	5	0	319	286
Seattle	7	6	0	352	344	New Orleans	7	6	0	275	287
Kansas City	5	8	0	291	295	San Francisco	7	6	0	332	245
San Diego	5	8	0	293	352	Atlanta	6	7	0	294	307

*Qualified for playoffs

WEEK FOURTEEN

American Football Conference
Buffalo 14 at Kansas City 9
Cincinnati 23 at Pittsburgh 10
Cleveland 6 at Denver 27
Los Angeles Raiders 42 at San Diego 10
Miami 24 at Houston 17
New York Jets 10 at Baltimore 6

National Football Conference
Atlanta 21 at Washington 37
Chicago 28 at Green Bay 31
Los Angeles Rams 9 at Philadelphia 13
Minnesota 2 at Detroit 13
St Louis 10 at New York Giants 6
Tampa Bay 21 at San Francisco 35

Interconference Games
Dallas 35 at Seattle 10
New Orleans 0 at New England 7

Interconference Play
AFC 22, NFC 22

Kevin House

The Miami Dolphins won the AFC Eastern division title with a late surge after having trailed Houston, 0-14 and 7-17. They were joined in the playoffs by the Raiders, who overran San Diego to win the AFC Western division title. Elsewhere, there was a fair old scramble going on for the remaining six places. The Pittsburgh Steelers could well have seen a three-game lead evaporate, losing to Cincinnati, but the Browns failed to seize their opportunity, going down to Denver. Nonetheless, together with their conquerors and Buffalo, Cleveland remained as strong candidates for a playoff berth. Despite their comprehensive loss at the hands of Dallas, the Seahawks could not be discounted and, with a third consecutive win, the New York Jets were coming with a late run. In the meeting between the NFC Central division's co-leaders, Minnesota were restricted to a two-point safety by the Lions, who established a one-game lead. But the Green Bay Packers renewed their threat when James Lofton hauled in a 67-yard pass to establish field position for Jan Stenerud's winning field goal which sailed through the uprights as time ran out.

The NFC Western division picture cleared slightly in the sense that, by losing to Washington, the Atlanta Falcons slipped quietly out of contention. On the other hand, any one of the 49ers, the Rams and the Saints could still come away with the title. After two consecutive defeats, the San Francisco 49ers woke up to beat the Buccaneers, though they had to survive a fusillade of passes from Tampa Bay quarterback Jack Thompson. Earlier in the day, the Rams had appeared to be certain winners when Mike Lansford's field goal broke a 6-6 tie with less than two minutes to go. However, careless defensive play allowed Tony Woodruff in for the touchdown which ended Philadelphia's seven-game losing streak and dropped the Rams back into a tie for first place. The Saints missed their chance to join them by losing to New England in Foxboro, Massachusetts, where a first-quarter touchdown was the game's only scoring play.

Outstanding Individual Performances

Stacey Bailey (Atlanta) caught nine passes for 159 yards.

Kevin House (Tampa Bay) caught six passes for 156 yards including a 74-yard touchdown.

Todd Christensen (Los Angeles Raiders) caught eight passes for 140 yards and scored three touchdowns.

Gerry Ellis (Green Bay) rushed for 141 yards on 18 carries and scored one touchdown.

Earl Campbell (Houston) rushed for 138 yards on 28 carries and scored one touchdown.

Pete Johnson (Cincinnati) rushed for 126 yards on 38 carries and scored two touchdowns.

Tony Dorsett (Dallas) rushed for 117 yards on 26 carries and scored two touchdowns.

Randy White (Dallas) had 3½ quarterback sacks.

Pete Johnson ▶

STANDINGS

AFC East	W	L	T	PF	PA
†*Miami	10	4	0	324	212
Buffalo	8	6	0	259	297
New England	7	7	0	247	258
N.Y. Jets	7	7	0	292	263
Baltimore	6	8	0	225	323
AFC Central					
Pittsburgh	9	5	0	304	266
Cleveland	8	6	0	299	291
Cincinnati	6	8	0	315	273
Houston	1	13	0	244	414
AFC West					
†*L.A. Raiders	11	3	0	388	290
Denver	8	6	0	264	260
Seattle	7	7	0	362	379
Kansas City	5	9	0	300	309
San Diego	5	9	0	303	394

NFC East	W	L	T	PF	PA
*Dallas	12	2	0	452	287
*Washington	12	2	0	479	300
St Louis	6	7	1	309	397
Philadelphia	5	9	0	209	271
N.Y. Giants	3	10	1	233	299
NFC Central					
Detroit	8	6	0	315	249
Green Bay	7	7	0	396	407
Minnesota	7	7	0	283	315
Chicago	6	8	0	269	267
Tampa Bay	2	12	0	212	345
NFC West					
L.A. Rams	8	6	0	328	299
San Francisco	8	6	0	367	266
New Orleans	7	7	0	275	294
Atlanta	6	8	0	315	344

† Division Champions
* Qualified for playoffs

WEEK FIFTEEN

American Football Conference
Baltimore 19 at Denver 21
Cleveland 27 at Houston 34
Kansas City 38 at San Diego 41
Pittsburgh 34 at New York Jets 7

National Football Conference
Chicago 19 at Minnesota 13
Green Bay 12 at Tampa Bay 9 (OT)
New Orleans 20 at Philadelphia 17 (OT)
Washington 31 at Dallas 10

Interconference Games
Atlanta 24 at Miami 31
Detroit 9 at Cincinnati 17
New England 21 at Los Angeles Rams 7
St Louis 34 at Los Angeles Raiders 24
San Francisco 23 at Buffalo 10
Seattle 17 at New York Giants 12

Interconference Play
AFC 26, NFC 24

Quarterback Terry Bradshaw made a brief return to active duty for Pittsburgh and reminded us of what we had been missing, by feathering a brace of touchdown passes to set the Steelers on the road to a resounding victory and, with it, the AFC Central division title. Sadly, the great man was forced to make an early exit, with a recurrence of his elbow injury, and would take no further part in the season. Denver was the only other team to reach the playoffs on this penultimate weekend, though it needed an astonishing comeback against the Colts, who entered the final quarter with a 19-0 lead. Just over ten minutes remained when John Elway fired off the first of his three touchdown passes, and the clock had wound down to 44 seconds before Gerald Willhite made the game-winning touchdown reception. Of the AFC's remaining playoff contenders, New England's victory set up their final-week encounter with the Seahawks, who stayed alive with a win over the Giants. However, both Cleveland and Buffalo, though neither team was yet eliminated, surrendered the initiative with losses to Houston and San Francisco respectively.

On the other side of the coin, the 49ers settled into the driving seat in the NFC Western division where, even so, all was to be decided on the final weekend when much would depend on the outcome of the Rams-Saints game. Detroit's loss and Green Bay's overtime win at Tampa Bay stirred things up in the NFC Central division though, with two regular season victories over the Packers, the Lions only needed to win their final game to take the division title. In fine style, the Redskins avenged their earlier loss to the Dallas Cowboys and, more importantly, were now in pole position to win the division title, together with its bonus of home-field advantage throughout the playoff series.

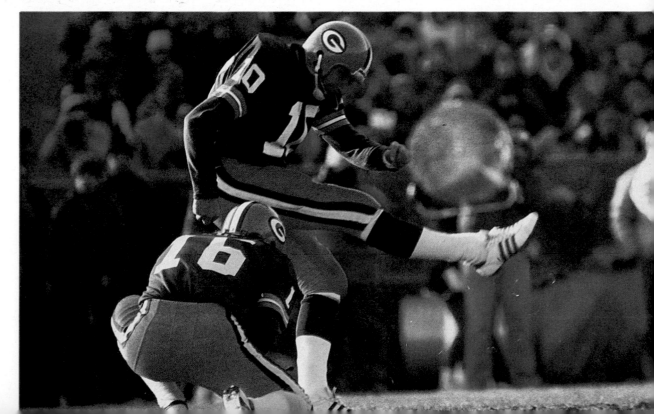

Outstanding Individual Performances

Jan Stenerud (Green Bay) kicked four field goals to establish a new NFL career record of 338.

William Andrews (Atlanta) rushed for 161 yards on 21 carries and scored one touchdown.

Mike Pruitt (Cleveland) rushed for 153 yards on 30 carries and scored three touchdowns.

Earl Campbell (Houston) rushed for 130 yards on 32 carries and scored one touchdown.

Matt Suhey (Chicago) rushed for 101 yards on 17 carries and *threw* a 74-yard touchdown pass.

Ottis Anderson (St Louis) rushed for 119 yards on 24 carries and scored one touchdown.

Carlos Carson (Kansas City) caught seven passes for 165 yards and scored one touchdown.

Kellen Winslow (San Diego) caught 14 passes for 162 yards and scored three touchdowns.

Tim Smith (Houston) caught seven passes for 150 yards and scored two touchdowns.

Johnny 'Lam' Jones (New York Jets) caught seven passes for 146 yards and scored one touchdown.

Bill Kenney (Kansas City) completed 31 of 41 passes for 411 yards and four touchdowns.

John Elway (Denver) completed 23 of 44 passes for 345 yards and three touchdowns.

◄ *Jan Stenerud* *Kellen Winslow*

STANDINGS

AFC East	W	L	T	PF	PA	NFC East	W	L	T	PF	PA
†*Miami	11	4	0	355	236	*Washington	13	2	0	510	310
Buffalo	8	7	0	269	320	*Dallas	12	3	0	462	318
New England	8	7	0	268	265	St Louis	7	7	1	343	421
N.Y. Jets	7	8	0	299	297	Philadelphia	5	10	0	226	291
Baltimore	6	9	0	244	344	N.Y. Giants	3	11	1	245	315
AFC Central						**NFC Central**					
†*Pittsburgh	10	5	0	338	273	Detroit	8	7	0	324	266
Cleveland	8	7	0	326	325	Green Bay	8	7	0	408	416
Cincinnati	7	8	0	332	282	Chicago	7	8	0	288	280
Houston	2	13	0	278	440	Minnesota	7	8	0	296	334
AFC West						Tampa Bay	2	13	0	221	357
†*L.A. Raiders	11	4	0	412	324	**NFC West**					
*Denver	9	6	0	285	279	San Francisco	9	6	0	390	276
Seattle	8	7	0	379	391	L.A. Rams	8	7	0	335	320
San Diego	6	9	0	344	432	New Orleans	8	7	0	295	311
Kansas City	5	10	0	338	350	Atlanta	6	9	0	339	375

† Division Champions
* Qualified for playoffs

WEEK SIXTEEN

American Football Conference
Denver 17 at Kansas City 48
Houston 10 at Baltimore 20
New England 6 at Seattle 24
New York Jets 14 at Miami 34
Pittsburgh 17 at Cleveland 30
San Diego 14 at Los Angeles Raiders 30

National Football Conference
Dallas 17 at San Francisco 42
Green Bay 21 at Chicago 23
Los Angeles Rams 26 at New Orleans 24
New York Giants 22 at Washington 31
Philadelphia 7 at St Louis 31
Tampa Bay 20 at Detroit 23

Interconference Games
Buffalo 14 at Atlanta 31
Cincinnati 14 at Minnesota 20

Interconference Play
AFC 26, NFC 26

Entering the final week of play, four AFC teams were in contention for the sole remaining wild card place in the playoffs. Buffalo, Cleveland and New England needed conditional wins. Cleveland needed a loss by Buffalo and New England to beat Seattle. New England had to beat Seattle and see Cleveland lose. Buffalo's fortunes lay in a loss by Cleveland and the unlikely event of a tie between New England and Seattle. Only the Seahawks were in control of their own destiny — for them, a win would do. In the NFC, five teams were competing for three places. Victories for Detroit and San Francisco would bring division titles and automatic entry to the playoffs. On the other hand, the Packers and the Rams had to win and then cross their fingers. The Packers needed either a loss by Detroit or a victory by the Rams. The Rams' only hope lay in beating the Saints, coupled with a loss by the Packers. The Saints had simply to beat the Rams.

In the event, Cleveland did win and Buffalo obliged them by losing to Atlanta but the Seahawks settled things by beating New England, later in the day. As it turned out Detroit and San Francisco were assured of playoff spots before they took to the field for, earlier in the day, both Green Bay and New Orleans had suffered heartbreaking last-minute defeats. The Packers went out to a field goal by Chicago's Bob Thomas with only ten seconds of the game remaining. New Orleans, however, seemed certain winners when, with just over one minute to go, they had the Rams pinned down on their own 20-yard line. But the Rams' quarterback,

Vince Ferragamo, completed six of seven quick passes, to set up Mike Lansford's 42-yard field goal with six seconds to spare. Detroit went on to beat Tampa Bay and later, on Monday evening, San Francisco pounded the lethargic Cowboys to take the NFC Western division title.

Outstanding Individual Performances

Ali Haji-Sheikh (New York Giants) kicked five field goals to establish an NFL single season record of 35.

William Andrews (Atlanta) rushed for 158 yards on 28 carries and scored two touchdowns.

Ottis Anderson (St Louis) rushed for 156 yards on 23 carries and scored one touchdown.

Walter Payton (Chicago) rushed for 148 yards on 30 carries.

George Rogers (New Orleans) rushed for 124 yards on 32 carries.

John Riggins (Washington) rushed for 122 yards on 30 carries and scored one touchdown.

Todd Christensen (Los Angeles Raiders) caught eight passes for 136 yards.

Steve Largent (Seattle) caught seven passes for 133 yards and scored one touchdown.

Byron Williams (New York Giants) caught eight passes for 124 yards.

Paul Coffman (Green Bay) caught four passes for 122 yards and scored one touchdown.

Brian Sipe (Cleveland) completed 14 of 22 passes for 199 yards and four touchdowns.

Tim Smith (Houston)
caught 8 passes for 69 yards.

Steve Largent

STANDINGS

AFC East	W	L	T	PF	PA	NFC East	W	L	T	PF	PA
†Miami	12	4	0	389	250	†Washington	14	2	0	541	333
New England	8	8	0	274	289	*Dallas	12	4	0	479	360
Buffalo	8	8	0	283	351	St Louis	8	7	1	374	428
Baltimore	7	9	0	313	331	Philadelphia	5	11	0	233	322
N.Y. Jets	7	9	0	264	354	N.Y. Giants	3	12	1	267	347
AFC Central						**NFC Central**					
†Pittsburgh	10	6	0	355	303	†Detroit	9	7	0	347	286
Cleveland	9	7	0	356	342	Green Bay	8	8	0	429	439
Cincinnati	7	9	0	346	302	Chicago	8	8	0	311	301
Houston	2	14	0	288	460	Minnesota	8	8	0	316	348
AFC West						Tampa Bay	2	14	0	241	380
†L.A. Raiders	12	4	0	442	338	**NFC West**					
*Seattle	9	7	0	403	397	†San Francisco	10	6	0	432	293
*Denver	9	7	0	302	327	*L.A. Rams	9	7	0	361	344
San Diego	6	10	0	358	462	New Orleans	8	8	0	319	337
Kansas City	6	10	0	386	367	Atlanta	7	9	0	370	389

† Division Champions
* Wild Card

WEEK SEVENTEEN —
WILD CARD WEEKEND

AFC Denver 7 at Seattle 31

When one team plays near flawless football and the other commits turnovers (fumbles and interceptions) when in scoring positions, the result is a virtual certainty. Such was the case in the Kingdome where, twice in the first half, Denver gave up the ball in the shadow of the Seahawks' goal posts. The first crucial turnover, on an interception by Seahawks cornerback Kerry Justin, led to Norm Johnson's 37-yard field goal, and the second, a fumble by Denver running back Gerald Willhite at the Seattle 4-yard line, meant that the Broncos again came away empty-handed. Even so, the teams went into the half-time break with Seattle leading only by a slender margin, 10-7. But then came the flawless football. Quarterback Dave Krieg, having his best game of the season, finished off Seattle's first drive of the second half with a touchdown pass to tight end Pete Metzelaars, breaking open what until then had been a close game. The Seahawks' defense then showed that it had learned the lessons of week twelve (they were beaten 38-27 by Denver) and firmed up to stifle the DeBerg — Watson passing threat. A fourth-quarter touchdown pass, to wide receiver Paul Johns, increased Seattle's lead to 24-7 and David Hughes's two-yard touchdown run put the result beyond doubt.

NFC Los Angeles Rams 24 at Dallas 17

A fumbled punt and three interceptions were to prove costly at Texas Stadium, where the Los Angeles Rams earned the dubious privilege of progressing to meet Washington in the subsequent NFC Divisional playoff game. As usual, the Cowboys fell behind, 0-7, and took some time to regroup before mounting a 70-yard drive to tie the scores at 7-7 going into half-time. Ominously, they took a 10-7 lead on Rafael Septien's 41-yard field goal and were on the point of re-establishing possession, after having held the Rams to less than ten yards on three downs. But Gary Allen fumbled the resulting punt and the Rams regained possession on the Dallas 16-yard line, from where quarterback Vince Ferragamo needed only one pass for the touchdown which took them into a 14-10 lead. Again the Cowboys drove down the field only to be halted by Jim Collins' interception on the Rams 43-yard line. Once more Ferragamo completed the return march with a touchdown pass, to give the Rams a 21-10 cushion. Still the Cowboys were not done and, this time, had

penetrated to the Rams' 23-yard line before LeRoy Irvin picked off a Danny White pass and scampered 94 yards to set up Mike Lansford's field goal, stretching the lead to 24-10. A late Dallas touchdown merely salvaged a little dignity.

Outstanding Individual Performances

Eric Dickerson (Los Angeles Rams) rushed for 99 yards on 23 carries.

Curt Warner (Seattle) rushed for 99 yards on 23 carries.

Tony Hill (Dallas) caught nine passes for 115 yards and scored one touchdown.

Dave Krieg (Seattle) completed 12 of 13 passes for 200 yards and three touchdowns.

Vince Ferragamo (Los Angeles Rams) completed 15 of 30 passes for 162 yards and three touchdowns.

LeRoy Irvin (Los Angeles Rams) returned an interception 94 yards.

Eric Dickerson ▼   *Dave Krieg* ►

WEEK EIGHTEEN —
DIVISIONAL PLAYOFFS
American Football Conference

Seattle 27 at Miami 20

It was no surprise when the Miami Dolphins began their bid for a repeat appearance in the Super Bowl, by driving 80 yards for the opening touchdown and, at the time, a missed extra point attempt seemed not so serious. However, Zachary Dixon returned the subsequent kickoff 59 yards and, six plays later, the Seahawks were leading 7-6 on Cullen Bryant's 6-yard touchdown reception. Nonetheless, after having dominated for the greater part, the Dolphins went into halftime with a 13-7 lead. Yet this was a Seattle team which had twice beaten the mighty Los Angeles Raiders and, now showing little respect for the much-vaunted Dolphins defense, they fought back into the lead with a touchdown by Curt Warner. One point became four points of daylight after Norm Johnson's fourth-quarter field goal and then, just when the Seahawks fans might have considered cautiously uncrossing their fingers, apparent disaster struck. A Dave Krieg pass was intercepted and returned to the Seattle 16-yard line, from where the Dolphins needed only three plays to go ahead, 20-17. But the Seahawks would not stay down. Curt Warner's second touchdown, completing a five-play 66-yard drive, restored their lead at 24-20, and Johnson's second field goal, in between two Miami fumbles, brought Seattle a deserved 27-20 victory. For the first time in their eight-year history, the Seahawks were off to the AFC Championship Game.

Curt Warner

◄ *John Riggins*

Pittsburgh 10 at Los Angeles Raiders 38

For just the few opening minutes, it might have been the Steelers of old who slashed 78 yards through the Raiders defense, to leave themselves on fourth down with only two inches to go for a touchdown. Yet, surprisingly, Steeler head coach Chuck Noll ignored the option of going for the morale-boosting touchdown and, instead, took the easy three-point field goal. Hardly believing their luck, the Raiders then went to town. Marcus Allen ran riot and quarterback Jim Plunkett approached perfection, directing an offense which rattled up 31 points without any semblance of a reply. When it did come, on a 58-yard touchdown reception by John Stallworth, the game had long since ceased to be a contest. Even then, the Raiders had the last say with a Frank Hawkins touchdown to make the score, at 38-10, a true reflection of their superiority.

National Football Conference

Los Angeles Rams 7 at Washington 51

'We had a hot day,' said head coach Joe Gibbs, after his Redskins had trampled the Rams, 51-7, to stroll serenely into the NFC Championship Game.

John Riggins warmed up for the 49ers with three touchdowns; Art Monk caught passes for two more and cornerback Darrell Green returned an interception 72 yards, to complete a six-touchdown romp. Revelling in the protection afforded by his enormous offensive line, Joe Theismann was at his best and passed for 302 yards, 171 of which were to 'Downtown' Charlie Brown. By contrast, Rams running back Eric Dickerson was held to only 16 yards rushing on ten carries and Vince Ferragamo, who completed fewer than half of his passes, was sacked three times and threw three interceptions.

Detroit 23 at San Francisco 24

In a game which came to life only after three quarters, the 49ers scraped through to their second NFC Championship Game in three years when Detroit's Eddie Murray missed a 43-yard field goal, with only eleven seconds to go. Despite the fact that quarterback Gary Danielson had thrown five pass interceptions, Detroit entered the final quarter still within striking distance, 9-17 down. Undaunted, Danielson completed three key passes in a 73-yard drive which was finished off by Billy Sims' 11-yard touchdown run. Again it was Sims who put Detroit into the lead, 23-17, after a Joe Montana pass had been intercepted and returned to the San Francisco 26-yard line. But then it was Montana's turn to redeem himself, as he completed six consecutive passes, the last one to Freddie Solomon in the end zone, to regain the lead at 24-23. Only one minute and 23 seconds remained when the Lions embarked on their final drive which placed them on the San Francisco 25-yard line with the clock showing eleven seconds. But poor Murray, who had earlier set an NFL playoff record with a successful attempt from 54 yards out, fluffed the kick, sending the 49ers on to Washington and the Lions back home to Detroit.

Outstanding Individual Performances

Marcus Allen (Los Angeles Raiders) rushed for 121 yards on 13 carries and scored two touchdowns.

John Riggins (Washington) rushed for 119 yards on 25 carries and scored three touchdowns.

Billy Sims (Detroit) rushed for 114 yards on 20 carries and scored two touchdowns.

Curt Warner (Seattle) rushed for 113 yards on 29 carries and scored two touchdowns.

Charlie Brown (Washington) caught six passes for 171 yards.

Mark Duper (Miami) caught nine passes for 117 yards and scored one touchdown.

WEEK NINETEEN – CONFERENCE CHAMPIONSHIPS
National Football Conference

San Francisco 21 at Washington 24

For three-quarters of the National Football Conference Championship Game, it was business as usual in Washington, where the Redskins gave notice of their intention of holding on to their NFL title with a comprehensive dominance of San Francisco. Twice John Riggins had blasted into the end zone, and Joe Theismann had connected with wide receiver Charlie Brown on a touchdown play covering 70 yards. Entering the final quarter with a 21-0 lead, the Redskins had no cause for concern when a display of 49er defiance moved the ball 79 yards, ending with Mike Wilson's touchdown, to open San Francisco's account. Mark Moseley's subsequent failure on a field goal attempt was hardly a tragedy, since the 49ers would have to restart from their 24-yard line. But, one play later, the alarm bells were ringing. Joe Montana had burned the Redskins secondary with a 76-yard touchdown bomb to Freddie Solomon, bringing the 49ers to within seven points. Quite suddenly, the Redskins were looking human and thoughts turned to week one of the regular season, when they had 'blown' a 23-3 lead over Dallas. Just over two minutes later, they were in a condition of 'red alert'. The 49ers had needed only four plays to complete a stunning comeback to tie the scores with Mike Wilson's second touchdown reception. But that was to be their lot for the day. The reigning Super Bowl Champions regrouped and drove systematically down the field to establish position for Mark Moseley's 25-yard field goal attempt. Unlike his four previous efforts, this one split the uprights and, with just 40 seconds to go, there would be no 49er reply.

American Football Conference

Seattle 14 at Los Angeles Raiders 30

For the Seattle Seahawks, the season came to a very abrupt end in the Los Angeles Coliseum, where the Raiders mounted a show of awesome offense and overpowering defense to sweep into Super Bowl XVIII. Young Seahawks quarterback Dave Krieg completed just three of nine passes and had been intercepted three times before being replaced by Jim Zorn in the third quarter. Rookie sensation Curt Warner was similarly ineffective, rushing for a mere 26 yards on eleven carries. Only towards the end of the third period did Seattle establish any consistency, driving 74 yards in ten

plays for their opening score, an 11-yard touchdown reception by Dan Doornink. But by then, the Raiders had scored 27 points to which three more would shortly be added with a Chris Bahr field goal. Marcus Allen, meanwhile, was relaxing after having rushed for 154 yards as his contribution to an offensive total of 401 yards, compared with the Seahawks' 167. Five pass interceptions and four quarterback sacks, all registered by the 'Silver and Black', told the story of a defense whose only acts of generosity came late in the game, when thoughts were focussed on a fourth Raiders Super Bowl appearance. The final word on an outstanding team effort came from defeated head coach Chuck Knox, who reflected: 'They have excellent personnel and they're well-coached. I think that the Raiders are capable of giving the Washington Redskins all they want...'

Outstanding Individual Performances

Marcus Allen (Los Angeles Raiders) rushed for 154 yards on 25 carries.

John Riggins (Washington) rushed for 123 yards on 36 carries and scored two touchdowns.

Charlie Brown (Washington) caught five passes for 137 yards including a 70-yard touchdown.

Malcolm Barnwell (Los Angeles Raiders) caught five passes for 116 yards.

Joe Montana (San Francisco) completed 27 of 48 passes for 347 yards and three touchdowns.

Charlie Brown

Frank Hawkins

SUPER BOWL XVIII

Los Angeles Raiders v Washington Redskins

Tampa, Florida, January 22nd, 1984

The Redskins had ended the regular season with the NFC's best ever won-lost record of 14-2 (both their losses were by one-point margins) and, including past and subsequent playoff victories, entered Super Bowl XVIII having lost only three out of their last 34 games. With 24 rushing touchdowns, John Riggins had set NFL records, both in this category and in the one which combines rushing and pass receiving, surpassing the previous marks of 19 and 23 respectively. More importantly, and in character, the foot-slogging infantryman of the regular season had become the stormtrooper of the playoffs. Kicker Mark Moseley, too, had entered the record book with 161 of his team's 541 regular season points, the latter establishing yet another NFL record. The ebullient Joe Theismann was at his superb best, connecting with his big-play wide receiver, 'Downtown' Charlie Brown, and the silky-smooth Art Monk, in a passing offense which was no less spectacular for its metronomic regularity. On defense, only Mat Mendenhall was absent from the forward group of seven (linemen and linebackers) which started in Super Bowl XVII. They had mounted a charge which led to 51 quarterback sacks and ranked number one in the NFL against the rushing offense, yielding, on average, only 80·6 yards per game. Their defensive secondary however, was less secure and relied heavily on the experience of free safety Mark Murphy and the raw speed of cornerback Darrell Green.

The Raiders had eased into the season with four comfortable wins, including the valuable scalp of Miami, before losing their own to the Redskins. There followed a shaky period, throughout which they were not helped by niggling injuries which slowed down several key players, such as Marcus Allen, Cliff Branch, Matt Millen and Ted Hendricks. There had been uncertainty at quarterback, too, where Jim Plunkett lost both his form and his starting place to Marc Wilson. It was during this time that they were defeated twice by Seattle but, equally, they (just about) handled the Cowboys and won four crucial nail-biters. By playoff time, however, they were ready to take on all-comers and dismissed their AFC challengers with consummate ease. Jim Plunkett was back at the controls, Marcus Allen had rediscovered the electrifying form of his rookie year, Cliff Branch had that characteristic bounce in his step and Matt Millen was once again breathing fire. Moreover the All Pro cornerback, Mike Haynes, had been acquired from New England to join All Pro Lester Hayes, Pro Bowler Vann McElroy and Mike Davis in what was now the NFL's best defensive secondary. But could even their best efforts keep the likes of Theismann, Brown and Monk quiet? And how does anybody stop John Riggins in the playoffs?

One thing was for certain — there was universal agreement that Super Bowl XVIII brought together the two finest teams in football.

The Vince Lombardi Trophy

THE GAME

Scoring By Quarters

1st Quarter
Los Angeles: Derrick Jensen, recovery of a blocked punt in the end zone; Bahr kick with 10:08 remaining.
Los Angeles 7 — Washington 0

2nd Quarter
Los Angeles: Cliff Branch, 12-yard pass from Plunkett; Bahr kick with 9:14 remaining.
Los Angeles 14 — Washington 0
Washington: Mark Moseley, 24-yard field goal with 3:05 remaining.
Los Angeles 14 — Washington 3
Los Angeles: Jack Squirek, 5-yard pass interception return; Bahr kick with 0:07 remaining.
Los Angeles 21 — Washington 3

3rd Quarter
Washington: John Riggins, 1-yard run; Moseley's kick blocked with 10:56 remaining.
Los Angeles 21 — Washington 9
Los Angeles: Marcus Allen, 5-yard run; Bahr kick with 7:06 remaining.
Los Angeles 28 — Washington 9
Los Angeles: Marcus Allen, 74-yard run; Bahr kick with 0:00 remaining.
Los Angeles 35 — Washington 9

4th Quarter
Los Angeles: Chris Bahr, 21-yard field goal with 2:24 remaining.
Los Angeles 38 — Washington 9

Even before the fateful Washington punt which led to the first score, the Raiders defense had already announced its presence. John Riggins had been made to work hard to gain ten yards on his first three carries and, on three subsequent plays, Mike Haynes had unilaterally imposed a close-season on pass receiving. Seconds later, a poor block by Otis Wonsley allowed Derrick Jensen through to charge down Jeff Hayes's punt and recover the ball in the end zone. (A similar disaster for the Raiders was averted when their punter, Ray Guy, made a spectacular one-handed catch in the second quarter.) Cliff Branch's touchdown reception in the second quarter was a classic demonstration of the art by the old master. In perfect unison with the movements of his co-wide receiver, Malcolm Barnwell, he went to work on cornerback Anthony Washington, feigning a move to the outside before slanting inside to make the reception unopposed. Mark Moseley's 24-yard field goal brought the Redskins to within eleven points and it was a not unacceptable deficit that they appeared to be taking into half-time when Joe Theismann, operating from his own 12-yard line, dropped back to pass on a play which had worked against the Raiders during the regular season. But his gentle floater was picked off and returned into the end zone by Jack Squirek, who had anticipated that very possibility.

It was a more decisive Washington which opened the second half with a 70-yard drive, completed by John Riggins' 1-yard smash for their first touchdown. Yet, somehow, their special team

Marcus Allen

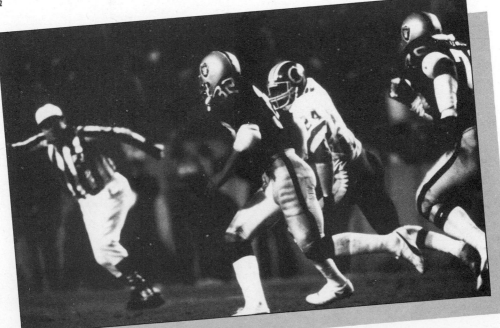

Joe Washington (25) in trouble

Joe Theismann (7) going down

Opening Scene at Super Bowl XVIII ▶

managed to make a hash of the extra point attempt and, four minutes later, the Raiders had dismissed any suggestion of a Redskins comeback. Aided by a pass interference ruling, the Raiders drove 70 yards for Marcus Allen's first touchdown, which he scored with a wicked sidestep to leave three defenders banging helmets. Allen's second, putting the result beyond doubt, covered 74 yards (as the crow flies) but was closer to 100 yards when his tour of the Raiders backfield was taken into account. Intending to sweep left but seeing the way barred, he reversed field before knifing through an inviting gap up the middle and on into the distant end zone. Chris Bahr's field goal completed a day

on which (almost) everything went right for the Raiders.

Even in defeat, however, the 1983 Washington Redskins will endure as one of the best teams in the history of the NFL. And by that measure, just how good were the 1983 Los Angeles Raiders?

Outstanding Individual Performances

Marcus Allen (Los Angeles Raiders), who was voted the game's Most Valuable Player, rushed for 191 yards on 20 carries and scored two touchdowns.

Cliff Branch (Los Angeles Raiders) caught six passes for 94 yards and scored one touchdown.

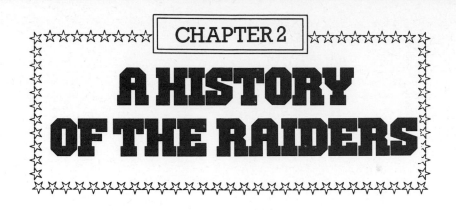

CHAPTER 2

A HISTORY OF THE RAIDERS

In the summer of 1959, the twelve-team National Football League was a prosperous, highly-tuned organization which could look forward to its fortieth season with unqualified optimism. Its treasure chest of memories overflowed with the legendary exploits of great players and teams. The Chicago Bears had already gained seven NFL Championships and, for the Green Bay Packers, Vince Lombardi was founding, arguably, a third dynasty which would swell their haul of six to eleven by the end of 1967. There had been many 'greatest games ever played', the most recent of which was Baltimore's dramatic sudden-death overtime victory over the New York Giants in the 1958 NFL Championship Game, watched by a television audience of 50,000,000 people. (It is widely accepted that, more than any other, it was this game which brought pro football home to the American public.) The League had, too, fought off the challenges from rival organizations on four separate occasions, always emerging essentially unscathed and even enriched when, following the collapse of the All America Football Conference in 1949, they had opened their doors to the Cleveland Browns and the San Francisco 49ers. (A third team, the Baltimore Colts, folded in 1950. The current team of the same name, which joined the NFL in 1953, was an entirely different outfit.)

It was, then, a daunting prospect faced by Lamar Hunt, when he founded and organized the six-team American Football League in August, 1959. Joining Hunt's Dallas Texans (they are now known as the Kansas City Chiefs) were teams from Denver, Houston, Los Angeles (later of San Diego), Minneapolis-St Paul and New York city. Buffalo and Boston appeared shortly afterwards, but the membership fell to seven when the Minneapolis-St Paul group sought entry into the NFL. It was then that Barron Hilton, owner of the far-flung Los Angeles Chargers and who was anxious to establish some 'local' competition, urged that the AFL place a franchise on the West Coast. His views were shared by AFL Commissioner Joe Foss and accordingly, on 30 January 1960, a team representing the city of Oakland, California, belatedly made up the numbers. And for three seasons, that's about all they did. Certainly, their opening 6-8-0 record looks respectable enough but, outside of a 14-13 upset victory over the eventual AFL Champion Houston Oilers, they were generally outclassed. In 1961 they slumped to 2-12-0 and, a year later, avoided the ultimate indignity only by winning on the final weekend.

Yet such a disappointing start was hardly surprising. By the time they joined the league, the AFL

Al Davis

Jim Otto

player draft had taken place and the best available talent had been creamed off. Oakland formed its initial squad by picking from the rosters of the other seven teams which, of course, were able to protect their best players. One refers to the team as 'Oakland' because they hadn't yet arrived at a nickname. They considered the 'Señors' and even the 'Dons' (both names reflecting the Spanish traditions of the area) before settling for the 'Raiders'. They had no stadium of their own and were obliged to cross the Oakland Bay Bridge into San Francisco, where they shared Kezar Stadium with the glamorous 49ers of the NFL. However, whereas the 49ers attracted an average of over 52,000 fans per game, the Raiders' total for their seven 'home' games was a mere 53,537. The figure did not improve when they moved to Candlestick Park (still in San Francisco) in 1961 and, at the end of a season when the financial deficit had risen to $1,000,000, only Ed McGah and Wayne Valley remained of the original eight-man syndicate of owners. Nevertheless, by the beginning of the 1962 season, there were signs of a change for the better. The city of Oakland was considering building an NFL-sized stadium and the Raiders had found an interim home on their own side of the bridge. Frank Youell Field was nothing more than a small high school facility and seated only 20,000 yet, despite the Raiders' poor playing performance, the average attendance rose from the 7,655 of 1961 to almost eleven thousand. The citizens of Oakland were warming to their team.

By now, the fans would have recognised at least a few players of some quality. Indeed, center Jim Otto was a future member of the Pro Football Hall of Fame, Wayne Hawkins was a dependable guard and Clem Daniels was emerging as one of the AFL's better running backs. Their original quarterback, a young Tom Flores (he is now the Raiders' head coach), rated highly though, in 1962, an extended illness threatened to end his brief career. Even so, the roster as a whole was still very weak and, of equal significance, the team were without a head coach. In turn, Eddie Erdelatz, Marty Feldman (no jokes please) and Bill 'Red' Conkright, had tried and failed. But the solution to this and, as it turned out, all the other problems, was just around the corner. In January 1963, Al Davis arrived to take control. A former assistant coach with the Chargers, the 33-year old Davis was already widely acknowledged as a coaching genius, but it was as an autocrat that he set about restructuring the club from top to bottom. Then it was Davis the charmer who won over a cynical press and, most important of all, Davis the inspirational leader who gave his players a reason for believing in themselves. He was also quite a fair horse trader, acquiring wide receiver Art Powell, formerly of the New York Titans (they were later known as the Jets), and middle linebacker Archie Matsos from the Buffalo Bills. It was Davis who changed the team colours from gold and black to silver and black. With a healthy Tom Flores resuming at quarterback, the Raiders powered to a 10-4-0 record, winning both games against the eventual AFL Champion San Diego Chargers, yet falling short of the playoffs by one game.

AFL Final Standings — 1963
Eastern Division

	W	L	T
Boston Patriots	7	6	1
Buffalo Bills	7	6	1
Houston Oilers	6	8	0
New York Jets	5	8	1

Western Division

	W	L	T
San Diego Chargers	11	3	0
Oakland Raiders	10	4	0
Kansas City Chiefs	5	7	2
Denver Broncos	2	11	1

AFL Championship Game:
San Diego 51 — Boston 10

Fred Biletnikoff

For three subsequent years, the Raiders were competitive but so too were both the Chargers and the Chiefs who, between them, won the first seven Western Division Championships. It was a period in which Davis revealed his ability to handle what some people might call 'high spirited lads' who had been unable to settle with other teams. Defensive ends Ben Davidson, formerly of Green Bay and Washington, and Ike Lassiter of the Broncos, were two such players. In addition, Davis was building from the collegiate draft. Defensive back Kent McCloughan, linebacker Gus Otto and the tackles, Harry Schuh and Bob Svihus, joined a squad which was beginning to look as threatening as its uniform. Fred Biletnikoff, a rookie in 1965, was perhaps not the fastest player of all time, but he wore the 'Silver and Black' with honour and left the game, after fourteen seasons, as the fourth most productive wide receiver (in terms of passes caught), and awaits his invitation to enter the Pro Football Hall Of Fame. If the Raiders squad was not yet complete, their new stadium was and, in 1966, they moved into the 54,000-seat Oakland-Alameda County Coliseum.

For a short time in this same year, Davis left the club to succeed Joe Foss as AFL Commissioner but, following the AFL-NFL merger agreement which took place in June, he returned to the Raiders as Managing General Partner. John Rauch, who had taken over as head coach, retained his appointment, leaving Davis free for his executive duties and, of course, to keep an eye on the market place. In 1967, he made what appeared to be a surprising trade, dealing Flores and Powell to Buffalo in exchange for wide receiver Glenn Bass and an exciting young quarterback, Daryle Lamonica. Wide receiver Bill Miller came from the same source. Not yet done, he acquired cornerback Willie Brown from Denver, and the 39-year-old quarterback-kicker, George Blanda, many of whose greatest moments were yet to come. Both Brown and Blanda are now enshrined in the Pro Football Hall Of Fame. In the 1967 season, Blanda was the AFL leading scorer, with 20 field goals and 56 extra points. Lamonica was the leading passer, and was subsequently voted the AFL Player of The Year. The Raiders were unstoppable and swept to their first Western division title, with a 13-1-0 record, before thrashing the Oilers, 40-7, in the AFL Championship Game to earn the right to represent the AFL in Super Bowl II. Here, though, they were comfortably beaten, 33-14, by the NFL's Green Bay Packers. It had been a disappointing end to the season, but they were the Champions of the AFL, and from now on would always be the team to beat.

The Raiders continued in the same vein throughout the 1968 season but could never quite shake off the Kansas City Chiefs and, at the end of the regular season, the two were tied for the Western division title — there would have to be a divisional playoff. By now, the Raiders and the Chiefs had built up a rivalry of some proportions, from which their respective fans were not to be excluded. Each team had beaten the other during the regular season and a close game was expected. However, that probability was dismissed in the first quarter, when the Raiders scored 21 points before coasting to an easy 41-6 victory. Once again, the Raiders were in the AFL Championship Game, where they would face quarterback Joe Namath and his New York Jets. Earlier in the regular season, they had played each other in the celebrated 'Heidi Game', remembered not least by the NBC Television network controller. The Jets were leading, 32-29, with only one minute and five seconds of the game remaining when, thinking that the game was as good as over, NBC switched to their showing of 'Heidi', a story for children. But the Raiders came back with two late touchdowns to score a dramatic

Daryle 'The Mad Bomber' Lamonica

43-32 victory, the best part of which was missed by many millions of irate viewers. NBC were left with their red faces and a jammed switchboard. In the Championship Game however, it was the Jets who came from behind and then held on to win a 27-23 thriller.

There were changes at the top in 1969, when the 32-year old John Madden succeeded John Rauch, becoming pro football's youngest head coach. It was a year in which quarterback Lamonica well and truly endorsed his nickname 'The Mad Bomber', teaming up with Fred Biletnikoff and a sensational young wide receiver, Warren Wells (Wells caught 47 passes at the astonishing average of 26·8 yards per reception). This time, the Raiders edged the Chiefs out of first place by one game though, under the AFL's new format, both teams progressed to the playoffs. Whilst the Chiefs had to travel to New York city to play the Jets, the Raiders hosted the Eastern division runners up, the Houston Oilers. For the Oilers the game turned out to be an experience which they would not wish to repeat. Lamonica, who had thrown six touchdown passes (in one half) against Buffalo in the regular season, repeated the dose (though he spread them out a bit) in a 56-7 blowout over the luckless Oilers. Once again, the Raiders would meet their arch rivals, the Chiefs, who had scored a close 13-6 victory over the Jets. It was a Championship Game in which the Raiders never really got going. Wells was unable to play and, in the early going, Lamonica suffered an injury to his hand. However, the teams were level, 7-7, midway in the third quarter, and the Chiefs were in big trouble at 3rd and 14 on their own 2-yard line. But quarterback Len Dawson expertly evaded the Raiders rush, in his own end zone, before drilling a 35-yard pass to Otis Taylor, whose never-to-be-forgotten reception sparked a 98-yard touchdown drive. Lamonica was subsequently intercepted three times to complete a miserable day for the Raiders, who limped off on the wrong end of a 17-7 score. To rub salt into the wound, the Chiefs went on to victory over the Vikings in Super Bowl IV.

Following this latest disappointment, the Raiders were some way short of being the overpowering regular season force in 1970, when they played in the AFC Western division of the expanded National Football League. Certainly, Lamonica was the AFC leading passer and Hewritt Dixon came third in the AFC list of leading rushers but, for a five-game period, they were kept afloat only by the veteran skills of the evergreen George Blanda, whose last-minute heroics attracted the attentions of a nation. He threw two touchdown passes in their

John Madden

three points. However the Colts, too, had their master practitioner, the fabled Johnny Unitas no less, and it was the great man's 68-yard touchdown pass to Ray Perkins which extended their lead to a game-winning ten points.

Well into the 1971 season, the Raiders were on course for a fifth consecutive Western division title, with a record of 7-1-2 after ten weeks, but they won only one of the remaining four games and gave way to the Chiefs. Lamonica had slipped a little but Biletnikoff was the AFC leading receiver and, with the senior running backs injured, Marv Hubbard staked his claim for a starting place. The end of the 1972 regular season, however, found them back on top of the division. The Chiefs meanwhile were just beginning to lapse into a decline from which they have yet to emerge. Several exciting new players were breaking into the starting lineup, particularly on defense. Otis Sistrunk, Art Thoms and Tony Cline were on the defensive line; Phil Villapiano and Gerald Irons were notoriously strong tacklers at linebacker and, behind them, Jack 'Monster Man' Tatum was no less formidable than George Atkinson and Willie Brown in the defensive secondary. Fred Biletnikoff was again the AFC leading receiver; Lamonica had reproduced his old form to come second in the AFC list of leading passers and, for the second year in a row, Hubbard was the third leading AFC rusher. They must have fancied their chances in the opening playoff game against Pittsburgh. Indeed, with only seconds to play, they were leading, 7-6, and had the Steelers in a hopeless position at 4th down and miles to go on their own 40-yard line. The Steelers' owner, Art Rooney, had even begun making his way to the locker room to commiserate with his lads. But Terry Bradshaw's desperation pass to John 'Frenchy' Fuqua was tipped and, it was argued, touched Jack Tatum before falling into the arms of running back Franco Harris, who ran the remaining 42 yards for the winning touchdown. The legality of the pass reception hinged on Tatum having touched the ball and, even though he denies it to this day, the officials ruled that he had made contact. Harris had won the game with what forever will be known as 'The Immaculate Reception'.

The 1972 playoff game marked the beginning of the AFC's most bitterly contested rivalry. For the next four seasons, the Raiders won the Western division title almost as of right and, each year, came up against the Steelers in the playoffs (there had also been a few regular season battles). In 1973, the Raiders gained revenge with a 33-14 victory in the divisional playoff game only to lose, 27-10, to Miami in the AFC Championship Game. The following year, they met in the AFC Championship Game,

31-14 victory over Pittsburgh and went on to kick a 48-yard goal, with only three seconds left, to earn a 17-17 tie with Kansas City. It couldn't happen a third time but it did, again with three seconds remaining, when he kicked a 52-yard field goal to bring a 23-20 victory over Cleveland. It was no surprise, the following week, when he took over at quarterback to ignite a comeback which saw the Raiders beat Denver, 24-19. Finally, he kicked a 19-yard field goal, as usual with four seconds to go, to beat San Diego by the score of 20-17. Now the unchallenged leader of America's over-40s set, he had given the Raiders a slender lead which they just maintained to win the division title with an 8-4-2 record. In the divisional playoff game against an improving Miami team, the Raiders showed signs of a return to form, with Lamonica's 82-yard touchdown pass to wide receiver Rod Sherman providing the margin in a 21-14 win. For the fourth consecutive year, the Raiders were one victory away from a trip to the Super Bowl yet, for the third year in a row, they came away empty-handed. But they were not disgraced in a 27-17 loss to the Baltimore Colts. George Blanda replaced Lamonica in the second quarter and tied the scores at 10-10, with a 48-yard field goal and a 38-yard touchdown pass to Biletnikoff. With a fourth-quarter touchdown pass to Warren Wells, he brought the Raiders to within won 24-13 by the Steelers who went on to victory in Super Bowl IX. Again, in the AFC Championship Game of 1975, the Steelers came out on top, winning 16-10 on the way to retaining their Super Bowl Championship. However 1976 belonged to the Raiders, who finally went all the way. In the AFC Championship Game, the Steelers were without their starting running backs, Franco Harris and Rocky Bleier, and could make little progress against the Raiders defense, which was at its best. On the other hand, the Raiders offense generally outsmarted the 'Steel Curtain' and they ran out easy winners by the score of 24-7.

There were several new faces in the starting lineup which faced the Minnesota Vikings in Super Bowl XI. In contrast to Lamonica, whom he had

replaced in 1973, quarterback Ken 'The Snake' Stabler was a crafty, ice-cool, medium range passer, who would chip away at the margins of the opposing defense. Fred Biletnikoff had a new partner in wide receiver Cliff Branch, a sprinter of Olympic calibre. Dave Casper would be many an expert's tight end of the 1970s. Mark van Eeghen, Pete Banaszak and Clarence Davis were solid running backs who operated behind an awesome offensive line which featured the left-side domination of tackle Art Shell and guard Gene Upshaw. The defense was a demolition mob. One look from defensive left end John Matuszak (6ft 8in, 290 lb) could turn a man into stone, that is, if a glance from defensive right end Otis Sistrunk had not already done so. Ted 'Mad Stork' Hendricks had brought

George Blanda

his All Pro quality to the linebacking quartet and Alonzo 'Doctor Death' Thomas was another in the Atkinson-Tatum mold, playing alongside the classy Willie Brown in the defensive secondary.

The Vikings' best chance came late in the first quarter, when they blocked Ray Guy's punt and recovered the ball on the Raiders' 3-yard line. However, two plays later, the Raiders recovered Brent McClanahan's fumble and then drove 90 yards for Errol Mann's field goal. Touchdowns by Casper and Banaszak (the extra point was missed) and a further field goal gave the Raiders a 19-0 lead in the third quarter. The Vikings somehow regained consciousness and opened their account with a touchdown reception by Sammy White, but their slim hopes were dashed by further touchdowns from Banaszak and Willie Brown, the latter running 75 yards after intercepting Fran Tarkenton's pass. A Minnesota touchdown, with 25 seconds to go, was of no consequence and, by the score of 32-14, the Raiders were Champions of The World. Rushing for 137 yards on 16 carries, Clarence Davis had his best day as a pro but Fred Biletnikoff, two of whose four pass receptions

◄ *Jack 'Monster Man' Tatum*   *John Matuszak*

bordered on the miraculous, was voted the game's Most Valuable Player.

The Raiders came up against trouble from an unexpected source in 1977. They won the first four games with ease, extending their sequence of consecutive victories to 17, before being hammered, 30-7 by Denver, who intercepted Stabler seven times. The compliment was later returned but, at the end of the regular season, the Raiders trailed the Broncos by one game and had to settle for a Wild Card berth in the playoffs. Dave Casper caught three touchdown passes in an exciting 37-31 overtime victory over Baltimore, in a divisional playoff game which was seen as good preparation for the AFC Championship Game, when the Raiders would surely settle this matter with Denver. However, the Broncos were to have something to say about that. Their offense was no great shakes but their defense, nicknamed the 'Orange Crush', had conceded the fewest points in the AFC. Casper continued in prime form, catching two touchdown passes, but the Raiders could manage only 17 points in answer to Denver's 20 and joined the other 26 teams who did not win the Super Bowl.

Horror of horrors, for the next two years, the Raiders did not reach the playoffs. In 1978, even though they trailed Denver by only one game in the Western division, their 9-7-0 record was not good enough for a Wild Card spot and, in 1979, under new head coach Tom Flores, an identical record earned them only fourth place in the division. There had to be changes. Stabler was traded to Houston, in exchange for Dan Pastórini, and Dave Casper followed shortly afterwards. Kenny King, a former Houston player, joined Mark van Eeghen in the Raiders' backfield and wide receiver Bob Chandler arrived from Buffalo, determined to prove that he was still one of the best around. Hardly had Pastorini begun to settle in when he was injured against the Chiefs, in a loss which dropped the Raiders to a worrying 2-3 record after the first five weeks. There were even rumours of a morale problem in the clubhouse. It was then that yet another Al Davis reclamation project stepped in to take his chance.

Jim Plunkett was the 1970 Heisman Trophy winner and had been selected overall first by New England in the 1971 collegiate draft. Despite starting regularly, he never quite reached the heights expected of him and, after five years, he was traded to San Francisco. After two modest years he was discarded and, with his career apparently in tatters, must have been surprised when he was picked up by the Raiders, who needed a third-string quarterback. For two further years, he did little more than warm the substitutes'

bench, throwing only fifteen passes in total. Now in his tenth year as a pro, he was being given his last chance – and he took it. Under Plunkett's leadership, the Raiders won nine of their last eleven games to enter the playoffs as one of two AFC Wild Cards. Bob Chandler had been a revelation and Kenny King had turned out to be a more than useful all-purpose running back. In the Wild Card game, Houston were swept aside, 27-7. Stabler was sacked seven times, twice by cornerback Lester Hayes who also returned an interception for a touchdown. The divisional playoff game against Cleveland, when the temperature fell to −37°F, was a close one. Indeed, with the Browns within comfortable field goal range, late in the fourth quarter, the Raiders were on the point of being eliminated. But, inexplicably, quarterback Brian Sipe went for the end zone, where his pass was intercepted by safety Mike Davis to preserve a 14-12 victory. At San Diego in the AFC Championship Game, the Chargers fought back to within four points after trailing 28-7; however, with superb play mixing by Plunkett, the Raiders controlled the ball through virtually the whole of the last quarter to win, 34-27.

The Philadelphia Eagles came into Super Bowl XV as slight favourites, having beaten the Raiders, 10-7, in the regular season. However, they were the other team in what turned out to be a one-sided affair, won 27-10 by the Raiders. Eagles quarterback Ron 'The Polish Rifle' Jaworski was intercepted three times, all by linebacker Rod Martin. Mark van Eeghen rushed for 80 yards and Kenny King broke the Super Bowl record with a touchdown reception on play which covered 80 yards. Completing 13 of 21 passes for 261 yards and three touchdowns, Jim Plunkett was voted the game's Most Valuable Player and, for the second time, Al Davis could go out and order another batch of Super Bowl rings.

After this, 1981 was a letdown. Injuries to several key players exposed a shortage of reserve strength and, with a record of 7-9-0, the Raiders had their first losing season since 1964. Even Plunkett fell from grace and was replaced by Marc Wilson. However, the veteran signal caller was back at the controls in 1982, quarterbacking a team which had found a new home in Los Angeles. The injured players were restored to full fitness and rejoined a team which was strengthened by a new running

Rod Martin intercepts in Super Bowl XV

back star. Marcus Allen had won the Heisman Trophy at the University of Southern California but was regarded with scepticism by the pro scouts, and two other running backs had been taken before Davis picked him up, 10th in round one of the collegiate draft. He turned out to be the rookie sensation of the year, scoring 14 touchdowns to lead the entire NFL in the strike-shortened 9-game season. It looked as if the Raiders would do likewise when they led the AFC with an 8-1-0 record and had little trouble beating Cleveland, 27-10, in round one of the playoffs. But an untidy, hesitant performance was not good enough against the Jets and, with a 17-14 defeat, their season came to an end.

The story of 1983's epic campaign has been told in chapter one of this book. After establishing an early lead and then hanging on during mid-season, the Raiders dismantled Washington to win their third Super Bowl Championship and now trail only the Steelers, who have won four. The message for 1984 is short and sweet: 'Look out Pittsburgh, here come the Silver and Black.'

RAIDERS RECORD 1960-83

Year	Won	Lost	Tied	PF	PA	Postseason Losses
1960	6	8	0	319	388	
1961	2	12	0	237	458	
1962	1	13	0	213	370	
1963	10	4	0	363	288	
1964	5	7	2	303	350	
1965	8	5	1	298	239	
1966	8	5	1	315	288	
1967 (a)(b)	13	1	0	468	233	Green Bay 33 — Oakland 14: Super Bowl II
1968 (a)	12	2	0	453	233	N.Y. Jets 27 — Oakland 23: AFL Championship Game
1969 (a)	12	1	1	377	242	Kansas City 17 — Oakland 7: AFL Championship Game
1970 (c)	8	4	2	300	293	Baltimore 27 — Oakland 17: AFC Championship Game
1971	8	4	2	344	278	
1972 (c)	10	3	1	365	248	Pittsburgh 13 — Oakland 7: Divisional Playoff
1973 (c)	9	4	1	292	175	Miami 27 — Oakland 10: AFC Championship Game
1974 (c)	12	2	0	355	228	Pittsburgh 24 — Oakland 13: AFC Championship Game
1975 (c)	11	3	0	375	255	Pittsburgh 16 — Oakland 10: AFC Championship Game
1976 (c)(d)	13	1	0	350	237	
1977 (e)	11	3	0	351	230	Denver 20 — Oakland 17: AFC Championship Game
1978	9	7	0	311	283	
1979	9	7	0	365	337	
1980 (e)(d)	11	5	0	364	306	
1981	7	9	0	273	343	
1982 (f)	8	1	0	260	200	N.Y. Jets 17 — Los Angeles 14: Second Round Playoff
1983 (c)(d)	12	4	0	442	338	

(a) AFL Western Division Champion
(b) AFL Champion
(c) AFC Western Division Champion
(d) Super Bowl Champion
(e) AFC Wild Card
(f) Best regular season record, AFC.

Raiders Players in the Pro Football Hall Of Fame

George Blanda, Quarterback-Kicker (1967-75)
Willie Brown, Cornerback (1967-78)
Ron Mix, Tackle (1971)
Jim Otto, Center (1960-74)

Willie Brown

Tom Flores

CHAPTER 3

HOW THE SEASON WORKS

The National Football League consists of twenty-eight teams divided into two Conferences, the American Football Conference (AFC) and the National Football Conference (NFC). Each Conference has fourteen teams, and is subdivided into three unequal Divisions. These are essentially based on sensible geographical considerations but also take into account the traditional rivalries which were in existence when the expanded NFL was restructured in 1970. The teams are listed below in order of their final 1983 standings since, for those in a five-team division, this is of importance in arriving at a team's schedule (fixture list) for 1984.

AMERICAN FOOTBALL CONFERENCE

Eastern Division

	W	L	T
Miami	12	4	0
New England	8	8	0
Buffalo	8	8	0
Baltimore	7	9	0
New York Jets	7	9	0

Central Division

	W	L	T
Pittsburgh	10	6	0
Cleveland	9	7	0
Cincinnati	7	9	0
Houston	2	14	0

Western Division

	W	L	T
Los Angeles Raiders	12	4	0
*Seattle	9	7	0
*Denver	9	7	0
San Diego	6	10	0
Kansas City	6	10	0

NATIONAL FOOTBALL CONFERENCE

Eastern Division

	W	L	T
Washington	14	2	0
*Dallas	12	4	0
St Louis	8	7	1
Philadelphia	5	11	0
New York Giants	3	12	1

Central Division

	W	L	T
Detroit	9	7	0
Green Bay	8	8	0
Chicago	8	8	0
Minnesota	8	8	0
Tampa Bay	2	14	0

Western Division

	W	L	T
San Francisco	10	6	0
*Los Angeles Rams	9	7	0
New Orleans	8	8	0
Atlanta	7	9	0

*Wild Card qualifiers for the Playoffs

THE SCHEDULE

A team always plays twelve games against others from within its own Conference. Equally, all except the fifth-placed teams will play four games against teams from the rival Conference (they are known as interconference games), specifically to allow fans in the cities of one Conference the opportunity of seeing star players and teams of the other Conference. A team's schedule depends on whether it plays in a four-team or a five-team Division and, if the latter, on its final standing in that Division.

Four-Team Division

A typical 1984 schedule, e.g. for the Cincinnati Bengals, appears below. It is set out, deliberately not in chronological order, to emphasise that the schedule has a quite definite structure.

CINCINNATI BENGALS (AFC Central)

Cleveland Browns	AFC Central	Home
Cleveland Browns	AFC Central	Away
Houston Oilers	AFC Central	Home
Houston Oilers	AFC Central	Away
Pittsburgh Steelers	AFC Central	Home
Pittsburgh Steelers	AFC Central	Away
Buffalo Bills	AFC East	Home
New England Patriots	AFC East	Away
New York Jets	AFC East	Away
Kansas City Chiefs	AFC West	Home
Seattle Seahawks	AFC West	Home
Denver Broncos	AFC West	Away
Atlanta Falcons	NFC West	Home
Los Angeles Rams	NFC West	Home
New Orleans Saints	NFC West	Away
San Francisco 49ers	NFC West	Away

The Bengals will always play their division rivals, Cleveland, Houston and Pittsburgh, both home and away. The flavour of intra-conference competition is maintained by six games, every year, against teams from outside their Division but within their Conference. There will always be three games against the AFC East and three against the AFC West. Again, every year, there will be four games against teams from a particular Division of the rival Conference, based on a three-year cycle. In 1984, they play against the NFC West; in 1985 they will play teams from the NFC East and in 1986, the NFC Central. A complete list of opponents, other than those within a team's own division, is arrived at by applying the following formula. The letters and numbers refer to Conference, Division and final 1983 standing in that division. Thus, the Washington Redskins, who are in the National Conference, Eastern Division and finished first in that division, are identified as NE-1. Equally, the Kansas City Chiefs, who are in the American Conference, Western Division and finished 5th in that division, are identified by AW-5.

AFC EAST-AE

AE-1		AE-2		AE-3		AE-4		AE-5	
A	H	A	H	A	H	A	H	A	H
NE-1	NE-2	NE-2	NE-1	NE-1	NE-2	NE-2	NE-1	AC-2	AC-1
NE-3	NE-4	NE-4	NE-3	NE-3	NE-4	NE-4	NE-3	AC-4	AC-3
AC-1	AC-4	AC-2	AC-3	AC-3	AC-2	AC-4	AC-1	AW-5	AW-5
AW-4	AW-1	AW-3	AW-2	AW-2	AW-3	AW-1	AW-4	NC-5	NE-5

AFC CENTRAL-AC

AC-1		AC-2		AC-3		AC-4	
A	H	A	H	A	H	A	H
AE-5	AW-5	AW-5	AE-5	AE-5	AW-5	AW-5	AE-5
NW-1	NW-2	NW-2	NW-1	NW-1	NW-2	NW-2	NW-1
NW-3	NW-4	NW-4	NW-3	NW-3	NW-4	NW-4	NW-3
AE-4	AE-1	AE-3	AE-2	AE-2	AE-3	AE-1	AE-4
AW-1	AW-4	AW-2	AW-3	AW-3	AW-2	AW-4	AW-1

AFC WEST-AW

AW-1		AW-2		AW-3		AW-4		AW-5	
A	H	A	H	A	H	A	H	A	H
NC-1	NC-2	NC-2	NC-1	NC-1	NC-2	NC-2	NC-1	AC-1	AC-2
NC-3	NC-4	NC-4	NC-3	NC-3	NC-4	NC-4	NC-3	AC-3	AC-4
AE-1	AE-4	AE-2	AE-3	AE-3	AE-2	AE-4	AE-1	AE-5	AE-5
AC-4	AC-1	AC-3	AC-2	AC-2	AC-3	AC-1	AC-4	NE-5	NC-5

NFC EAST-NE

	NE-1		NE-2		NE-3		NE-4		NE-5	
	A	**H**	**A**	**H**	**A**	**H**	**A**	**H**	**A**	**H**
	AE-2	AE-1	AE-1	AE-2	AE-2	AE-1	AE-1	AE-2	NW-2	NW-1
	AE-4	AE-3	AE-3	AE-4	AE-4	AE-3	AE-3	AE-4	NW-4	NW-3
	NW-1	NW-4	NW-2	NW-3	NW-3	NW-2	NW-4	NW-1	NC-5	NC-5
	NC-4	NC-1	NC-3	NC-2	NC-2	NC-3	NC-1	NC-4	AE-5	AW-5

NFC CENTRAL-NC

	NC-1		NC-2		NC-3		NC-4		NC-5	
	A	**H**	**A**	**H**	**A**	**H**	**A**	**H**	**A**	**H**
	AW-2	AW-1	AW-1	AW-2	AW-2	AW-1	AW-1	AW-2	NW-1	NW-2
	AW-4	AW-3	AW-3	AW-4	AW-4	AW-3	AW-3	AW-4	NW-3	NW-4
	NE-1	NE-4	NE-2	NE-3	NE-3	NE-2	NE-4	NE-1	NE-5	NE-5
	NW-4	NW-1	NW-3	NW-2	NW-2	NW-3	NW-1	NW-4	AW-5	AE-5

NFC WEST-NW

	NW-1		NW-2		NW-3		NW-4	
	A	**H**	**A**	**H**	**A**	**H**	**A**	**H**
	NE-5	NC-5	NC-5	NE-5	NE-5	NC-5	NC-5	NE-5
	AC-2	AC-1	AC-1	AC-2	AC-2	AC-1	AC-1	AC-2
	AC-4	AC-3	AC-3	AC-4	AC-4	AC-3	AC-3	AC-4
	NE-4	NE-1	NE-3	NE-2	NE-2	NE-3	NE-1	NE-4
	NC-1	NC-4	NC-2	NC-3	NC-3	NC-2	NC-4	NC-1

Five-Team Division

Concentrating now on the AFC Western Division, the schedules for each of the top four teams have an identical structure and will always include a full programme of home and away games against the other four teams in the Division. In addition, every year, each of the top four will play two games against AFC Central teams and two against the AFC East. Again, they will play each of the top four teams in the NFC Central Division as part of their three-year cycle of interconference games. In 1985 they will play against teams from the NFC Western Division and in 1986, the NFC East. The 1984 schedule for the Los Angeles Raiders is set out, again not in chronological order.

LOS ANGELES RAIDERS (AFC West)

Denver Broncos	AFC West	Home
Denver Broncos	AFC West	Away
Kansas City Chiefs	AFC West	Home
Kansas City Chiefs	AFC West	Away
San Diego Chargers	AFC West	Home
San Diego Chargers	AFC West	Away
Seattle Seahawks	AFC West	Home
Seattle Seahawks	AFC West	Away
Pittsburgh Steelers	AFC Central	Home
Houston Oilers	AFC Central	Away
Indianapolis Colts	AFC East	Home
Miami Dolphins	AFC East	Away
Green Bay Packers	NFC Central	Home
Minnesota Vikings	NFC Central	Home
Chicago Bears	NFC Central	Away
Detroit Lions	NFC Central	Away

Still in the AFC, the two fifth-placed teams in the Eastern and Western Divisions (last year they were the New York Jets and Kansas City respectively) will each play eight games against teams within their own Divisions and will always play single games against each of the four AFC Central Division teams. Over in the NFC, the corresponding fifth-placed teams (the New York Giants and Tampa Bay) each play eight games against teams within their own Divisions and will always play single games against the four NFC West teams. Beyond these, for all four of the fifth-placed teams, there is a little relief. Each team is guaranteed home and away games against the other fifth-placed team in its own Conference, together with single games against the two fifth-placed teams from the rival Conference. The schedule structures are:

New York Jets (AFC East)

AFC East	8 games
AFC Central	4 games
Kansas City	Home
Kansas City	Away
New York Giants	Home
Tampa Bay	Away

New York Giants (NFC East)

NFC East	8 games
NFC West	4 games

Tampa Bay	Home
Tampa Bay	Away
Kansas City	Home
New York Jets	Away

Kansas City (AFC West)

AFC West	8 games
AFC Central	4 games
New York Jets	Home
New York Jets	Away
New York Giants	Away
Tampa Bay	Home

Tampa Bay (NFC Central)

NFC Central	8 games
NFC West	4 games
New York Giants	Home
New York Giants	Away
New York Jets	Home
Kansas City	Away

THE PLAYOFFS

On completion of the regular season, each Conference holds an elimination competition known as the Playoffs. The teams involved are the three Division winners and two Wild Card teams namely, those two, other than the Division winners, who have the best won-lost-tied records. The two Wild Card teams play each other to decide which one advances to join the three Division winners in the Divisional Playoffs (semi-final games). The results of the 1983 American Football Conference playoffs are set out as follows:—

Wild Card Game
Denver 7 at Seattle 31
(Seattle secured home-field advantage via the tie-breaking procedure.)

Divisional Playoffs
Seattle 27 at Miami 20
Pittsburgh 10 at Los Angeles Raiders 38
(Miami and the Los Angeles Raiders secured home-field advantage by having superior regular season records.)

Conference Championship Game
Seattle 14 at Los Angeles Raiders 30
The Los Angeles Raiders advanced to Super Bowl XVIII as AFC Champions.

TIE-BREAKING PROCEDURES

It is often necessary to separate two or even more teams, who have identical records, not only for the Division title but also for the Wild Card places. For this, selection is made by applying one or more of the several sets of criteria, which are listed as follows:

Teams in the same Division
A: *Two Teams*
1. Head-to-head (best record in games played between the two teams)
2. Best record in games played within the Division
3. Best record in games played within the Conference
4. Best record in common games
5. Best net points scored in Division games (just like goal difference in soccer)
6. Best net points in all games

B: *Three or More Teams* (if two teams remain tied after all other teams are eliminated, the tie-breaking procedure reverts to A:1.)
1. Head-to-head (best record in games played between the teams)
2. Best record in games played within the Division
3. Best record in games played within the Conference
4. Best record in common games
5. Best net points in Division games
6. Best net points in all games

Tie Breaker for the Wild Card places
(a) If the teams are from the same Division, the Division tie-breaker is applied.
(b) If the teams are from different Divisions, the following procedure is adopted.
C: *Two Teams*
1. Head-to-head (if they have played each other)
2. Best record in games played within the Conference
3. Best record in common games (minimum of four)
4. Best average net points in Conference games
5. Best net points in all games

D: *Three or More Teams* (If two teams remain tied after all other teams are eliminated, the tie-breaking procedure reverts to A: 1, or C: 1, whichever is applicable.)
1. Head-to-head sweep (this applies only if one team has beaten all the others or if one team has lost to all the others.)
2. Best record in games played within the Conference
3. Best record in common games (minimum of four)
4. Best average net points in Conference games
5. Best net points in all games

Thankfully, in 1984 the application of this, the world's most complicated formula, was necessary only to identify the two AFC Wild Card teams. Seattle, Denver and Cleveland had identical 9-7-0 records, but Cleveland had been beaten by both Seattle and Denver and were thus eliminated (D: 1). Seattle and Denver were left as the two Wild Cards, with Seattle gaining the home-field advantage by having registered a superior record in games played within the Division (A: 2).

THE SUPER BOWL

Though the obvious comparison is with the FA Cup Final, the Super Bowl is more sensibly seen as the culmination of an end-of-season elimination competition, involving the Champions of six mini leagues together with the Wild Card teams, the latter being considered, perhaps, as potential giant killers (the Raiders won Super Bowl XV after gaining entry to the playoffs as a Wild Card). Unlike for the FA Cup Final, the Super Bowl venue changes from year to year and, since the site is chosen some three years in advance, it is possible for one team to be playing 'at home'. Surprisingly, this has never occurred, though when the Rams played in Super Bowl XIV at Pasadena, they were only an hour's drive from downtown Los Angeles. In selecting the venue, great importance is placed on the likelihood of good weather. Conseqently, with the exception of Pontiac Silverdome (this is a domed stadium), all past Super Bowl stadia have been in the 'sunshine' belt, stretching from Florida to California. Super Bowl XIX will be played at Stanford Stadium, Palo Alto, California, and XX at the New Orleans Superdome.

THE PRO BOWL

This annual game between the two representative teams from each Conference is a lovely way to end the season. Basking in the sunshine of Honolulu, Hawaii, 50,000 fans have the opportunity of watching the NFL's very best talent, selected by a poll of players, coaches, administrators and sports journalists. Despite fielding eight members of the victorious Los Angeles Raiders squad, in 1984 the AFC fell foul of Washington's Joe Theismann, who completed 21 of 27 passes for 242 yards and three touchdowns, in the NFC's record 45-3 victory.

Bill Kenney (AFC) drops back to pass in the 1984 Pro Bowl

AFC — NFC Pro Bowl Results — NFC leads series 9-5					
YEAR	DATE	WINNER	LOSER	SITE	ATTENDANCE
1984	Jan. 29	NFC 45	AFC 3	Honolulu	50,445
1983	Feb. 6	NFC 20	AFC 19	Honolulu	47,201
1982	Jan. 31	AFC 16	NFC 13	Honolulu	49,521
1981	Feb. 1	NFC 21	AFC 7	Honolulu	47,879
1980	Jan. 27	NFC 37	AFC 27	Honolulu	48,060
1979	Jan. 29	NFC 13	AFC 7	Los Angeles	46,281
1978	Jan. 23	NFC 14	AFC 13	Tampa	51,337
1977	Jan. 17	AFC 24	NFC 14	Seattle	64,151
1976	Jan. 26	NFC 23	AFC 20	New Orleans	30,546
1975	Jan. 20	NFC 17	AFC 10	Miami	26,484
1974	Jan. 20	AFC 15	NFC 13	Kansas City	66,918
1973	Jan. 21	AFC 33	NFC 28	Dallas	37,091
1972	Jan. 23	AFC 26	NFC 13	Los Angeles	53,647
1971	Jan. 24	NFC 27	AFC 6	Los Angeles	48,222

PRO BOWL ROSTERS
(Starters in Capitals)

OFFENSE	American Football Conference		National Football Conference	
Wide Receivers	CARLOS CARSON	Kansas City	JAMES LOFTON	Green Bay
	CRIS COLLINSWORTH	Cincinnati	MIKE QUICK	Philadelphia
	Wes Chandler	San Diego	Roy Green	St. Louis
	Mark Duper	Miami	Charlie Brown	Washington
Tight End	TODD CHRISTENSEN	L.A. Raiders	PAUL COFFMAN	Green Bay
	Kellen Winslow	San Diego	Doug Cosbie	Dallas
Tackles	ANTHONY MUNOZ	Cincinnati	JOE JACOBY	Washington
	MARVIN POWELL*	N.Y. Jets	MIKE KENN	Atlanta
	Brian Holloway	New England	Jackie Slater	L.A. Rams
	Henry Lawrence**	L.A. Raiders		
Guards	JOHN HANNAH*	New England	KENT HILL	L.A. Rams
	CHRIS HINTON	Baltimore	RUSS GRIMM	Washington
	Ed Newman	Miami	R.C. Thielemann	Atlanta
	Bob Kuechenberg**	Miami		
Center	DWIGHT STEPHENSON	Miami	JEFF BOSTIC	Washington
	Mike Webster	Pittsburgh	Larry McCarren	Green Bay
Quarterback	DAN MARINO*	Miami	JOE THEISMANN	Washington
	Dan Fouts	San Diego	Joe Montana	San Francisco
	Bill Kenney**	Kansas City		
Running Backs	EARL CAMPBELL	Houston	ERIC DICKERSON	L.A. Rams
	CURT WARNER	Seattle	WILLIAM ANDREWS	Atlanta
	Tony Collins	New England	Tony Dorsett	Dallas
	Joe Cribbs	Buffalo	Walter Payton	Chicago

DEFENSE				
Defensive Ends	DOUG BETTERS	Miami	LEE ROY SELMON	Tampa Bay
	HOWIE LONG	L.A. Raiders	ED JONES	Dallas
	Mark Gastineau	N.Y. Jets	Fred Dean*	San Francisco
			William Gay**	Detroit
Defensive Tackles	BOB BAUMHOWER	Miami	DOUG ENGLISH	Detroit
	FRED SMERLAS	Buffalo	RANDY WHITE	Dallas
	Joe Klecko	N.Y. Jets	Dave Butz	Washington
Outside Linebackers	CHIP BANKS	Cleveland	LAWRENCE TAYLOR	N.Y. Giants
	ROD MARTIN	L.A. Raiders	HUGH GREEN	Tampa Bay
	Ted Hendricks	L.A. Raiders	Rickey Jackson	New Orleans
Middle Linebacker	JACK LAMBERT	Pittsburgh	MIKE SINGLETARY	Chicago
	Randy Gradishar	Denver	Harry Carson	N.Y. Giants
Safeties	DERON CHERRY	Kansas City	MARK MURPHY	Washington
	KENNY EASLEY	Seattle	NOLAN CROMWELL	L.A. Rams
	Vann McElroy	L.A. Raiders	Dwight Hicks	San Francisco
Cornerbacks	GARY GREEN	Kansas City	RONNIE LOTT	San Francisco
	LESTER HAYES	L.A. Raiders	EVERSON WALLS	Dallas
	Louis Wright*	Denver	Mark Haynes	N.Y. Giants
	Ray Clayborn**	New England		
Placekicker	GARY ANDERSON	Pittsburgh	ALI HAJI-SHEIKH	N.Y. Giants
Punter	RICH CAMARILLO	New England	CARL BIRDSONG	St. Louis
Kick/Punt Returner	GREG PRUITT	L.A. Raiders	BILLY JOHNSON	Atlanta

* Unable to play   ** Replacement

Starting this year, the Pro Bowl coaches will be those of the teams which lost in the Conference Championship games. Thus in 1984 Chuck Knox (Seattle) coached the AFC and Bill Walsh (San Francisco) coached the NFC.

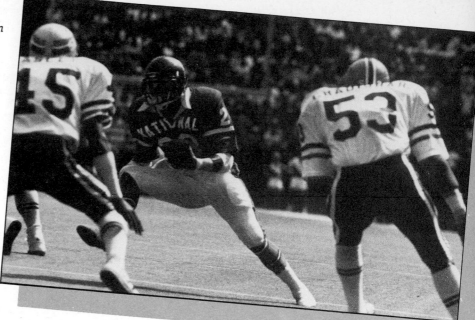

Eric Dickerson (NFC) in action in the 1984 Pro Bowl

THE ALL PRO TEAM

The major periodicals and news services (AP and UPI) each produce what they consider to be the best team selected from the whole NFL. Not everyone would agree with me, but here is my dream team.

All Pro
Jack Lambert

Wide Receivers	Wes Chandler	San Diego
	James Lofton	Green Bay
Tight End	Kellen Winslow	San Diego
Tackles	Anthony Munoz	Cincinnati
	Marvin Powell	New York Jets
Guards	John Hannah	New England
	Ed Newman	Miami
Center	Dwight Stephenson	Miami
Quarterback	Joe Theismann	Washington
Running Backs	Earl Campbell	Houston
	Walter Payton	Chicago
Defensive Ends	Lee Roy Selmon	Tampa Bay
	Howie Long	Los Angeles Raiders
Defensive Tackles	Bob Baumhower	Miami
	Randy White	Dallas
Outside Linebackers	Lawrence Taylor	New York Giants
	Chip Banks	Cleveland
Inside Linebackers	Jack Lambert	Pittsburgh
	Mike Singletary	Chicago
Safeties	Nolan Cromwell	Los Angeles Rams
	Kenny Easley	Seattle
Cornerbacks	Lester Hayes	Los Angeles Raiders
	Mike Haynes	Los Angeles Raiders
Placekicker	Nick Lowery	Kansas City
Punter	Ray Guy	Los Angeles Raiders
Punt Returner	Billy Johnson	Atlanta
Kick Returner	Mike Nelms	Washington
Head Coach	Don Shula	Miami

CHAPTER 4
ALL TIME RECORDS

CHAMPIONS 1921-1983

National Football League 1921-1969 (Until 1933 based solely on regular season play)

1921	Chicago Staleys
1922	Canton Bulldogs
1923	Canton Bulldogs
1924	Cleveland Bulldogs
1925	Chicago Cardinals
1926	Frankford Yellowjackets
1927	New York Giants
1928	Providence Steamroller
1929	Green Bay Packers
1930	Green Bay Packers
1931	Green Bay Packers
1932	Chicago Bears 9 Portsmouth Spartans 0 (Championship Playoff)
1933	Chicago Bears 23 New York Giants 21
1934	New York Giants 30 Chicago Bears 13
1935	Detroit Lions 26 New York Giants 7
1936	Green Bay Packers 21 Boston Redskins 6
1937	Washington Redskins 28 Chicago Bears 21
1938	New York Giants 23 Green Bay Packers 17
1939	Green Bay Packers 27 New York Giants 0
1940	Chicago Bears 73 Washington Redskins 0
1941	Chicago Bears 37 New York Giants 9
1942	Washington Redskins 14 Chicago Bears 6
1943	Chicago Bears 41 Washington Redskins 21
1944	Green Bay Packers 14 New York Giants 7
1945	Cleveland Rams 15 Washington Redskins 14
1946	Chicago Bears 24 New York Giants 14
1947	Chicago Cardinals 28 Philadelphia Eagles 21
1948	Philadelphia Eagles 7 Chicago Cardinals 0
1949	Philadelphia Eagles 14 Los Angeles Rams 0
1950	Cleveland Browns 30 Los Angeles Rams 28
1951	Los Angeles Rams 24 Cleveland Browns 17
1952	Detroit Lions 17 Cleveland Browns 7
1953	Detroit Lions 17 Cleveland Browns 16
1954	Cleveland Browns 56 Detroit Lions 10
1955	Cleveland Browns 38 Los Angeles Rams 14
1956	New York Giants 47 Chicago Bears 7
1957	Detroit Lions 59 Cleveland Browns 14
1958	Baltimore Colts 23 New York Giants 17
1959	Baltimore Colts 31 New York Giants 16

1960	Philadelphia Eagles 17 Green Bay Packers 13
1961	Green Bay Packers 37 New York Giants 0
1962	Green Bay Packers 16 New York Giants 7
1963	Chicago Bears 14 New York Giants 10
1964	Cleveland Browns 27 Baltimore Colts 0
1965	Green Bay Packers 23 Cleveland Browns 12
1966	Green Bay Packers 34 Dallas Cowboys 27
1967	Green Bay Packers 21 Dallas Cowboys 17
1968	Baltimore Colts 34 Cleveland Browns 0
1969	Minnesota Vikings 27 Cleveland Browns 7

American Football League 1960-69

1960	Houston Oilers 24 Los Angeles Chargers 16
1961	Houston Oilers 10 San Diego Chargers 3
1962	Dallas Texans 20 Houston Oilers 17
1963	San Diego Chargers 51 Boston Patriots 10
1964	Buffalo Bills 20 San Diego Chargers 7
1965	Buffalo Bills 23 San Diego Chargers 0
1966	Kansas City Chiefs 31 Buffalo Bills 7
1967	Oakland Raiders 40 Houston Oilers 7
1968	New York Jets 27 Oakland Raiders 23
1969	Kansas City Chiefs 17 Oakland Raiders 7

Conference Champions 1970-83

NFC

1970	Dallas Cowboys 17 San Francisco 49ers 10
1971	Dallas Cowboys 14 San Francisco 49ers 3
1972	Washington Redskins 26 Dallas Cowboys 3
1973	Minnesota Vikings 27 Dallas Cowboys 10
1974	Minnesota Vikings 14 Los Angeles Rams 10
1975	Dallas Cowboys 37 Los Angeles Rams 7
1976	Minnesota Vikings 24 Los Angeles Rams 13
1977	Dallas Cowboys 23 Minnesota Vikings 6
1978	Dallas Cowboys 28 Los Angeles Rams 0
1979	Los Angeles Rams 9 Tampa Bay Buccaneers 0
1980	Philadelphia Eagles 20 Dallas Cowboys 7
1981	San Francisco 49ers 28 Dallas Cowboys 27
1982	Washington Redskins 31 Dallas Cowboys 17
1983	Washington Redskins 24 San Francisco 49ers 21

Philadelphia Eagles Championship team 1948

AFC

1970	Baltimore Colts 27	Oakland Raiders 17	
1971	Miami Dolphins 21	Baltimore Colts 0	
1972	Miami Dolphins 21	Pittsburgh Steelers 17	
1973	Miami Dolphins 27	Oakland Raiders 10	
1974	Pittsburgh Steelers 24	Oakland Raiders 13	
1975	Pittsburgh Steelers 16	Oakland Raiders 10	
1976	Oakland Raiders 24	Pittsburgh Steelers 7	
1977	Denver Broncos 20	Oakland Raiders 17	
1978	Pittsburgh Steelers 34	Houston Oilers 5	
1979	Pittsburgh Steelers 27	Houston Oilers 13	
1980	Oakland Raiders 34	San Diego Chargers 27	
1981	Cincinnati Bengals 27	San Diego Chargers 7	
1982	Miami Dolphins 14	New York Jets 0	
1983	Los Angeles Raiders 30	Seattle Seahawks 14	

Super Bowl 1966-83

SB	Winner		Loser		Stadium	Attendance
I	Green Bay	35	Kansas City	10	Los Angeles Coliseum	61,946
II	Green Bay	33	Oakland	14	Miami Orange Bowl	75,546
III	New York Jets	16	Baltimore	7	Miami Orange Bowl	75,389
IV	Kansas City	23	Minnesota	7	New Orleans Tulane Stadium	80,562
V	Baltimore	16	Dallas	13	Miami Orange Bowl	79,204
VI	Dallas	24	Miami	3	New Orleans Tulane Stadium	81,023
VII	Miami	14	Washington	7	Los Angeles Coliseum	90,182
VIII	Miami	24	Minnesota	7	Houston Rice Stadium	71,882
IX	Pittsburgh	16	Minnesota	6	New Orleans Tulane Stadium	80,997
X	Pittsburgh	21	Dallas	17	Miami Orange Bowl	80,107
XI	Oakland	32	Minnesota	14	Pasadena Rose Bowl	103,438
XII	Dallas	27	Denver	10	New Orleans Superdome	75,583
XIII	Pittsburgh	35	Dallas	31	Miami Orange Bowl	79,484
XIV	Pittsburgh	31	Los Angeles Rams	19	Pasadena Rose Bowl	103,985
XV	Oakland	27	Philadelphia	10	New Orleans Superdome	76,135
XVI	San Francisco	26	Cincinnati	21	Pontiac Silverdome	81,270
XVII	Washington	27	Miami	17	Pasadena Rose Bowl	103,667
XVIII	Los Angeles Raiders	38	Washington	9	Tampa Stadium	72,920

ALL TIME INDIVIDUAL RECORDS
(Regular Season)

Career Best

SEASONS PLAYED	26	George Blanda
GAMES PLAYED	340	George Blanda
POINTS	2,002	George Blanda (9-TD, 943-EP, 335-FG)
EXTRA POINTS	943	George Blanda
FIELD GOALS	338	Jan Stenerud
TOUCHDOWNS		
Rushing and Pass Receiving	126	Jim Brown (106-R, 20-PR)
Rushing	106	Jim Brown
Pass Receiving	99	Don Hutson
Passes Thrown	342	Fran Tarkenton
By Interception Return	9	Ken Houston
By Punt Return	8	Jack Christiansen
By Kick Return	6	Ollie Matson
		Gale Sayers
		Travis Williams
By Fumble Recovery Return	4	Bill Thompson
YARDAGE		
Rushing	12,312	Jim Brown
Pass Receiving	11,834	Don Maynard
Passing	47,003	Fran Tarkenton

Chicago running back Gale Sayers   *Green Bay end Don Hutson*

HOW MANY TIMES

Pass Receptions	649	Charley Taylor
Passes Completed	3,686	Fran Tarkenton
Interceptions	81	Paul Krause

MOST SEASONS LEADING LEAGUE

Points	5	Don Hutson, Green Bay 1940-44
		Gino Cappelletti, Boston 1961, 1963-66
Extra Points	8	George Blanda, Chicago Bears 1956, Houston 1961-62, Oakland 1967-69, 1972, 1974
Field Goals	5	Lou Groza, Cleveland Browns 1950, 1952-54, 1957
Touchdowns	8	Don Hutson, Green Bay 1935-38, 1941-44
Touchdowns, Rushing	5	Jim Brown, Cleveland Browns 1957-59, 1963, 1965
Touchdowns, Pass Receiving	9	Don Hutson, Green Bay 1935-38, 1940-44
Touchdowns, Passes Thrown	4	Johnny Unitas, Baltimore 1957-60
		Len Dawson, Dallas Texans 1962, Kansas City 1963, 1965-66
Yards, Rushing	8	Jim Brown, Cleveland Browns 1957-61, 1963-65
Yards, Pass Receiving	7	Don Hutson, Green Bay 1936, 1938-39, 1941-44
Yards, Passing	5	Sonny Jurgensen, Philadelphia, 1961-62, Washington 1966-67, 1969
Pass Receptions	8	Don Hutson, Green Bay 1936-37, 1939, 1941-45
Passes Completed	5	Sammy Baugh, Washington 1937, 1943, 1945, 1947-48

Season Best

POINTS	176	Paul Hornung, Green Bay (15-TD, 41-EP, 15-FG)
EXTRA POINTS	64	George Blanda, Houston 1961
FIELD GOALS	34	Jim Turner, N.Y. Jets 1968

TOUCHDOWNS

Rushing and Pass Receiving	24	John Riggins, Washington 1983 (24-R)
Rushing	24	John Riggins, Washington 1983
Pass Receiving	17	Don Hutson, Green Bay 1942
		Elroy 'Crazylegs' Hirsch, L.A. Rams 1951
		Bill Groman, Houston 1961
Passes Thrown	36	George Blanda, Houston 1961
		Y.A. Tittle, N.Y. Giants 1963
By Interception Return	4	Ken Houston, Houston 1971
		Jim Kearney, Kansas City 1972
By Punt Return	4	Jack Christiansen, Detroit 1951
		Rick Upchurch, Denver 1976
By Kick Return	4	Travis Williams, Green Bay 1967
		Cecil Turner, Chicago 1970
By Fumble Recovery Return	2	By many players

YARDAGE

Rushing	2,003	O.J. Simpson, Buffalo 1973
Pass Receiving	1,746	Charley Hennigan, Houston 1961
Passing	4,802	Dan Fouts, San Diego 1981

HOW MANY TIMES

Pass Receptions	101	Charley Hennigan, Houston 1964
Passes Completed	360	Dan Fouts, San Diego 1981
Interceptions	14	Dick 'Night Train' Lane, L.A. Rams 1952

Game Best

POINTS	40	Ernie Nevers (6-TD, 4-EP), Chicago Cardinals v Chicago Bears 1929
EXTRA POINTS	9	Pat Harder, Chicago Cardinals v N.Y. Giants 1948
		Bob Waterfield, L.A. Rams v Baltimore 1950
		Charlie Gogolak, Washington v N.Y. Giants 1966
FIELD GOALS	7	Jim Bakken, St. Louis v Pittsburgh 1967

TOUCHDOWNS

Rushing and Pass Receiving   6   Ernie Nevers (6-R), Chicago Cardinals v Chicago Bears 1929
Dub Jones (4-R, 2-PR), Cleveland v Chicago Bears 1951
Gale Sayers (4-R, 1-PR, 1-K Ret) Chicago Bears
v San Francisco 1965

Rushing   6   Ernie Nevers, Chicago Cardinals v Chicago Bears 1929
Pass Receiving   5   Bob Shaw, Chicago Cardinals v Baltimore 1950
Kellen Winslow, San Diego v Oakland 1981

Passes Thrown   7   Sid Luckman, Chicago Bears v N.Y. Giants 1943
Adrian Burk, Philadelphia v Washington 1954
George Blanda, Houston v N.Y. Titans 1961
Y.A. Tittle, N.Y. Giants v Washington 1962
Joe Kapp, Minnesota v Baltimore 1969

YARDAGE

Rushing   275   Walter Payton, Chicago Bears v Minnesota 1977
Pass Receiving   303   Jim Benton, Cleveland Rams v Detroit 1945
Passing   554   Norm Van Brocklin, L.A. Rams v N.Y. Yanks 1951

HOW MANY TIMES

Rushing Attempts   43   Butch Woolfolk, N.Y. Giants v Philadelphia 1983
Pass Receptions   18   Tom Fears, L.A. Rams v Green Bay 1950
Passes Completed   42   Richard Todd, N.Y. Jets v San Francisco 1980
Interceptions   4   By many players

LONGEST

Touchdown Rushing   99 yds   Tony Dorsett, Dallas v Minnesota 1982
Touchdown Pass Receiving   99 yds   Andy Farkas (from Filchock) Washington v Pittsburgh 1939
Bob Mitchell (from Izo) Washington v Cleveland 1963
Pat Studstill (from Sweetan) Detroit v Baltimore 1966
Gerry Allen (from Jurgensen) Washington v Chicago 1968
Cliff Branch (from Plunkett) L.A. Raiders v Washington 1983

Field Goal   63 yds   Tom Dempsey, New Orleans v Detroit 1970
Punt Return (All TDs)   98 yds   Gil LeFebvre, Cincinnati v Brooklyn 1933
Charlie West, Minnesota v Washington 1968
Dennis Morgan, Dallas v St Louis 1974

Kick Return (All TDs)   106 yds   Al Carmichael, Green Bay v Chicago Bears 1956
Noland Smith, Kansas City v Denver 1967
Roy Green, St Louis v Dallas 1979

Interception Return (All TDs)   102 yds   Bob Smith, Detroit v Chicago Bears 1949
Erich Barnes, N.Y. Giants v Dallas 1961
Gary Barbaro, Kansas City v Seattle 1977
Louis Breeden, Cincinnati v San Diego 1981

Fumble Recovery Return (TD)   104 yds   Jack Tatum, Oakland v Green Bay 1972

TEAM RECORDS

MOST CHAMPIONSHIPS   11   Green Bay, 1929-31, 1936, 1939, 1944, 1961-62, 1965-67
   8   Chicago Bears, 1921, 1932-33, 1940-41, 1943, 1946, 1963
   4   N.Y. Giants, 1927, 1934, 1938, 1956
Detroit, 1935, 1952-53, 1957
Cleveland Browns, 1950, 1954-55, 1964
Baltimore, 1958-59, 1968, 1970
Pittsburgh, 1974-75, 1978-79

MOST CONSECUTIVE GAMES WON (inc. playoffs)   18   Chicago Bears, 1933-34 and 1941-42 Miami, 1972-73
MOST CONSECUTIVE GAMES WON (exc. playoffs)   17   Chicago Bears 1933-34
MOST CONSECUTIVE GAMES LOST   26   Tampa Bay, 1976-77
MOST POINTS IN A SEASON   541   Washington, 1983
FEWEST POINTS IN A SEASON   37   Cincinnati-St Louis, 1934
MOST POINTS IN A GAME   72   Washington v N.Y. Giants, 1966
MOST POINTS (BOTH TEAMS) IN A GAME   113   Washington v N.Y. Giants, 1966
FEWEST POINTS (BOTH TEAMS) IN A GAME   0   Many teams; last time N.Y. Giants v Detroit 1943

ALL TIME TOP TWENTY
(1983 Active players in capitals)

All Time Leading Rushers

		Yrs.	Att.	Yds.	Av.	TDs
1.	Jim Brown	9	2,359	12,312	5·2	106
2.	FRANCO HARRIS	12	2,881	11,950	4·1	91
3.	WALTER PAYTON	9	2,666	11,625	4·4	78
4.	O.J. Simpson	11	2,404	11,236	4·7	61
5.	JOHN RIGGINS	12	2,413	9,436	3·9	82
6.	Jim Taylor	10	1,941	8,597	4·4	83
7.	Joe Perry	14	1,737	8,378	4·8	53
8.	TONY DORSETT	7	1,834	8,336	4·5	53
9.	EARL CAMPBELL	6	1,883	8,296	4·4	69
10.	Larry Csonka	11	1,891	8,081	4·3	64
11.	Leroy Kelly	10	1,727	7,274	4·2	74
12.	John Henry Johnson	13	1,571	6,803	4·3	48
13.	CHUCK MUNCIE	8	1,547	6,651	4·3	71
14.	MARK VAN EEGHEN	10	1,652	6,650	4·0	37
15.	Lawrence McCutcheon	10	1,521	6,578	4·3	26
16.	Lydell Mitchell	9	1,675	6,534	3·9	30
17.	Floyd Little	9	1,641	6,323	3·8	43
18.	Don Perkins	8	1,500	6,217	4·1	42
19.	OTTIS ANDERSON	5	1,401	6,190	4·4	34
20.	Ken Willard	10	1,622	6,105	3·8	45

All Time Leading Receivers

		Yrs.	No.	Yds.	Av.	TDs
1.	Charley Taylor	13	649	9,110	14·0	79
2.	Don Maynard	15	633	11,834	18·7	88
3.	Ray Berry	13	631	9,275	14·7	68
4.	CHARLIE JOINER	15	596	9,981	16·7	50
5.	HAROLD CARMICHAEL	13	589	8,978	15·2	79
	Fred Biletnikoff	14	589	8,974	15·2	76
7.	HAROLD JACKSON	15	579	10,372	17·9	76
8.	Lionel Taylor	10	567	7,195	12·7	45
9.	Lance Alworth	11	542	10,266	18·9	85
10.	Bobby Mitchell	11	521	7,954	15·3	65
11.	Billy Howton	12	503	8,459	16·8	61
12.	Tommy McDonald	12	495	8,410	17·0	84
13.	Ahmad Rashad	10	495	6,831	13·8	44
14.	DREW PEARSON	11	489	7,822	16·0	48
15.	Don Hutson	11	488	7,991	16·4	99
16.	Jackie Smith	16	480	7,918	16·5	40
17.	Art Powell	10	479	8,046	16·8	81
18.	CLIFF BRANCH	12	474	8,284	17·5	67
	Boyd Dowler	12	474	7,270	15·4	40
20.	STEVE LARGENT	8	471	7,608	16·2	60

All Time Leading Scorers

		Yrs.	TDs.	EPs	FGs	Total
1.	George Blanda	26	9	943	335	2,002
2.	JAN STENERUD	17	0	509	338	1,523
3.	Jim Turner	16	1	521	304	1,439
4.	Jim Bakken	17	0	534	282	1,380
5.	Fred Cox	15	0	519	282	1,365
6.	Lou Groza	17	1	641	234	1,349
7.	Gino Cappelletti*	11	42	350	176	1,130
8.	MARK MOSELEY	13	0	378	242	1,104

Charlie Joiner

9.	Don Cockroft	13	0	432	216	1,080
10.	Garo Yepremian	14	0	444	210	1,074
11.	Bruce Gossett	11	0	374	219	1,031
12.	Sam Baker	15	2	428	179	977
13.	Lou Michaels**	13	1	386	187	955
14.	Roy Gerela	11	0	351	184	903
15.	Bobby Walston	12	46	365	80	881
16.	Pete Gogolak	10	0	344	173	863
17.	Errol Mann	11	0	315	177	846
18.	Don Hutson	11	105	172	7	823
19.	Paul Hornung	9	62	190	66	760
20.	Tony Fritsch	11	0	287	157	758

* Includes four two-point conversions

** Includes a safety recorded in 1965 when Michaels played as a defensive end

ALL TIME PASSER RATINGS

(Minimum 1,500 attempts)

		Yrs.	Att.	Comp.	Yds.	TDs	Int.	Rating
1.	JOE MONTANA	5	1,645	1,045	11,979	78	44	89·8
2.	DANNY WHITE	8	1,710	1,029	13,174	98	79	84·2
3.	Roger Staubach	11	2,958	1,685	22,700	153	109	83·5
4.	Sonny Jurgensen	18	4,262	2,433	32,224	255	189	82·8
5.	Len Dawson	19	3,741	2,136	28,711	239	183	82·6
6.	KEN ANDERSON	13	4,145	2,452	30,390	184	146	82·0
7.	DAN FOUTS	11	3,873	2,268	30,114	182	168	81·1
8.	Fran Tarkenton	18	6,467	3,686	47,003	342	266	80·5
9.	Bart Starr	16	3,149	1,808	24,718	152	138	80·3
10.	Johnny Unitas	18	5,186	2,830	40,239	290	253	78·2
	Bert Jones	10	2,551	1,430	18,190	124	101	78·2
12.	Otto Graham	6	1,565	872	13,499	88	94	78·1
13.	Frank Ryan	13	2,133	1,090	16,042	149	111	77·7
14.	JOE THEISMANN	10	2,824	1,594	20,041	128	109	77·4
15.	Bob Griese	14	3,429	1,926	25,092	192	172	77·3
16.	KEN STABLER	14	3,723	2,237	27,599	192	217	76·2
17.	Norm Van Brocklin	12	2,895	1,553	23,611	173	178	75·3
18.	Sid Luckman	12	1,744	904	14,686	137	132	75.0
	BRIAN SIPE	10	3,439	1,944	23,713	154	149	75·0
20.	Don Meredith	9	2,308	1,170	17,199	135	111	74·7

Joe Montana

PASSES COMPLETED	No.	YARDS PASSING	Yards	TOUCHDOWN PASSES	No.
1. Fran Tarkenton	3,686	1. Fran Tarkenton	47,003	1. Fran Tarkenton	342
2. Johnny Unitas	2,830	2. Johnny Unitas	40,239	2. Johnny Unitas	290
3. JIM HART	2,590	3. JIM HART	34,639	3. Sonny Jurgensen	255
4. John Brodie	2,469	4. John Hadl	33,503	4. John Hadl	244
5. KEN ANDERSON	2,452	5. Sonny Jurgensen	32,224	5. Len Dawson	239
6. Sonny Jurgensen	2,433	6. John Brodie	31,548	6. George Blanda	236
7. Roman Gabriel	2,366	7. Norm Snead	30,797	7. John Brodie	214
8. John Hadl	2,363	8. KEN ANDERSON	30,390	8. TERRY BRADSHAW	212
9. Norm Snead	2,276	9. DAN FOUTS	30,114	Y.A. Tittle	212
10. DAN FOUTS	2,268	10. Roman Gabriel	29,444	10. JIM HART	209
11. KEN STABLER	2,237	11. Len Dawson	28,711	11. Roman Gabriel	201
12. Len Dawson	2,136	12. Y.A. Tittle	28,339	12. Norm Snead	196
13. Y.A. Tittle	2,118	13. TERRY BRADSHAW	27,989	Bobby Layne	196
14. Craig Morton	2,053	14. Craig Morton	27,908	14. Bob Griese	192
15. TERRY BRADSHAW	2,025	15. Joe Namath	27,663	KEN STABLER	192
16. JOE FERGUSON	1,997	16. KEN STABLER	27,599	16. Sammy Baugh	187
17. ARCHIE MANNING	1,959	17. George Blanda	26,920	17. KEN ANDERSON	184
18. BRIAN SIPE	1,944	18. Bobby Layne	26,768	18. Craig Morton	183
19. Bob Griese	1,926	19. JOE FERGUSON	25,599	19. DAN FOUTS	182
20. George Blanda	1,911	20. Bob Griese	25,092	20. Babe Parilli	176

INDEX OF RETIRED PLAYERS LISTED IN ALL TIME STATISTICS

ALLEN Gerry, Baltimore (1966), Washington (1967-69)

ALWORTH Lance, San Diego (1962-70), Dallas (1971-72)

BAKER Sam, Washington (1953 and 1956-59), Cleveland (1960-61), Dallas (1962-63) Philadelphia (1964-69)

BAKKEN Jim, St Louis (1962-78)

BARBARO Gary, Kansas City (1976-82)

BARNES Erich, Chicago Bears (1958-60), N.Y. Giants (1961-64), Cleveland (1965-71)

BAUGH Sammy, Washington (1937-52)

BENTON, Jim, Cleveland Rams (1938-42 and 1944-47), Chicago Bears (1943)

BERRY Raymond, Baltimore (1955-67)

BILETNIKOFF Fred, Oakland (1965-78)

BLANDA George, Chicago Bears (1949-58), Houston (1960-66), Oakland (1967-75)

BRODIE John, San Francisco (1957-73)

BROWN Jim, Cleveland (1957-65)

BURK Adrian, Baltimore (1950), Philadelphia (1951-56)

CAPPELLETTI Gino, Boston (later known as New England) (1960-70)

CARMICHAEL Al, Green Bay (1953-58), Denver (1960-61)

CHRISTIANSEN Jack, Detroit (1951-58)

COCKROFT Don, Cleveland (1968-80)

CONERLY Charlie, N.Y. Giants (1948-61)

COX Fred, Minnesota (1963-77)

CSONKA Larry, Miami (1968-74 and 1979) N.Y. Giants (1976-77)

DAWSON Len, Pittsburgh (1957-59), Cleveland (1960-61), Kansas City (1962-75)

DEMPSEY Tom, New Orleans (1969-70), Philadelphia (1971-74), Cleveland (1975-76), Houston (1977), Buffalo (1978-79)

DOWLER Boyd, Green Bay (1959-69), Washington (1971)

FARKAS Andy, Washington (1938-44), Detroit (1945)

FEARS Tom, L.A. Rams (1948-56)

FILCHOCK Frank, Pittsburgh (1938), Washington (1938-41 and 1944-45), N.Y. Giants (1946), Baltimore (1950)

FOREMAN Chuck, Minnesota (1973-79), New England (1980)

FRITSCH Tony, Dallas (1971-73 and 1975), Houston (1976-81), New Orleans (1982)

GABRIEL Roman, L.A. Rams (1962-72), Philadelphia (1973-77)

GERELA Roy, Houston (1969-70), Pittsburgh (1971-78)

GOGOLAK Charley, Washington (1966-68), New England (1970-72)

GOGOLAK Pete, Buffalo (1964-65), N.Y. Giants (1966-74)

GOSSETT Bruce, L.A. Rams (1964-69), San Francisco (1970-74)

GRAHAM Otto, Cleveland Browns (1946-55)

GRIESE Bob, Miami (1967-80)

GROMAN Bill, Houston (1960-62 and 1966), Denver (1963), Buffalo (1964-65)

GROZA Lou, Cleveland Browns (1945-59 and 1961-67)

HADL John, San Diego (1962-72), L.A. Rams (1973-74), Green Bay (1974-75), Houston (1976-77)

HARDER Pat, Chicago Cardinals (1946-50), Detroit (1951-53)

HENNIGAN Charley, Houston (1960-66)

HIRSCH Elroy 'Crazylegs', Chicago Rockets (AAFC) (1946-48), L.A. Rams (1949-57)

HORNUNG Paul, Green Bay (1957-62 and 1964-66)

HOUSTON Ken, Houston (1967-72), Washington (1973-80)

HOWTON Billy, Green Bay (1952-58), Cleveland (1959), Dallas (1960-63)

HUTSON Don, Green Bay (1935-45)

IZO George, St Louis (1960), Washington (1961-64), Detroit (1965), Pittsburgh (1966)

JOHNSON John Henry, San Francisco (1954-56), Detroit (1957-59), Pittsburgh (1960-65) Houston (1966)

JONES Bert, Baltimore (1973-81), L.A. Rams (1982)

JONES Dub, Cleveland (1948-55)

JURGENSEN Sonny, Philadelphia (1957-63), Washington (1964-74)

KAPP Joe, Minnesota (1967-69), Boston Patriots (1970)

KEARNEY Jim, Detroit (1965-66), Kansas City (1967-75), New Orleans (1976)

KELLY Leroy, Cleveland (1964-73)

KRAUSE Paul, Washington (1964-67), Minnesota (1968-79)

LANE Dick 'Night Train', L.A. Rams (1952-53), Chicago Cardinals (1954-59), Detroit (1960-65)

LAYNE Bobby, Chicago Bears (1948), N.Y. Giants (1949), Detroit (1950-58), Pittsburgh (1958-62)

LeFEBVRE Gil, Cincinnati Reds (1933)

LITTLE Floyd, Denver (1967-75)

LUCKMAN Sid, Chicago Bears (1939-50)

MANN Errol, Green Bay (1968), Detroit (1969-76), Oakland (1976-78)

MATSON Ollie, Chicago Cardinals (1952 and 1954-58), L.A. Rams (1959-62), Detroit (1963), Philadelphia (1964)

MAYNARD Don, N.Y. Jets (1960-72), St Louis (1973)

McCUTCHEON Lawrence, L.A. Rams (1972-79), Denver (1980), Seattle (1980), Buffalo (1981)

McDONALD Tommy, Philadelphia (1957-63), Dallas (1964), L.A. Rams (1965-66)

MEREDITH Don, Dallas (1960-68)

MICHAELS Lou, L.A. Rams (1958-60), Pittsburgh (1961-63), Baltimore (1964-69), Green Bay (1971)

MITCHELL Bobby, Cleveland (1958-61), Washington (1962-68)

MITCHELL Lydell, Baltimore (1972-77), San Diego (1978-79)

MORGAN Dennis, Dallas (1974), Philadelphia (1975)

MORRALL Earl, San Francisco (1956), Pittsburgh (1957-58), Detroit (1958-64), N.Y. Giants (1965-67), Baltimore (1968-71), Miami (1972-76)

MORTON Craig, Dallas (1965-74), N.Y. Giants (1974-76), Denver (1977-82)

NAMATH Joe, N.Y. Jets (1965-76), L.A. Rams (1977)

NEVERS Ernie, Duluth Eskimos (1926-27), Chicago Cardinals (1929-31)

PARILLI Babe, Green Bay (1952-53 and 1956-58), Cleveland (1956), Oakland (1960), New England (1961-67), N.Y. Jets (1968-69)

PERKINS Don, Dallas (1961-68)

PERRY Joe, San Francisco (1948-60 and 1963), Baltimore (1961-62)

POWELL Art, Philadelphia (1959), N.Y. Titans (1960-62), Oakland (1963-66), Buffalo (1967)

RASHAD Ahmad, St Louis (1972-73), Buffalo (1974-75), Minnesota (1976-82)

RYAN Frank, L.A. Rams (1958-61), Cleveland (1962-68), Washington (1969-70)

SAYERS Gale, Chicago (1965-71)

SHAW Bob, L.A. Rams (1945-49), Chicago Cardinals (1950)

SIMPSON O.J., Buffalo (1969-77), San Francisco (1978-79)

SIPE Brian, Cleveland (1974-83)

SMITH Bob, Detroit (1949-54)

SMITH Jackie, St Louis (1963-77), Dallas (1978)

SMITH Noland, Kansas City (1967-69), San Francisco (1969)

SNEAD Norm, Washington (1961-63), Philadelphia (1964-70), Minnesota (1971), N.Y. Giants (1972-74 and 1976), San Francisco (1974-75)

STARR Bart, Green Bay (1956-71)

STAUBACH Roger, Dallas (1969-79)

STUDSTILL Pat, Detroit (1961-67), L.A. Rams (1968-71)

SWEETAN Karl, Detroit (1966-67), New Orleans (1968), L.A. Rams (1969-70)

TARKENTON Fran, Minnesota (1961-66 and 1972-78), N.Y. Giants (1967-71)

TATUM Jack, Oakland (1971-79), Houston (1980)

TAYLOR Charley, Washington (1964-77)

TAYLOR Jim, Green Bay (1958-66), New Orleans (1967)

TAYLOR Lionel, Chicago Bears (1959), Denver (1960-66), Houston (1967-68)

THOMPSON Bill, Denver (1969-81)

TITTLE Y.A., Baltimore (1948-51), San Francisco (1951-60), N.Y. Giants (1961-64)

TURNER Cecil, Chicago (1968-73)

TURNER Jim, N.Y. Jets (1964-70), Denver (1971-79)

UNITAS Johnny, Baltimore (1956-72), San Diego (1973)

VAN BROCKLIN Norm, L.A. Rams (1949-57), Philadelphia (1958-60)

WALSTON Bobby, Philadelphia (1951-62)

WATERFIELD Bob, Cleveland Rams (1945), L.A. Rams (1946-52)

WEST Charlie, Minnesota (1968-73), Detroit (1974-77), Denver (1978-79)

WILLARD Ken, San Francisco (1965-73)

WILLIAMS Travis, Green Bay (1967-70), L.A. Rams (1971)

YEPREMIAN Garo, Miami (1970-78), New Orleans (1979), Tampa Bay (1980-81)

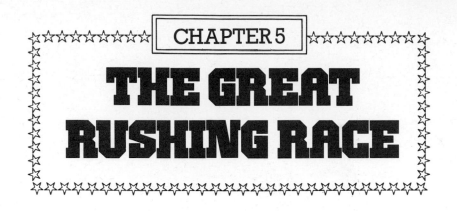

CHAPTER 5

THE GREAT RUSHING RACE

JIM BROWN

In December 1965, running back Jim Brown, of the Cleveland Browns, was in the final stages of topping up an NFL ground-gaining record, thought then and for most of the time since to be unapproachable. Playing in his 118th consecutive regular season game, he was coming to the end of a nine-year career during which he had rushed for

Jim Brown

eight yards short of seven miles, much of which had been gained with half the opposition hanging around his neck, midriff and ankles. In addition, he had caught 262 passes for 2,499 yards which, together with 648 yards gained on punt and kick returns, produced the grand total of 15,459 yards. On the way he had left a bucketful of supplemental, though only barely less remarkable, reminders of his greatness for those who would dare contemplate the attempt to scale Brown's mountain. Seven times he had rushed for over 1,000 yards in a season, and he almost made it nine out of nine, falling short by only 58 yards and a mere 4 yards, in 1957 and 1962 respectively. At the time, he was the only man to have gained over 2,000 yards in a season, combining rushing and pass receiving but excluding punt and kick returns. In four separate games, he had rushed for over 200 yards — and this at a time when no other player had done it more than once. He broke the 100-yard barrier 58 times, a figure more than twice that hitherto achieved by any other player. He had rushed for 106 touchdowns, some 29 more than by Green Bay's Jim Taylor who, at that time, lay second in this category. Furthermore, his total haul of 126 touchdowns (20 were by pass reception) was comfortably in excess of Lenny Moore's (Baltimore) 106 (Moore retired with 113 TDs). Had there been a mark for style, he would surely have ranked alongside Jayne Torvill and Christopher Dean. More than any other of Brown's staggering achievements however, it is the coveted 12,312 career rushing yardage record which, for almost two decades, has lured a succession of the NFL's elite infantrymen almost to the point of destruction, both of body and will.

The impressions of two young lads, one fifteen and the other eleven, in that December of 1965, are not recorded but, coming on nineteen years later, they will shortly re-engage in the titanic struggle from which one will emerge to claim his crown.

FRANCO HARRIS

Franco Harris was the fifteen-year old who was soon to have his first taste of national acclaim as a High School All-America at Rancocas Valley High in Mt. Holly, New Jersey. Naturally, he went on to enrol at one of the nation's college football power-houses, Penn State University, where he teamed up with Lydell Mitchell, who was the perfect foil for his style of play. However, despite rushing for a career 2,002 yards at an average of 5·3 yards per carry, and scoring 24 touchdowns, to become the eighth leading rusher in the team's history, he never quite reached the heights expected of him and was considered by some pro scouts to be inferior to his partner. But Chuck Noll, head coach of the Pittsburgh Steelers, thought differently. For three years, Noll had been patiently assembling a squad of outstanding young players and he seized the opportunity to take Harris in the first round of the 1972 collegiate draft. (He was the 13th player and the first running back selected overall.) Shortly to embark on their 40th season in the NFL, the

Franco Harris

Steelers had never won a championship of any kind but, with the not inconsiderable contributions of this exciting rookie running back, they won the AFC Central Division title. Even though he had started in only two of the first seven games, Harris was the fourth leading AFC rusher with 1,055 yards at an average of 5·6 yards per carry, the latter which still exists as the second highest figure ever achieved by a 1,000-yard rookie. (The prodigious average of 9·9 yards on 101 carries, by Beattie Feathers in 1934, is never likely to be challenged.)

With seven 100-yard games, he led the entire NFL and, with six consecutive 100-yard perform-ances, joined Jim Brown in the record book. (The existing record of seven consecutive 100-yard games is held jointly by O.J. Simpson and Earl Campbell.) Any doubts about his ability as a big-play running back were dispelled by his 75-yard touchdown run against Cleveland. Still not done, he made the 'Immaculate Reception', follow-ing a deflected Terry Bradshaw pass, to score the winning touchdown as time ran out in the Divisional Playoff game against the Raiders. A 21-17 loss to

Franco Harris

Miami in the AFC Championship Game brought an end to the season for the Steelers but not for Harris who, as AFC Rookie of the Year, was named to the AFC Pro Bowl squad for the first of nine consecutive times. The year 1972 had been one in which he established standards of which he would only rarely fall short. His twelve-year career has brought him to within 362 yards of the mighty Jim Brown.

Not surprisingly, the Steelers too have prospered, winning eight AFC Central Division titles en route to a record four Super Bowl Championships. Over nineteen playoff games, Harris has set NFL rushing records for most carries (400), yards (1,556), touchdowns (16) and, with 102 points (he scored one touchdown by pass reception), he trails George Blanda by only 13. Again, in Super Bowl play, he leads with most career rushing attempts (101), points (24) and touchdowns (4). In Super Bowl IX, he was voted the game's Most Valuable Player, having rushed for 158 yards on 34 carries, to establish records which fell only to a superhuman performance by the indestructable John Riggins in Super Bowl XVII. (The current record of 191 yards belongs to Marcus Allen of the Raiders.)

Harris does have his detractors, who would measure his achievements by comparison with the fleet-footed, more elusive running backs such as Gale Sayers and O.J. Simpson of old, and the likes of Tony Dorsett and Earl Campbell of the present day. Indeed, Harris has had only two gains of over 70 yards and he has never cracked the single game 200-yard barrier, unlike O.J. Simpson, who achieved the feat six times. In 1980, even his durability was questioned when this most punishing of roles appeared to be having its irreversible effect. But he roared back defiantly in 1981, with 987 yards, and was on schedule for 1,070 yards over the nine games of the strike-shortened 1982 season. In 1983, with his target within sight if not grasp, he became the only man ever to log eight 1,000-yard seasons, relegating Brown to second place in this category. Common sense suggests that a 34-year old running back will need six more games to surpass 12,312 yards but, when that man is called Franco Harris, you begin to think that perhaps five might be enough.

WALTER PAYTON

At eleven years old, Walter Payton had little interest in football and it was only when in his junior (penultimate) year in High School that he was persuaded to give the game a try. Before this, he could often be found in the gymnasium where his exceptional strength and co-ordination made him a 'natural' for the parallel bars. With his inherent speed and uncanny knack of wrong-footing would-be tacklers, he was soon equally at home on the gridiron. Surprisingly, he was overlooked by the major college talent spotters, and yet it mattered little to this modest young man. For him, Jackson State University, in his home state of Mississippi, was good enough. However, very quickly and throughout his college career, he would have to accept the attentions of a football world whose eyes were focused with astonishment on the most prolific scorer in the history of the National Collegiate Athletic Association (NCAA). He scored 66 touchdowns and rushed for 3,563 yards at an average of 6.1 yards per attempt. Kicking 53 PATs and five field goals, he amassed a total of 464 points. In addition, he caught 27 passes for 474 yards, was a respectable punter and returned kicks at the quite staggering average of 43 yards per attempt. Were all this not enough, he completed 14 out of 19 passes, four of which were for touchdowns. He even found time to graduate with a B.A. in special

education, as an expression of his interest in young people which would develop in later years. But first, he took his extraordinary skills into the NFL.

In the 1975 collegiate draft, the Chicago Bears had some anxious moments as the three teams before them, Atlanta, Dallas and Baltimore, made their selections. But then came their turn which they used to make Payton the first running back drafted (he was fourth overall). His name was thus added to the honour roll of all time great running backs who have played for George Halas's Bears. He would follow where 'Red' Grange, 'Bronko' Nagurski, Bill Osmanski and latterly, Gale Sayers, had gone before. However, unlike another former Bears rookie, Beattie Feathers, who has a special place in the game's history, Payton's first season was modest (he rushed for 679 yards). But in 1976, he rushed for the first of six consecutive 1,000-yard seasons to gain the first of five successive NFC rushing titles, matching Jim Brown's (NFL) dominance which had begun nineteen years earlier. Over this period, a place in both the Pro Bowl and All Pro squads was a formality and yet, still in 1976, his first thoughts were for that group of players whose praises often go unsung. To each of his offensive linemen, he gave a gold watch inscribed with the words: 'Thanks for the 1,000-yard season'. Even after his unspectacular rookie season, Jim Brown had remarked that he had never seen a running back with better instincts (for the slightest opening) and now, O.J. Simpson, who was still playing, offered his congratulations and added: 'Before your career is over, all my records will be gone and forgotten.'

Not long afterwards, on 20 November 1977, those words had a ring of truth when, against the Minnesota Vikings, Payton rushed for 275 yards to break O.J.'s single game record of 273. Furthermore, needing 599 yards with four games remaining, he was within striking distance of Simpson's single season record of 2,003 yards. He entered the final game, against the Giants in New York city, knowing that some 200 yards would be enough. Coincidentally, on near enough the same date in 1973, Simpson had done just that, in New York city but against the Jets, to establish the record. Even the weather was the same, a driving snowstorm, when Payton took to the field for the final assault. But unlike O.J., he could not master the elements and, by the end, had fallen short by 151 yards. Even so, his 1,852-yard haul was the third highest in NFL history, behind Simpson and Jim Brown's 1,863 (Earl Campbell has since registered 1,934 yards). Furthermore, he became the third player, following Brown and Simpson, to gain over 2,000 yards in a season, combining rushing and

pass receiving only (Simpson had done it twice). It was a performance which earned him the title of NFL Most Valuable Player at the youngest ever age of 23.

It is fair to assert that, had the Bears not been going through and extended lean period, many more honours would have come his way. Indeed, that he has maintained his sequence of 1,000-yard seasons throughout this time (excluding the nine-

game 1982 season), only serves to underline his greatness. Equally, unlike virtually all the modern specialist running backs, this multi-talented player could have dominated in any era. An outstanding blocker, he has also thrown five touchdown passes and would surely have been the ideal tailback (the forerunner of the modern quarterback), operating from the single wing formation used by most pro teams until the early 1940s. In addition, he has

Walter Payton

Career Rushing Statistics Compared

JIM BROWN

Year	Att.	Yds.	Ave.	Long	TDs
1957	202	942	4·7	69t	9
1958	257	1,527	5·9	65t	17
1959	290	1,329	4·6	70t	14
1960	215	1,257	5·8	71t	9
1961	305	1,408	4·6	38	8
1962	230	996	4·3	31	13
1963	291	1,863	6·4	80t	12
1964	280	1,446	5·2	71	7
1965	289	1,544	5·3	67	17

FRANCO HARRIS

Year	Att.	Yds.	Ave.	Long	TDs
1972	188	1,056	5·6	75t	10
1973	188	698	3·7	35	3
1974	208	1,006	4·8	54	5
1975	262	1,246	4·8	36	10
1976	289	1,128	3·9	30	14
1977	300	1,162	3·9	61t	11
1978	310	1,082	3·5	37	8
1979	267	1,186	4·4	71	11
1980	208	789	3·8	26	4
1981	242	987	4·1	50	8
1982	140	604	4·3	21	2
1983	279	1,007	3·6	19	5

WALTER PAYTON

Year	Att.	Yds.	Ave.	Long	TDs
1975	196	679	3·5	54t	7
1976	311	1,390	4·5	60	13
1977	339	1,852	5·5	73	14
1978	333	1,395	4·2	76	11
1979	369	1,610	4·4	43t	14
1980	317	1,460	4·6	69t	6
1981	339	1,222	3·6	39	6
1982	148	596	4·0	26	1
1983	314	1,421	4·5	49t	6

caught 328 passes for nine touchdowns, the longest covering 75 yards.

Glancing back to 1981 however, the bare statistics suggested that even his powers were on the wane — his 1,222 rushing yards were at the hard-earned average of 3·6 yards per carry. But all suggestion of that was emphatically dismissed when, in 1983, he rushed and caught passes to exceed 2,000 yards for the second time, joining O.J. Simpson and William Andrews (Atlanta). It brought him to within 207 yards of Jim Brown's combined yardage record of 15,459 (this includes punt and kick returns). More importantly though, he is now only 687 yards adrift of the magic number, 12,312.

It is most unlikely that he will win the initial race but, barring injury and with age on his side, he could well be ahead when, with Franco Harris, he completes the lap of honour.

CHAPTER 6

AMERICAN FOOTBALL CONFERENCE

TEAM RANKINGS

| | OFFENSE | | | | | | DEFENSE | | | | | |
	Total Yds.	Rushing	Passing	Points For	%Interceptions	%Sacked	Total Yds.	Rushing	Passing	Points Against	% Intercepted	%Sacks
*Baltimore	10	1	14	14	13	13	11	7	11	10	9	5
Buffalo	13	12	7	12	8	4	12	13	10	9	14	13
Cincinnati	7	7	6	8	3	7	1	1	1	3	8	7
Cleveland	4	10	3	6	9	3	5	6	6	8	7	12
Denver	14	11	9	10	6	12	9	4	12	5	5	11
Houston	12	9	11	11	14	8	10	14	2	13	12	9
Kansas City	3	14	2	4	2	5	7	10	7	11	2	10
L.A. Raiders	2	4	4	1	7	10	3	2	8	7	10	2
Miami	8	5	8	3	1	2	4	5	5	1	3	4
New England	6	3	12	13	5	11	8	11	9	2	11	8
N.Y. Jets	5	8	5	9	10	6	6	12	4	6	6	3
Pittsburgh	11	2	13	7	12	14	2	3	3	4	1	1
San Diego	1	13	1	5	11	1	13	8	13	14	13	14
Seattle	9	6	10	2	4	9	14	9	14	12	4	6

*Baltimore are now known as the Indianapolis Colts

AFC PASSERS

	Att	Comp	% Comp	Yards	Ave Gain	TD	% TD	Long	Int	Pct Int	Rating Points
Marino, Dan, *Mia.*	296	173	58.4	2210	7.47	20	6.8	t85	6	2.0	96.0
Krieg, Dave, *Sea.*	243	147	60.5	2139	8.80	18	7.4	t50	11	4.5	95.0
Fouts, Dan, *S.D.*	340	215	63.2	2975	8.75	20	5.9	t59	15	4.4	92.5
Anderson, Ken, *Cin.*	297	198	66.7	2333	7.86	12	4.0	t80	13	4.4	85.6
Plunkett, Jim, *Raiders*	379	230	60.7	2935	7.74	20	5.3	t99	18	4.7	82.7
Grogan, Steve, *N.E.*	303	168	55.4	2411	7.96	15	5.0	t76	12	4.0	81.4
Kenney, Bill, *K.C.*	603	346	57.4	4348	7.21	24	4.0	53	18	3.0	80.8
DeBerg, Steve, *Den.*	215	119	55.3	1617	7.52	9	4.2	54	7	3.3	79.9
Sipe, Brian, *Clev.*	496	291	58.7	3566	7.19	26	5.2	t66	23	4.6	79.1
Todd, Richard, *Jets*	518	308	59.5	3478	6.71	18	3.5	t64	26	5.0	70.3
Ferguson, Joe, *Buff.*	508	281	55.3	2995	5.90	26	5.1	t43	25	4.9	69.3
Zorn, Jim, *Sea.*	205	103	50.2	1166	5.69	7	3.4	43	7	3.4	64.8
Pagel, Mike, *Balt.*	328	163	49.7	2353	7.17	12	3.7	t72	17	5.2	64.0
Luck, Oliver, *Hou.*	217	124	57.1	1375	6.34	8	3.7	66	13	6.0	63.4
Stoudt, Cliff, *Pitt.*	381	197	51.7	2553	6.70	12	3.1	52	21	5.5	60.6
Luther, Ed, *S.D.*	287	151	52.6	1875	6.53	7	2.4	46	17	5.9	56.6
Elway, John, *Den.*	259	123	47.5	1663	6.42	7	2.7	t49	14	5.4	54.9

AFC RECEIVERS

	No	Yards	Ave	Long	TD
Christensen, Todd, *Raiders*	92	1247	13.6	45	12
Newsome, Ozzie, *Clev.*	89	970	10.9	t66	6
Winslow, Kellen, *S.D.*	88	1172	13.3	46	8
Smith, Tim, *Hou.*	83	1176	14.2	t47	6
Carson, Carlos, *K.C.*	80	1351	16.9	t50	7
Largent, Steve, *Sea.*	72	1074	14.9	t46	11
Allen, Marcus, *Raiders.*	68	590	8.7	36	2
Collinsworth, Cris, *Cin.*	66	1130	17.1	63	5
Joiner, Charlie, *S.D.*	65	960	14.8	t33	3
Walker, Wesley, *Jets*	61	868	14.2	t64	7
Watson, Steve, *Den.*	59	1133	19.2	t78	5
Morgan, Stanley, *N.E.*	58	863	14.9	t50	2
Chandler, Wes, *S.D.*	58	845	14.6	t44	5
Cribbs, Joe, *Buff.*	57	524	9.2	t33	7
Nathan, Tony, *Mia.*	52	461	8.9	25	1
Duper, Mark, *Mia.*	51	1003	19.7	t85	10
Marshall, Henry, *K.C.*	50	788	15.8	52	6
Harper, Bruce, *Jets*	48	413	8.6	33	2
Brown, Theotis, *K.C.*	47	418	8.9	53	2
Jones, 'Lam', *Jets*	43	734	17.1	t50	4
Curtis, Isaac, *Cin.*	42	571	13.6	t80	2
Kreider, Steve, *Cin.*	42	554	13.2	54	1
Ross, Dan, *Cin.*	42	483	11.5	30	3
Muncie, Chuck, *S.D.*	42	396	9.4	27	1
Warner, Curt, *Sea.*	42	325	7.7	28	1
Upchurch, Rick, *Den.*	40	639	16.0	40	2
Branch, Cliff, *Raiders*	39	696	17.8	t99	5
Sweeney, Calvin, *Pitt.*	39	577	14.8	42	5
Moore, Nat, *Mia.*	39	558	14.3	t66	6
Logan, Dave, *Clev.*	37	627	16.9	34	2
Hancock, Anthony, *K.C.*	37	584	15.8	50	1
Young, Charle, *Sea.*	36	529	14.7	47	2
Jones, Bobby, *Clev.*	36	507	14.1	t32	4
Lewis, Frank, *Buff.*	36	486	13.5	t27	3
Hunter, Tony, *Buff.*	36	402	11.2	t40	3
Butler, Jerry, *Buff.*	36	385	10.7	25	3
Barnwell, Malcolm, *Raiders*	35	513	14.7	41	1
Cunningham, Bennie, *Pitt.*	35	442	12.6	29	3
Johns, Paul, *Sea.*	34	486	14.3	t30	4
Harris, Franco, *Pitt.*	34	278	8.2	t29	2
Moore, Booker, *Buff.*	34	199	5.9	21	1
Sievers, Eric, *S.D.*	33	452	13.7	28	3
Dierking, Scott, *Jets*	33	275	8.3	19	0
Barkum, Jerome, *Jets*	32	385	12.0	34	1
Dressel, Chris, *Hou.*	32	316	9.9	t35	4
Jackson, Billy, *K.C.*	32	243	7.6	29	0
Alexander, Charles, *Cin.*	32	187	5.8	14	0
Paige, Stephone, *K.C.*	30	528	17.6	43	6
Franklin, Byron, *Buff.*	30	452	15.1	t43	4
Henry, Bernard, *Balt.*	30	416	13.9	t40	4
Pruitt, Mike, *Clev.*	30	157	5.2	21	2
Holt, Harry, *Clev.*	29	420	14.5	t48	3
Rose, Joe, *Mia.*	29	345	11.9	37	3
Walker, Dwight, *Clev.*	29	273	9.4	35	1
Scott, Willie, *K.C.*	29	247	8.5	22	6
Porter, Tracy, *Balt.*	28	384	13.7	38	0
Thomas, Ken, *K.C.*	28	236	8.4	25	1
Collins, Anthony, *N.E.*	27	257	9.5	20	0
Abercrombie, Walter, *Pitt.*	26	391	15.0	t51	3

Todd Christensen

	No	Yards	Ave	Long	TD
Shuler, Mickey, *Jets*	26	272	10.5	28	1
Bouza, Matt, *Balt.*	25	385	15.4	26	0
Sherwin, Tim, *Balt.*	25	358	14.3	30	0
Brammer, Mark, *Buff.*	25	215	8.6	21	2
Brooks, James, *S.D.*	25	215	8.6	36	0
Green, Boyce, *Clev.*	25	167	6.7	33	1
Dickey, Curtis, *Balt.*	24	483	20.1	t72	3
Ramsey, Derrick, *N.E.*	24	335	14.0	39	6
Doornink, Dan, *Sea.*	24	328	13.7	47	2
McMillan, Randy, *Balt.*	24	195	8.1	27	1
Johnson, Dan, *Mia.*	24	189	7.9	33	4
Renfro, Mike, *Hou.*	23	316	13.7	t38	2
Holohan, Pete, *S.D.*	23	272	11.8	35	2

AFC RUSHERS

Chuck Muncie

	Att	Yards	Ave	Long	TD
Warner, Curt, *Sea.*	335	1449	4.3	60	13
Campbell, Earl, *Hou.*	322	1301	4.0	42	12
Pruitt, Mike, *Clev.*	293	1184	4.0	27	10
Cribbs, Joe, *Buff.*	263	1131	4.3	45	3
Dickey, Curtis, *Balt.*	254	1122	4.4	56	4
Collins, Anthony, *N.E.*	219	1049	4.8	t50	10
Allen, Marcus, *Raiders*	266	1014	3.8	19	9
Harris, Franco, *Pitt.*	279	1007	3.6	19	5
Muncie, Chuck, *S.D.*	235	886	3.8	t34	12
McMillan, Randy, *Balt.*	198	802	4.1	t39	5
Johnson, Pete, *Cin.*	210	763	3.6	t16	14
Winder, Sammy, *Den.*	196	757	3.9	52	3
Franklin, Andra, *Mia.*	224	746	3.3	18	8
Nathan, Tony, *Mia.*	151	685	4.5	40	3
McNeil, Freeman, *Jets*	160	654	4.1	19	1
Pollard, Frank, *Pitt.*	135	608	4.5	32	4
Crutchfield, Dwayne, *Jets-Hou.*	140	578	4.1	17	3
Tatupu, Mosi, *N.E.*	106	578	5.5	55	4
Hawkins, Frank, *Raiders*	110	526	4.8	32	6
Alexander, Charles, *Cin.*	153	523	3.4	12	3
Brooks, James, *S.D.*	127	516	4.1	61	3
Jackson, Billy, *K.C.*	152	499	3.3	19	2
Green, Boyce, *Clev.*	104	497	4.8	29	3
Brown, Theotis, *Sea.–K.C.*	130	481	3.7	t49	8
Stoudt, Cliff, *Pitt.*	77	479	6.2	23	4
Abercrombie, Walter, *Pitt.*	112	446	4.0	t50	4
Pagel, Mike, *Balt.*	54	441	8.2	33	0
Weathers, Robert, *N.E.*	73	418	5.7	77	1
Overstreet, David, *Mia.*	85	392	4.6	44	1
van Eeghen, Mark, *N.E.*	95	358	3.8	11	2
Harper, Bruce, *Jets*	51	354	6.9	t78	1
Moriarty, Larry, *Hou.*	65	321	4.9	80	3
Hughes, David, *Sea.*	83	313	3.8	26	1
King, Kenny, *Raiders*	82	294	3.6	16	1
Moore, Booker, *Buff.*	60	275	4.6	21	0
Wilson, Stanley, *Cin.*	56	267	4.8	18	1
Poole, Nathan, *Den.*	81	246	3.0	19	4
Preston, Dave, *Den.*	57	222	3.9	28	1
Moore, Alvin, *Balt.*	57	205	3.6	13	1
Bennett, Woody, *Mia.*	49	197	4.0	25	2
Willhite, Gerald, *Den.*	43	188	4.4	t24	3
Leaks, Roosevelt, *Buff.*	58	157	2.7	12	1

	Att	Yards	Ave	Long	TD
Kinnebrew, Larry, *Cin.*	39	156	4.0	17	3
Pruitt, Greg, *Raiders*	26	154	5.9	18	2
Anderson, Ken, *Cin.*	22	147	6.7	29	1
Craft, Donald, *Hou.*	55	147	2.7	8	0
Elway, John, *Den.*	28	146	5.2	23	1
Wilson, Marc, *Raiders*	13	122	9.4	23	0
Schonert, Turk, *Cin.*	29	117	4.0	15	2
Thomas, Jewerl, *K.C.*	44	115	2.6	11	0
Dierking, Scott, *Jets*	28	113	4.0	31	3
Grogan, Steve, *N.E.*	23	108	4.7	17	2
Todd, Richard, *Jets*	35	101	2.9	17	0
Walker, Dwight, *Clev.*	19	100	5.3	15	0
Doornink, Dan, *Sea.*	40	99	2.5	9	2
Parros, Rick, *Den.*	30	96	3.2	13	1
Smith, Sherman, *S.D.*	24	91	3.8	20	0
Ferguson, Joe, *Buff.*	20	88	4.4	19	0
Bryant, Cullen, *Sea.*	27	87	3.2	9	0
Hector, Johnny, *Jets*	16	85	5.3	42	0
Plunkett, Jim, *Raiders*	26	78	3.0	20	0
Woodley, David, *Mia.*	19	78	4.1	15	0
Barber, Marion, *Jets*	15	77	5.1	13	1
Tate, Rodney, *Cinc.*	25	77	3.1	13	0
Williams, Newton, *Balt.*	28	77	2.8	13	0
Zorn, Jim, *Sea.*	30	71	2.4	t18	1
Kenney, Bill, *K.C.*	23	59	2.6	11	3
Sipe, Brian, *Clev.*	26	56	2.2	9	0
Krieg, Dave, *Sea.*	16	55	3.4	t10	2

Jim Zorn

AFC KICKERS

	XP	XPA	FG	FGA	PTS
Anderson, Gary, *Pitt.*	38	39	27	31	119
Lowery, Nick, *K.C.*	44	45	24	30	116
Bahr, Chris, *Raiders*	51	53	21	27	114
Allegre, Raul, *Balt.*	22	24	30	35	112
Johnson, Norm, *Sea.*	49	50	18	25	103
Bahr, Matt, *Clev.*	38	40	21	24	101
von Schamann, Uwe, *Mia.*	45	48	18	27	99
Karlis, Rich, *Den.*	33	34	21	25	96
Benirschke, Rolf, *S.D.*	43	45	15	24	88
Breech, Jim, *Cin.*	39	41	16	23	87
Kempf, Florian, *Hou.*	33	34	17	21	84
Leahy, Pat, *Jets*	36	37	16	24	84
Danelo, Joe, *Buff.*	33	34	10	20	63
Steinfort, Fred *Buff.–N.E.*	17	18	7	21	38
Smith, John, *N.E.*	12	15	3	6	21
Cox, Steve, *Clev.*	0	0	1	1	3
Zendejas, Joaquin, *N.E.*	3	4	0	1	3

AFC KICKOFF RETURNERS

	No	Yards	Ave	Long	TD
Walker, Fulton, *Mia.*	36	962	26.7	78	0
Brown, Steve, *Hou.*	31	795	25.6	t93	1
Williams, Kendall, *Balt.*	20	490	24.5	90	0
Dixon, Zachary, *Balt.–Sea*	51	1171	23.0	t94	1
Springs, Kirk, *Jets*	16	364	22.8	64	0
Williams, Van, *Buff.*	22	494	22.5	60	0
Brown, Preston, *Jets*	29	645	22.2	46	0
Montgomery, Cle, *Raiders*	21	464	22.1	48	0

	No	Yards	Ave	Long	TD
Smith, Ricky, *N.E.*	42	916	21.8	53	0
Walker, Dwight, *Clev.*	29	627	21.6	38	0
Green, Boyce, *Clev.*	17	350	20.6	30	0
Thomas, Zack, *Den.*	28	573	20.5	42	0
Riddick, Robb, *Buff.*	28	568	20.3	49	0
Wilson, Steve, *Den.*	24	485	20.2	32	0
Pruitt, Greg, *Raiders*	31	604	19.5	42	0
Odom, Henry, *Pitt.*	39	756	19.4	35	0
Brooks, James, *S.D.*	32	607	19.0	34	0
Porter, Ricky, *Balt.*	18	340	18.9	28	0
Roaches, Carl, *Hou.*	34	641	18.9	t97	1
Hancock, Anthony, *K.C.*	29	515	17.8	33	0
Anderson, Larry, *Balt.*	18	309	17.2	26	0
Harris, Tim, *Pitt.*	18	289	16.1	32	0
(Non-Qualifiers)					
Laird, Bruce, *S.D.*	15	342	22.8	41	0
Brown, Theotis, *K.C.*	15	301	20.1	46	0
Simmons, John, *Cin.*	14	317	22.6	36	0
Hector, Johnny, *Jets*	14	274	19.6	45	0
Verser, David, *Cin.*	13	253	19.5	29	0
Tate, Rodney, *Cin.*	13	218	16.8	23	0
Hughes, David, *Sea.*	12	282	23.5	35	0
Hall, Dino, *Clev.*	11	237	21.5	28	0
Jackson, Earnest, *S.D.*	11	201	18.3	32	0
Mosley, Mike, *Buff.*	9	236	26.2	33	0
Walls, Herkie, *Hou.*	9	110	12.2	25	0
Wilson, Stanley, *Cin.*	7	161	23.0	32	0
Horton, Ray, *Cin.*	5	128	25.6	49	0
Williams, Dokie, *Raiders*	5	88	17.6	19	0
McPherson, Miles, *S.D.*	5	77	15.4	19	0
Jones, Cedric, *N.E.*	4	63	15.8	23	0
Lane, Eric, *Sea.*	4	58	14.5	18	0
Kozlowski, Mike, *Mia.*	4	50	12.5	23	0
Dressel, Chris, *Hou.*	4	40	10.0	13	0
Lee, Keith, *N.E.*	4	40	10.0	19	0
Weathers, Robert, *N.E.*	3	68	22.7	29	0
McAlister, Ken, *Sea.*	3	59	19.7	22	0
Weathers, Clarence, *N.E.*	3	58	19.3	33	0
Mullen, Davlin, *Jets*	3	57	19.0	26	0
Williams, Ben, *Buff.*	3	56	18.7	23	0
Jodat, Jim, *S.D.*	3	45	15.0	18	0
Young, Andre, *S.D.*	3	41	13.7	19	0
Roquemore, Durwood, *K.C.*	3	36	12.0	13	0
Nathan, Tony, *Mia.*	3	15	5.0	12	0
Cherry, Deron, *K.C.*	2	54	27.0	31	0
Moore, Alvin, *Balt.*	2	40	20.0	23	0
Ferguson, Vagas, *Clev.*	2	36	18.0	27	0
Smith, Sherman, *S.D.*	2	32	16.0	21	0
Nicolas, Scott, *Clev.*	2	29	14.5	15	0
Tice, Mike, *Sea.*	2	28	14.0	19	0
Moriarty, Larry, *Hou.*	2	25	12.5	16	0
Millen, Matt, *Raiders*	2	19	9.5	10	0
Talley, Darryl, *Buff.*	2	9	4.5	5	0
Studdard, Dave, *Den.*	2	8	4.0	8	0
Heflin, Vince, *Mia.*	1	27	27.0	27	0
Clayton, Mark, *Mia.*	1	25	25.0	25	0
Martin, Mike, *Cin.*	1	19	19.0	19	0
Harper, Bruce, *Jets*	1	16	16.0	16	0
Scales, Dwight, *S.D.*	1	16	16.0	16	0
Tullis, Willie, *Hou.*	1	16	16.0	16	0

Carlos Carson

	No	Yards	Ave	Long	TD
Bingham, Craig, *Pitt.*	1	15	15.0	15	0
Carson, Carlos, *K.C.*	1	12	12.0	12	0
Hunt, Daryl, *Hou.*	1	12	12.0	12	0
McCloskey, Mike, *Hou.*	1	11	11.0	11	0

AFC PUNTERS

	No	Yards	Long	Ave	Total Punts	TB	Blk	Opp Ret	Ret Yds	In 20	Net Ave
Stark, Rohn, *Balt.*	91	4124	68	45.3	91	9	0	55	642	20	36.3
Camarillo, Rich, *N.E.*	81	3615	70	44.6	81	11	0	48	392	25	37.1
Buford, Maury, *S.D.*	63	2763	60	43.9	63	8	0	35	299	13	36.6
Roby, Reggie, *Mia.*	74	3189	64	43.1	75	11	1	32	229	26	36.5
Guy, Ray, *Raiders*	78	3336	67	42.8	78	10	0	35	334	17	35.9
Colquitt, Craig, *Pitt.*	80	3352	58	41.9	80	7	0	44	418	20	34.9
McInally, Pat, *Cin.*	67	2804	60	41.9	69	9	2	41	310	13	33.5
Prestridge, Luke, *Den.*	87	3620	60	41.6	87	7	0	55	524	19	34.0
Gossett, Jeff, *Clev.*	70	2854	60	40.8	70	8	0	30	309	17	34.1
Arnold, Jim, *K.C.*	93	3710	64	39.9	93	6	0	54	559	21	32.6
Ramsey, Chuck, *Jets*	81	3218	56	39.7	82	5	1	47	367	17	33.5
Cater, Greg, *Buff.*	89	3533	60	39.7	89	7	0	42	403	24	33.6
James, John, *Hou.*	79	3136	53	39.7	80	8	1	47	354	12	32.8
West, Jeff, *Sea.*	79	3118	56	39.5	79	10	0	36	185	25	34.6

AFC PUNT RETURNERS

	No	FC	Yards	Ave	Long	TD
Springs, Kirk, *Jets*	23	4	287	12.5	t76	1
Pruitt, Greg, *Raiders*	58	18	666	11.5	t97	1
Johns, Paul, *Sea*	28	5	316	11.3	t75	1
Thomas, Zack, *Den.*	33	9	368	11.2	t70	1
Smith, Ricky, *N.E.*	38	12	398	10.5	55	0
Martin, Mike, *Cin.*	23	3	227	9.9	19	0
Clayton, Mark, *Mia.*	41	11	392	9.6	t60	1
Skansi, Paul, *Pitt.*	43	9	363	8.4	57	0
Smith, J.T., *K.C.*	26	5	210	8.1	19	0
Roaches, Carl, *Hou.*	20	9	159	8.0	23	0
Brooks, James, *S.D.*	18	4	137	7.6	30	0
Hall, Dino, *Clev.*	39	12	284	7.3	19	0
Simmons, John, *Cin.*	25	2	173	6.9	43	0
Anderson, Larry, *Balt.*	20	4	138	6.9	20	0
Riddick, Robb, *Buff.*	42	5	241	5.7	24	0

AFC INTERCEPTORS

	No	Yards	Ave	Long	TD
Riley, Ken, *Cin.*	8	89	11.1	t42	2
McElroy, Vann, *Raiders*	8	68	8.5	28	0
Easley, Ken, *Sea.*	7	106	15.1	48	0
Cherry, Deron, *K.C.*	7	100	14.3	41	0
Mehl, Lance, *Jets*	7	57	8.1	t34	1
Walters, Danny, *S.D.*	7	55	7.9	33	0

	No	Yards	Ave	Long	TD
Sanford, Rick, *N.E.*	7	24	3.4	16	0
Brown, Dave, *Sea.*	6	83	13.8	37	0
Judson, William, *Mia.*	6	60	10.0	29	0
Green, Gary, *K.C.*	6	59	9.8	25	0
Wright, Louis, *Den.*	6	50	8.3	34	0
Horton, Ray, *Cin.*	5	121	24.2	t55	1
James, Roland, *N.E.*	5	99	19.8	46	0
Wilson, Steve, *Den.*	5	91	18.2	36	0
Tullis, Willie, *Hou.*	5	65	13.0	44	0
Small, Gerald, *Mia.*	5	60	12.0	28	0
Woods, Rick, *Pitt.*	5	53	10.6	31	0
Foley, Steve, *Den.*	5	28	5.6	16	0
Shell, Donnie, *Pitt.*	5	18	3.6	18	0
Harden, Mike, *Den.*	4	127	31.8	48	0
Roquemore, Durwood, *K.C.*	4	117	29.3	t42	1
Martin, Rod, *Raiders*	4	81	20.3	t40	2
Blackwood, Lyle, *Mia.*	4	77	19.3	45	0
Cousineau, Tom, *Clev.*	4	47	11.8	15	0
Burruss, Lloyd, *K.C.*	4	46	11.5	27	0
Lewis, Albert, *K.C.*	4	42	10.5	34	0
Simpson, Keith, *Sea.*	4	39	9.8	14	0
Smith, Dennis, *Den.*	4	39	9.8	23	0
Hatchett, Derrick, *Balt.*	4	36	9.0	25	0
Blount, Mel, *Pitt.*	4	32	8.0	21	0
Holmes, Johnny, *Jets*	3	107	35.7	t43	1
Smith, Lucious, *K.C.*	3	99	33.0	t58	1
Banks, Chip, *Clev.*	3	95	31.7	t65	1
Woodruff, Dwayne, *Pitt.*	3	85	28.3	47	0
Johnson, Ron, *Pitt.*	3	84	28.0	t34	1
Ray, Darrol, *Jets*	3	77	25.7	42	0
Lynn, Johnny, *Jets*	3	70	23.3	t42	1
Whitwell, Mike, *Clev.*	3	67	22.3	28	0
Merriweather, Mark, *Pitt.*	3	55	18.3	t31	1
Dixon, Hanford, *Clev.*	3	41	13.7	35	0
Freeman, Steve, *Buff.*	3	40	13.3	29	0
Glasgow, Nesby, *Balt.*	3	35	11.7	18	0
Kemp, Bobby, *Cin.*	3	26	8.7	26	0
Williams, Chris, *Buff.*	3	6	2.0	4	0
Blackwood, Glenn, *Mia.*	3	0	0.0	0	0
Anderson, Kim, *Balt.*	2	81	40.5	t71	1
Kozlowski, Mike, *Mia.*	2	73	36.5	t38	2
Hayes, Lester, *Raiders*	2	49	24.5	28	0
Young, Andre, *S.D.*	2	49	24.5	t40	1
Breeden, Louis, *Cin.*	2	47	23.5	39	0
Bokamper, Kim, *Mia.*	2	43	21.5	t24	1
Sanford, Lucius, *Buff.*	2	39	19.5	20	0
Kay, Bill, *Hou.*	2	31	15.5	27	0
Romes, Charles, *Buff.*	2	27	13.5	27	0
Griffin, Ray, *Cin.*	2	24	12.0	24	0
Jackson, Robert, *Cin.*	2	21	10.5	15	0

Jacob Green

	No	Yards	Ave	Long	TD
Keating, Chris, *Buff.*	2	20	10.0	17	0
Bracelin, Greg, *Balt.*	2	19	9.5	19	0
Delaney, Jeff, *Balt.*	2	16	8.0	11	0
Harris, John, *Sea.*	2	15	7.5	10	0
Fox, Tim, *S.D.*	2	14	7.0	14	0
Burroughs, Jim, *Balt.*	2	8	4.0	8	0
Jackson, Bobby, *Jets*	2	8	4.0	8	0
Schroy, Ken, *Jets*	2	6	3.0	4	0
Marion, Fred, *N.E.*	2	4	2.0	4	0
Bostic, Keith, *Hou.*	2	0	0.0	0	0
Burrell, Clinton, *Clev.*	2	0	0.0	0	0
Johnson, Lawrence, *Clev.*	2	0	0.0	0	0
Scott, Clarence, *Clev.*	2	0	0.0	0	0
Lambert, Jack, *Pitt.*	2	−1	−0.5	0	0
Green, Jacob, *Sea.*	1	73	73.0	t73	1
Clayton, Harvey, *Pitt.*	1	70	70.0	t70	1

BUFFALO BILLS AFC East

Address One Bills Drive, Orchard Park, New York 14127
Stadium Rich Stadium, Buffalo.
 Capacity 80,020 *Playing Surface* AstroTurf.
Team Colours Scarlet Red, Royal Blue and White.
Head Coach Kay Stephenson — second year.
Championships AFL 1964,'65; Division 1980.
History AFL 1960-69, AFC 1970—

Offense

In 1983, the offensive line played to a consistently high standard, despite being without right tackle Joe Devlin. With Tom Lynch substituting, they gave up only 37 quarterback sacks and their lowly ranking of 24th in the NFL for yards gained rushing is almost certainly a measure of the shortage of reserve support for running back Joe Cribbs. The departure of the latter for the USFL gives coach Stephenson a real headache, as Cribbs' obvious successor as the main rushing strike force, Booker Moore, has yet to fulfil his college promise. Drafted in the first round of 1981, Moore missed his entire rookie season with a rare nerve disorder, and made a cautious entry with 38 yards on 16 carries in 1982. His 275 yards gained at an average of 4·6 yards per carry, in 1983, are grounds for guarded optimism but he has still to show that he can lead a team into battle. Recognising the need, the Bills took Notre Dame running back Greg Bell with their first round option in the collegiate draft. Quarterback Joe Ferguson, entering his twelfth season, still has his good days (against Miami, he threw five touchdown passes) but is inconsistent and throws a few too many interceptions for comfort. He could be under pressure from Matt Kofler, who has shown good accuracy when given his few opportunities. A potentially fine receiving corps was hampered by injuries to both Frank Lewis, who has subsequently retired, and Jerry Butler — the latter's future is still uncertain. In their absence, Perry Tuttle, Mike Mosley and especially Byron Franklin (he caught 30 passes for 452 yards) made good contributions.

Another promising performance came from rookie tight end Tony Hunter, a first round pick, who caught 36 passes for 402 yards despite being bothered with shoulder and hamstring problems. He will be completely fit for 1984 and, together with Mark Brammer and Buster Barnett, gives the Bills solid depth at this position.

Defense

The Bills have slipped somewhat from their overall second ranking in 1982 to 24th in 1983, with injuries to key players again exposing a shortage of reserve strength. Left end Ben Williams is noted for his pass rushing and nose tackle Fred Smerlas confirmed his reputation, going to his fourth consecutive Pro Bowl, but only rarely were opposing quarterbacks placed under threat. Defensive end Sherman White was missed, as was the inside linebacker, Jim Haslett, in a linebacking quartet which is experienced but had a modest season defending against the run. One bright spot was the raw enthusiasm of the rookie outside linebacker, Darryl Talley, who recorded five quarterback sacks when entering the field on obvious passing downs. On paper at least, the defensive secondary ought to be good, and probably suffered from an inconsistent pass rush by the upfield players. Cornerbacks Mario Clark and Charles Romes have been around a bit and should be in their primes. Free safety Steve Freeman is well respected, and strong safety Mike Kennedy did a good job, substituting for the injured Rod Kush. Furthermore, the experienced Bill Hurley (ex Steelers) and Judson Flint (ex Browns) are available for emergency duty.

Special Teams

Both the kicker, Joe Danelo, and the punter, Greg Cater, will have to reassert themselves in training camp. Danelo, formerly of the Giants, and who replaced Fred Steinfort, kicked only 10 of 20 field goal attempts, and Cater had a modest punting average of 39·7 yards. Van Williams maintained a respectable 22·5-yard average returning kicks, with a longest of 60 yards, but Robb Riddick only just crept into the AFC list of qualifiers with his punt return average of 5·7 yards.

1984 DRAFT

Round	Name	Pos.	Ht.	Wt.	College
1.	Bell, Greg	RB	5-11	215	Notre Dame
2.	Richardson, Eric	WR	6-1	185	San Jose State
3.	Bellinger, Rodney	DB	5-8	184	Miami
3.	McNanie, Sean	DE	6-5	250	San Diego State
3.	Neal, Speedy	RB	6-1	250	Miami
4.	Brookins, Mitchell	WR	5-10	188	Illinois
5.	Kidd, John	P	6-2	200	Northwestern
6.	Slaton, Tony	C	6-3	260	Southern California
7.	David, Stan	DB	6-3	211	Texas Tech.
8.	Rayfield, Stacy	DB	6-1	195	Texas-Arlington
9.	Howell, Leroy	DE	6-4	228	Appalachian State
10.	Azelby, Joe	LB	6-2	226	Harvard
11.	White, Craig	WR	6-1	190	Missouri
12.	Davis, Russell	WR	6-5	215	Maryland

1984 SCHEDULE

September

2	NEW·ENGLAND	1:00
9	at St Louis	12:00
17	MIAMI	9:00
23	NEW YORK JETS	1:00
30	at Indianapolis	1:00

October

7	PHILADELPHIA	1:00
14	at Seattle	1:00
21	DENVER	1:00
28	at Miami	4:00
4	CLEVELAND	1:00

November

11	at New England	1:00
18	DALLAS	1:00
25	at Washington	1:00

December

2	INDIANAPOLIS	1:00
8	at New York Jets	12:30
16	at Cincinnati	1:00

Ben Williams

VETERAN ROSTER

No.	Name	Pos.	Ht.	Wt.	NFL Year	College
75	Acker, Bill	NT	6-2	255	5	Texas
84	Barnett, Buster	TE	6-5	225	4	Jackson State
73	Borchardt, Jon	G	6-5	255	6	Montana State
86	Brammer, Mark	TE	6-3	235	5	Michigan State
80	Butler, Jerry	WR	6-0	178	6	Clemson
67	Caldwell, Darryl	T	6-5	245	2	Tennessee State
7	Cater, Greg	P	6-0	191	5	Tennessee-Chattanooga
29	Clark, Mario	CB	6-2	195	9	Oregon
63	Cross, Justin	T	6-6	257	3	Western State, Colorado
18	Danelo, Joe	K	5-9	166	10	Washington State
89	Dawkins, Julius	WR	6-1	196	2	Pittsburgh
70	Devlin, Joe	T	6-5	250	9	Iowa
11	Dufek, Joe	QB	6-4	215	2	Yale
12	Ferguson, Joe	QB	6-1	195	12	Arkansas
	Flint, Judson	S	6-0	201	5	Memphis State
85	Franklin, Byron	WR	6-1	179	3	Auburn
22	Freeman, Steve	S	5-11	185	10	Mississippi State
53	Grant, Will	C	6-4	248	7	Kentucky
55	Haslett, Jim	LB	6-3	232	6	Indiana, Pa.
	Holt, Robert	WR	6-1	182	3	Baylor
25	Hooks, Roland	RB	6-0	195	9	North Carolina State
87	Hunter, Tony	TE	6-4	237	2	Notre Dame
47	Hurley, Bill	S	5-11	195	3	Syracuse
90	Hutchinson, Scott	DE	6-3	245	7	Florida
91	Johnson, Ken	DE	6-5	253	6	Knoxville
72	Jones, Ken	T	6-5	250	9	Arkansas State
50	Junkin, Trey	LB	6-2	221	2	Louisiana Tech.
52	Keating, Chris	LB	6-2	223	6	Maine
21	Kennedy, Mike	S	6-0	195	2	Toledo
43	Kilson, David	CB	6-1	200	2	Nevada-Reno
10	Kofler, Matt	QB	6-3	192	3	San Diego State
42	Kush, Rod	S	6-0	188	5	Nebraska-Omaha
48	Leaks, Roosevelt	FB	5-10	225	10	Texas
59	Lumpkin, Joey	LB	6-2	230	3	Arizona State
61	Lynch, Tom	T-G	6-5	250	8	Boston College
54	Marve, Eugene	LB	6-2	230	3	Saginaw Valley State
58	Merrill, Mark	LB	6-3	234	6	Minnesota
34	Moore, Booker	FB	5-11	224	3	Penn State
88	Mosley, Mike	WR	6-2	192	3	Texas A & M
38	Nixon, Jeff	S	6-3	190	6	Richmond
62	Parker, Ervin	LB	6-5	240	5	South Carolina State
	Payne, Jimmy	DE	6-3	264	1	Georgia
40	Riddick, Robb	RB	6-0	195	3	Millersville State
51	Ritcher, Jim	G-C	6-3	251	5	North Carolina State
26	Romes, Charles	CB	6-1	190	8	North Carolina Central
57	Sanford, Lucius	LB	6-2	216	7	Georgia Tech
76	Smerlas, Fred	NT	6-3	270	6	Boston College
56	Talley, Darryl	LB	6-3	231	2	West Virginia
	Taylor, Roger	T	6-6	271	3	Oklahoma State
24	Thompson, Gary	CB	6-0	180	2	Redwoods J.C.
81	Tuttle, Perry	WR	6-0	178	3	Clemson
	Valentine, Zack	LB	6-2	220	6	East Carolina
41	Villapiano, Phil	LB	6-2	225	13	Bowling Green
93	Virkus, Scott	DE	6-5	248	2	San Francisco C.C.
65	Vogler, Tim	G-C	6-3	245	6	Ohio State
45	Walterscheid, Len	S	5-11	190	8	Southern Utah State
83	White, Sherman	DE	6-5	250	13	California
77	Williams, Ben	DE	6-3	245	9	Mississippi
27	Williams, Chris	S	6-0	197	4	Louisiana State
23	Williams, Van	RB	6-0	208	2	Carson-Newman

INDIANAPOLIS COLTS AFC East

Address P.O. Box 20000, Indianapolis, Indiana 46220.
Stadium Hoosier Dome, Indianapolis.
 Capacity 61,000 *Playing Surface* AstroTurf
Team Colours Royal Blue, White and Silver.
Head Coach Frank Kush — third year.
Championships Super Bowl 1970; NFL 1958,'59,'68; Division 1975,'76,'77.
History NFL 1953-69, AFC 1970—
 (Until 1984, they were known as the Baltimore Colts. A team of the same name played in the AAFC, from 1947 to 1949, and in the NFL in 1950, at the end of which they went out of business.)

Offense

The Colts' return to competitiveness has begun with the formation of a good offensive line. Left tackle Karl Baldischwiler and right guard Steve Wright were inspired acquisitions from Detroit and Dallas respectively, and center Ray Donaldson is beginning to produce the consistency expected of a former number two draft pick. But the real surprise in 1983 was the instant maturity of left guard Chris Hinton, who was obtained in part exchange for quarterback John Elway and saved a few blushes by becoming a Pro Bowler in his rookie year. Running backs Curtis Dickey and Randy McMillan made sure that the efforts of the offensive line did not go unrewarded. Dickey, who had his first 1,000-yard season, is the more productive but, as a pair, they carried the Colts to first place in the AFC for yards rushing and trailed only Chicago in the NFL. Hoping to amplify this strength, offensive guard Ron Solt was the Colts second selection overall, but still in the first round of the 1984 collegiate draft. This extra first-round pick was another part of the Hinton-Elway trade (it belonged to Denver) and a good contribution from Solt will indeed make the transaction a good deal for the Colts. Two learning years after having been thrown in at the deep end, quarterback Mike Pagel has still not emerged from his apprenticeship, and yet has shown a good deal of composure and fortitude. He will, however, be pressed in training camp by Mark Herrmann, whose arrival from Denver in 1983 completed the payment for Elway. Wide receiver Ray Butler is of the highest class and was sorely missed last year when injury restricted his output to ten receptions for 207 yards. Tracy Porter and Bernard Henry ended the season as the starting pair in a passing offense which very much played second fiddle to the rushers. Equally, from the tight end position, there was only a modest yield — however Tim Sherwin will have gained confidence having doubled his career total with 25 receptions for 358 yards.

Defense

The defensive line is young and improving. Nose tackle Leo Wisniewski (he had five sacks) and defensive right end Steve Parker are solid, and left end Donnell Thompson is beginning to attract double-teaming from the opposition. They can be expected to improve. There is quite a fair quartet developing at linebacker where both Johnie Cooks and Barry Krauss are former first-round draft choices and seem on the verge of confirming that status. Vernon Maxwell (he had 11 sacks and 1 interception) was the 29th player overall to be selected in 1983 and is probably the fastest linebacker in the NFL. Greg Bracelin, who was picked up after being made available by the Raiders via the so-called 'waiver system', was a pleasant surprise, with 5½ sacks and two interceptions. In addition, the reserves, Cliff Odom, Gary Padjen and Ricky Jones, are no-nonsense tacklers. The departure of right cornerback Derrick Hatchett confirmed a suspected weakness in the defensive secondary as a whole, and Kush wasted no time in selecting Leonard Coleman with his first option in the collegiate draft. Even so, there is both stature and quality in the form of free safety Nesby Glasgow, who is the defensive captain, and left cornerback Jim Burroughs plays well enough to justify confidence in his future improvement.

Special Teams

Kicker Raul Allegre was another excellent acquisition from Dallas and forms a partnership with punter Rohn Stark in what must be the best young combination in the NFL. Allegre kicked 30 of 35 field goal attempts and Stark led the entire NFL with a gross average of 45·3 yards. Kendall Williams maintained the NFL's fourth best average returning kickoffs but the veteran punt returner, Larry Anderson, was disappointing and may be replaced.

1984 DRAFT

Round	Name	Pos.	Ht.	Wt.	College
1.	Coleman, Leonard	DB	6-1	195	Vanderbilt
1.	Solt, Ron	G	6-2	270	Maryland
2.	Winter, Blaise	DT	6-3	260	Syracuse
3.	Scott, Chris	DT	6-4	250	Purdue
4.	Curry, Craig	DB	5-11	190	Texas
4.	Wonsley, George	RB	5-9	200	Mississippi State
5.	Tate, Golden	WR	6-2	185	Tennessee State
5.	Call, Kevin	T	6-6	285	Colorado State
6.	Beverly, Dwight	RB	5-10	195	Illinois
8.	Daniel, Eugene	DB	5-10	180	Louisiana State
11.	Stowe, Bob	T	6-4	272	Illinois
12.	Hathaway, Steve	LB	6-3	215	West Virginia

Chris Hinton

1984 SCHEDULE

September
2	NEW YORK JETS	4:00
9	at Houston	3:00
16	ST. LOUIS	1:00
23	at Miami	4:00
30	BUFFALO	1:00

October
7	WASHINGTON	1:00
14	at Philadelphia	1:00
21	PITTSBURGH	1:00
28	at Dallas	12:00

November
4	SAN DIEGO	1:00
11	at New York Jets	1:00
18	NEW ENGLAND	1:00
25	at Los Angeles Raiders	1:00

December
2	at Buffalo	1:00
9	MIAMI	1:00
16	at New England	1:00

VETERAN ROSTER

No.	Name	Pos.	Ht.	Wt.	NFL Year	College
74	Abramowitz, Sid	T	6-5	280	2	Tulsa
2	Allegre, Raul	K	5-10	165	2	Texas
26	Anderson, Kim	CB-S	5-10	182	5	Arizona State
30	Anderson, Larry	S-KR	5-11	188	7	Louisiana Tech.
72	Baldischwiler, Karl	T	6-5	260	7	Oklahoma
97	Ballard, Quinton	NT	6-3	260	2	Elon College
81	Beach, Pat	TE	6-4	243	3	Washington State
90	Bell, Mark	DE	6-4	240	5	Colorado State
85	Bouza, Matt	WR	6-3	211	3	California
52	Bracelin, Greg	LB	6-1	210	5	California
45	Burroughs, James	CB	6-1	192	3	Michigan State
80	Butler, Ray	WR	6-2	195	5	USC
98	Cooks, Johnie	LB	6-4	243	3	Mississippi State
33	Dickey, Curtis	HB	6-0	209	5	Texas A & M
53	Donaldson, Ray	C	6-4	260	5	Georgia
50	Feasel, Grant	C	6-7	255	2	Abilene Christian
25	Glasgow, Nesby	FS	5-10	180	6	Washington
88	Henry, Bernard	WR	6-0	185	3	Arizona State
9	Herrmann, Mark	QB	6-4	184	4	Purdue
75	Hinton, Chris	G	6-4	265	2	Northwestern
57	Humiston, Mike	LB	6-3	238	4	Weber State
51	Jones, Ricky	LB	6-2	222	8	Tuskegee
29	Kafentzis, Mark	S	5-10	185	3	Hawaii
55	Krauss, Barry	LB	6-3	232	6	Alabama
56	Maxwell, Vernon	LB	6-2	225	2	Arizona State
32	McMillan, Randy	FB	6-0	220	4	Pittsburgh
76	Mills, Jim	T	6-8	270	2	Hawaii
23	Moore, Alvin	HB	6-0	197	2	Arizona State
84	Oatis, Victor	WR	5-11	178	2	Northwest Louisiana
49	Odom, Cliff	LB	6-2	225	4	Texas-Arlington
60	Padjen, Gary	LB	6-2	246	3	Arizona State
18	Pagel, Mike	QB	6-2	201	3	Arizona State
78	Parker, Steve	DE	6-3	235	2	Northwestern
20	Porter, Rick	HB	5-10	190	3	Slippery Rock
87	Porter, Tracy	WR	6-1	196	4	Louisiana State
35	Randle, Tate	CB	6-0	202	3	Texas Tech.
8	Reed, Mark	QB	6-3	195	3	Moorhead
83	Sherwin, Tim	TE	6-6	237	4	Boston College
54	Shiver, Sanders	LB	6-2	227	9	Carson-Newman
	Smith, Phil	WR	6-3	190	2	San Diego State
3	Stark, Rohn	P	6-3	195	3	Florida State
12	Taylor, Jim Bob	QB	6-2	205	2	Georgia Tech.
21	Thompson, Aundra	WR	6-1	186	8	East Texas State
99	Thompson, Donnell	DE	6-4	254	4	North Carolina
64	Utt, Ben	G	6-4	255	3	Georgia Tech.
71	Waechter, Henry	DE	6-5	270	3	Nebraska
44	Williams, Kendall	CB	5-9	185	2	Arizona State
39	Williams, Newton	FB	5-10	204	3	Arizona State
69	Wisniewski, Leo	NT	6-2	263	3	Penn State
73	Wright, Steve	G-T	6-5	263	4	Northern Iowa
86	Young, Dave	TE	6-5	240	3	Purdue

MIAMI DOLPHINS AFC East

Address 3550 Biscayne Boulevard, Miami, Florida 33137.
Stadium Orange Bowl, Miami.
Capacity 75,459 *Playing Surface* Grass (Prescription Athletic Turf).
Team Colours Aqua, Coral and White
Head Coach Don Shula — fifteenth year.
Championships Super Bowl 1972,'73; AFC 1971,'82; Division 1974,'79,'81,'83.
History AFL 1966-69, AFC 1970—

Offense

As one comes to expect of any team coached by Don Shula, the Dolphins have but few weaknesses. Center Dwight Stephenson, right guard Ed Newman and left guard Bob Kuechenberg, all went to the Pro Bowl and some would consider right tackle Eric Laakso unlucky not to have joined them. Collectively, they gave up just 23 quarterback sacks, tying with the Rams for the lowest number in the NFL. However, they were less successful clearing the way for the running backs, though this could be more a measure of a modest performance by Andra Franklin, who gained only 746 yards at the disappointing average of 3·3 yards per carry (he would be expected to gain over 1,000 yards.) The elusive Tony Nathan turned in a useful 685 yards at the healthy average of 4·5 yards per carry and the signs are that David Overstreet is adjusting to the demands of the NFL (he came from the Canadian Football League in 1983). Tommy Vigorito returns from injury to challenge alongside Woody Bennett, who is a valuable short-yardage specialist. Five quarterbacks had been selected in the 1983 collegiate draft before the Dolphins picked up Dan Marino (he was taken 27th overall), but he has fulfilled all their hopes. A rifle arm, an exceptionally quick release and an uncanny ability to read defenses, added up to a passer rating of 96·0 which was good enough to lead the AFC. Reserve quarterback Don Strock is vastly experienced and might well be a starter with other teams in the league. The versatile Tony Nathan led the team in number of passes

caught, but wide receiver Mark 'Super' Duper was only one behind with 51, at the excellent average of 19·7 yards, including an 85-yard touchdown against the Colts. It is interesting that Duper, who didn't catch a pass in his rookie year (1982), was regarded with 'some optimism' by the Dolphins in their pre-season review. The other starter, Nat Noore, clearly thrived on Duper's success and, together with Mark Clayton and the returning Jimmy Cefalo, makes up Miami's best set of wide receivers for some time. At tight end, both Joe Rose and Dan Johnson chip in with timely pass receptions, whilst Bruce Hardy is a good blocker.

Defense

The Dolphins led the entire NFL in fewest points allowed (250) and went some way towards correcting a weakness against the rush which was exploited by the Redskins in Super Bowl XVII. Of the defensive linemen, both left end Doug Betters, who had his best ever season with 16 sacks, and nose tackle Bob Baumhower went to the Pro Bowl. However, the right side of the defense was less effective, once more against rushing plays, and coach Shula admitted his concern by selecting linebackers, Jackie Shipp and Jay Brophy, with his first two options in the collegiate draft. Left outside linebacker Bob Brudzinski continues in prime form, as do Earnie Rhone and Charles Bowser, particularly against the pass. The defensive secondary is at times outstanding and could well be unchanged despite the availability of former starting cornerback Don McNeal. Cornerbacks William Judson and Gerald Small grabbed six and five interceptions respectively and the Blackwood brothers, Lyle and Glenn, are uncompromising tacklers in the safety positions.

Special Teams

Rookie punter Reggie Roby who, with a 43·1-yard gross average ranked fourth in the NFL, has emerged to complement the reliable kicking skills of Uwe von Schamann. Fulton Walker led the NFL with a 26·7-yard average for kick returns and Mark Clayton played his full part in a superb special team effort, returning punts for an average of 9·6 yards.

1984 DRAFT

Round	Name	Pos.	Ht.	Wt.	College
1.	Shipp, Jackie	LB	6-2	233	Oklahoma
2.	Brophy, Jay	LB	6-2	228	Miami
4.	Carter, Joe	RB	5-11	195	Alabama
5.	May, Dean	QB	6-5	215	Louisville
6.	Tatum, Rowland	LB	6-0	225	Ohio State
7.	Carvalho, Bernard	G	6-3	260	Hawaii
8.	Landry, Ronnie	RB	6-1	217	McNeese State
9.	Boyle, Jim	T	6-4	275	Tulane
10.	Chesley, John	TE	6-4	225	Oklahoma State
11.	Brown, Bud	DB		187	So. Mississippi
12.	Devane, William	DT	6-2	265	Clemson
12.	Weingrad, Mike	LB	6-1	225	Illinois

1984 SCHEDULE

September

2	at Washington	1:00
9	NEW ENGLAND	1:00
17	at Buffalo	9:00
23	INDIANAPOLIS	4:00
30	at St Louis	12:00

October

7	at Pittsburgh	1:00
14	HOUSTON	1:00
21	at New England	1:00
28	BUFFALO	1:00

November

4	at New York Jets	4:00
11	PHILADELPHIA	1:00
18	at San Diego	1:00
26	NEW YORK JETS	9:00

December

2	LOS ANGELES RAIDERS	4:00
9	at Indianapolis	1:00
17	DALLAS	9:00

Dan Marino (13) and Mark Duper (85)

VETERAN ROSTER

No.	Name	Pos.	Ht.	Wt.	NFL Year	College
70	Barnett, Bill	NT	6-4	260	5	Nebraska
73	Baumhower, Bob	NT	6-5	260	8	Alabama
34	Bennett, Woody	RB	6-2	222	6	Miami
91	Benson, Charles	DE	6-3	267	2	Baylor
75	Betters, Doug	DE	6-7	260	7	Nevada-Reno
47	Blackwood, Glenn	S	6-0	186	6	Texas
42	Blackwood, Lyle	S	6-1	188	12	Texas Christian
58	Bokamper, Kim	DE	6-6	250	8	San Jose State
56	Bowser, Charles	LB	6-3	222	3	Duke
51	Brown, Mark	LB	6-2	226	2	Purdue
59	Brudzinski, Bob	LB	6-4	230	8	Ohio State
81	Cefalo, Jimmy	WR	5-11	188	7	Penn State
71	Charles, Mike	DE	6-4	283	2	Syracuse
76	Clark, Steve	DE	6-4	255	3	Utah
83	Clayton, Mark	WR-PR	5-9	172	2	Louisville
77	Duhe, A.J.	LB	6-4	248	8	Louisiana State
85	Duper, Mark	WR	5-9	185	3	Northwestern Louisiana
61	Foster, Roy	T	6-4	275	3	USC
37	Franklin, Andra	FB	5-10	225	4	Nebraska
79	Giesler, Jon	T	6-4	260	6	Michigan
74	Green, Cleveland	T	6-3	262	6	Southern
84	Hardy, Bruce	TE	6-4	230	7	Arizona State
88	Heflin, Vince	WR	6-0	185	3	Central State, Ohio
53	Hester, Ron	LB	6-1	218	3	Florida State
31	Hill, Eddie	RB	6-2	210	6	Memphis State
11	Jensen, Jim	WR-QB	6-4	212	4	Boston University
87	Johnson, Dan	TE	6-3	245	2	Iowa State
49	Judson, William	CB	6-1	181	3	South Carolina State
40	Kozlowski, Mike	S	6-0	198	5	Colorado
67	Kuechenberg, Bob	G	6-2	255	15	Notre Dame
68	Laakso, Eric	T	6-4	265	7	Tulane
44	Lankford, Paul	S	6-1	178	3	Penn State
13	Marino, Dan	QB	6-3	214	2	Pittsburgh
28	McNeal, Don	CB	5-11	192	5	Alabama
89	Moore, Nat	WR	5-9	188	11	Florida
22	Nathan, Tony	HB	6-0	206	6	Alabama
64	Newman, Ed	G	6-2	255	12	Duke
20	Overstreet, David	HB	5-11	208	2	Oklahoma
55	Rhone, Earnie	LB	6-2	224	9	Henderson, Ark.
4	Roby, Reggie	P	6-2	243	2	Iowa
80	Rose, Joe	TE	6-3	230	5	California
	Shull, Steve	LB	6-1	220	5	William & Mary
48	Small, Gerald	CB	5-11	192	7	San Jose State
45	Sowell, Robert	CB	5-11	175	2	Howard
57	Stephenson, Dwight	C	6-2	255	5	Alabama
10	Strock, Don	QB	6-5	220	11	Virginia Tech.
52	Tautolo, Terry	LB	6-2	227	8	UCLA
54	Thomas, Rodell	LB	6-1	227	4	Alabama State
	Tilley, Emmett	LB	5-11	240	2	Duke
60	Toews, Jeff	G-C	6-3	255	6	Washington
32	Vigorito, Tommy	RB-KR	5-10	197	4	Virginia
5	von Schamann, Uwe	K	6-0	188	6	Oklahoma
41	Walker, Fulton	CB-KR	5-10	193	4	West Virginia

NEW ENGLAND PATRIOTS AFC East

Address Sullivan Stadium, Route 1, Foxboro, Mass. 02035.
Stadium Sullivan Stadium, Foxboro.
 Capacity 61,297 *Playing Surface* Super Turf.
Team Colours Red, Blue and White.
Head Coach Ron Meyer — third year.
Championships Division 1978.
History AFL 1960-69, AFC 1970—
 (Until 1971, they were known as the Boston Patriots.)

Offense

The offensive line is big, strong and highly effective on rushing plays, particularly on the left side, which features the Pro Bowlers, tackle Brian Holloway and guard John Hannah. Pete Brock is a dependable center and the 280-lb Ron Wooten has eased smoothly into a starting role inside right tackle Bob Cryder, who is even heavier at 293 lb. They have yet to establish consistent pass protection, however, and quarterback Steve Grogan went down under most of the 45 sacks yielded in 1983. Having suspect knees, this he can ill afford but, given adequate protection, he can riddle any defense with his 'bombs away' style, as he did in 1983 until being injured on week twelve against the Browns. His replacement, rookie Tony Eason, shows a good deal of class and gained valuable experience late in the season. With the arrival of wide receiver Irving Fryar, who was the overall number one selection in the 1984 collegiate draft, the prospects for the passing offense become really exciting. At the very least, he will deflect attention away from Stanley Morgan who, for so long, has been subjected to double coverage by defenders. Last year's third round selection, Stephen Starring, is a genuine big-play wide receiver (he averaged 22·9 yards on 17 receptions) and with 1983's number two pick, Darryal Wilson, returning from injury, Grogan could be spoilt for choice. There are no problems with the rushing offense in which Tony Collins has led the team for the last three years. Season 1983 saw his first 1,000-yard campaign, gained at the remarkable average of 4·8 yards per carry, and against

the Jets he rushed for 212 yards to break the Patriots' single game record of 208 yards, set by Jim Nance in 1966. There will be competition for the other spot following the retirement of Mark van Eeghen. Mosi Tatupu, who in 1983 averaged over five yards per carry for the third year in a row, would be an excellent replacement — even so, he will first have to stave off the challenge of Craig James who has arrived from the USFL (James partnered Eric Dickerson at Southern Methodist University).

Defense

The defense is inconsistent, but has all the pieces which need only come together to form one of the NFL's best. Despite the loss of defensive left end Ken Sims for almost all the season (he was the overall number one selection in 1982) and injuries to George Crump and nose tackle Lester Williams, the line remained competitive with right end Julius Adams as its cornerstone. With the return of Sims and Williams, Dennis Owens and Toby Williams will become the experienced reserves. Both Clayton Weishuhn and Andre Tippett are very fine young linebackers. Tippett showed his versatility when moving to an inside position, following injury to Steve Nelson, and Larry McGrew was an adequate replacement for Don Blackmon. Nelson and Blackmon will be back to complete what could be a marauding forward group of seven. Safeties Rick Sanford and Roland James were responsible for 12 of the Patriots' 17 interceptions (they caught 7 and 5 respectively) and though cornerback Ray Clayborn was empty-handed in this category, he played well enough to earn selection to the Pro Bowl as replacement for Louis Wright of Denver. Rookie cornerback Ronnie Lippett had the unenviable responsibility of filling in for the departed Mike Haynes (he went to the Raiders) and, by all accounts, is going to be a good one.

Special Teams

Kicker Joaquin Zendejas took over from Fred Steinfort, who had replaced John Smith. He faces the challenge from former Eagles kicker Tony Franklin. Rich Camarillo went to the Pro Bowl after averaging a gross 44·6 yards to rank second in the NFL. Ricky Smith does a respectable job returning both kickoffs and punts.

1984 DRAFT

Round	Name	Pos.	Ht.	Wt.	College
1.	Fryar, Irving	WR	5-11	195	Nebraska
2.	Williams, Ed	LB	6-2	238	Texas
3.	Williams, Jon	RB	5-9	202	Penn State
5.	Fairchild, Paul	G	6-3	260	Kansas
6.	Gibson, Ernest	DB	5-10	180	Furman
7.	Kallmeyer, Bruce	K	5-10	180	Kansas
7.	Williams, Derwin	WR			New Mexico
8.	Keyton, James	T	6-4	285	Arizona State
9.	Bolzan, Scott	T	6-4	280	Northern Illinois
9.	Windham, David	LB	6-2	235	Jackson State
11.	Flager, Charlie	G	6-3	259	Washington State
12.	Howell, Harper	TE	6-3	220	UCLA

1984 SCHEDULE

September
2	at Buffalo	1:00
9	at Miami	1:00
16		1:00
23	WASHINGTON	1:00
30	at New York Jets	1:00

October
7	at Cleveland	1:00
14	CINCINNATI	1:00
21	MIAMI	1:00
28	NEW YORK JETS	1:00

November
4	at Denver	2:00
11	BUFFALO	1:00
18	at Indianapolis	1:00
22	at Dallas	3:00
29	ST LOUIS	1:00

December
9	at Philadelphia	1:00
16	INDIANAPOLIS	1:00

Steve Grogan

VETERAN ROSTER

No.	Name	Pos.	Ht.	Wt.	NFL Year	College
85	Adams, Julius	DE	6-3	270	13	Texas Southern
55	Blackmon, Don	LB	6-3	245	4	Tulsa
58	Brock, Pete	C	6-5	275	9	Colorado
3	Camarillo, Rich	P	5-11	191	4	Washington
26	Clayborn, Ray	CB	6-0	186	8	Texas
33	Collins, Anthony	RB	5-11	203	4	East Carolina
91	Crump, George	DE	6-4	260	3	East Carolina
75	Cryder, Bob	T	6-4	293	7	Alabama
87	Dawson, Lin	TE	6-3	240	4	North Carolina State
47	Dombroski, Paul	CB	6-0	185	5	Linfield
11	Eason, Tony	QB	6-4	212	2	Illinois
	Franklin, Tony	K	5-8	182	6	Texas A & M
59	Golden, Tim	LB	6-2	220	3	Florida
14	Grogan, Steve	QB	6-4	210	10	Kansas State
68	Haley, Darryl	T	6-4	279	3	Utah
73	Hannah, John	G	6-3	265	12	Alabama
70	Henson, Luther	NT	6-0	275	3	Ohio State
76	Holloway, Brian	T	6-7	288	4	Stanford
51	Ingram, Brian	LB	6-4	230	3	Tennessee
	James, Craig	RB	6-1	215	R	Southern Methodist
38	James, Roland	S	6-2	191	5	Tennessee
83	Jones, Cedric	WR	5-11	184	3	Duke
19	Kerrigan, Mike	QB	6-3	190	2	Northwestern
22	Lee, Keith	S	5-11	193	4	Colorado State
42	Lippett, Ronnie	CB	5-11	180	2	Miami
31	Marion, Fred	S	6-2	196	3	Miami
50	McGrew, Larry	LB	6-5	233	4	USC
67	Moore, Steve	T	6-4	285	2	Tennessee State
86	Morgan, Stanley	WR	5-11	181	8	Tennessee
57	Nelson, Steve	LB	6-2	230	11	North Dakota State
98	Owens, Dennis	NT	6-1	252	3	North Carolina State
35	Peoples, George	RB	6-0	211	3	Auburn
88	Ramsey, Derrick	TE	6-5	235	7	Kentucky
52	Rembert, Johnny	LB	6-3	234	2	Clemson
94	Reynolds, Ed	LB	6-5	230	2	Virginia
65	Rogers, Doug	DE	6-5	255	3	Stanford
25	Sanford, Rick	S	6-1	192	6	South Carolina
77	Sims, Kenneth	DE	6-5	279	3	Texas
27	Smith, Ricky	CB-PR	6-0	174	3	Alabama State
81	Starring, Stephen	WR	5-10	172	2	McNeese State
30	Tatupu, Mosi	RB	6-0	227	7	USC
56	Tippett, Andre	LB	6-3	231	3	Iowa
82	Weathers, Clarence	WR	5-9	170	2	Delaware State
24	Weathers, Robert	RB	6-2	217	3	Arizona State
53	Weishuhn, Clayton	LB	6-2	220	3	Angelo State
62	Wheeler, Dwight	C-G	6-3	269	6	Tennessee State
80	Williams, Brooks	TE	6-4	226	7	North Carolina
72	Williams, Lester	NT	6-2	272	3	Miami
90	Williams, Toby	DE	6-3	254	2	Nebraska
	Wilson, Darryal	WR	6-0	182	2	Tennessee
61	Wooten, Ron	G	6-4	280	3	North Carolina
5	Zendejas, Joaquin	K	5-10	174	2	La Verne, Calif.

NEW YORK JETS AFC East

Address 598, Madison Avenue, New York, N.Y. 10022.
Stadium Giants Stadium, East Rutherford, N.J. 07073.
   Capacity 76,891 *Playing Surface* AstroTurf.
Team Colours Kelly Green and White.
Head Coach Joe Walton — second year.
Championships Super Bowl 1968.
History AFL 1960-69, AFC 1970—
   (Until 1963, they were known as the New York Titans.)

Offense

The Jets entered the 1983 season strongly fancied to win the AFC Championship, and it is against this background that an otherwise respectable performance must be described as disappointing. There is talent spread throughout the squad, not least on the offensive line which includes the All Pros, right tackle Marvin Powell and center Joe Fields. Elsewhere, left tackle Chris Ward is good and the others dependable. It is becoming more apparent that the Jets' system relies heavily, not only on the performance but also the very presence, of running back Freeman McNeil. He was the NFL Leading Rusher in 1982 and even though missing four complete games of the 1983 season, he still rushed for 654 yards at an average of 4·1 yards per carry. In his absence, Bruce Harper made good contributions, particularly with 118 yards on only nine carries against Buffalo and a career best 78-yard touchdown run against Atlanta. Indeed, his average of 6·9 yards per carry for the season is quite remarkable, but then he rushed a mere 51 times. The veteran Scott Dierking and the exciting young Dwayne Crutchfield have been traded, leaving Mike Augustyniak and Marion Barber in the competition for playing time. A healthy Freeman McNeil will certainly release the pressure on the passing offense, which will be without the services of quarterback Richard Todd (he has been traded to New Orleans). Here the Jets could be vulnerable, since Pat Ryan has completed only 48 passes in a six-year career, and last year's rookie, Ken O'Brien, has yet to have his first taste of competition. On the other hand, wide receiver Wesley Walker is a former Pro Bowler and Johnny 'Lam' Jones has become much more than an Olympic sprinter (he is a gold medallist) who catches the odd pass. Reserve Derrick Gaffney is certainly capable of hauling in the receptions if given the chance. The veteran tight end, Jerome Barkum, has retired, making way for Mickey Shuler and Tom Coombs to battle it out for a starting position.

Defense

Even without Abdul Salaam and Kenny Neil (they have been traded to San Diego), the defensive line will be as good as its nickname, 'The New York Sack Exchange', suggests. Left end Mark Gastineau remains as one of the NFL's most effective (and demonstrative) pass rushers although, under the new rules, he will have to tone down his post-sack celebrations. Joe Klecko will probably return to the right end position from where, in 1981, he recorded a club record 20½ sacks and earned a trip to the Pro Bowl. The departures of linebackers Ron Crosby and Stan Blinka place extra importance on the return of a healthy Greg Buttle to take his place alongside John Woodring, Bob Crable and Lance Mehl — the last-named had seven interceptions in 1983. With only modest reserve strength, the Jets took Kyle Clifton and Bobby Bell in draft rounds three and four respectively. Darrol Ray, Bobby Jackson and Ken Schroy form the basis of a solid defensive secondary — however the defections of Jerry Holmes and Jesse Johnson (both to the USFL) leave the Jets a little short if injuries strike.

Special Teams

Kicker Pat Leahy is steady but the punter, Chuck Ramsey, could do with two or three more yards on top of his 39·7 gross average. Kirk Springs was an unqualified success in his first season as kickoff and punt returner. His 22.8-yard average on kickoffs included a 64-yarder and, with an average of 12·5 yards, he led the AFC returning punts. Furthermore, a 76-yard punt return brought victory for the Jets over New Orleans.

1984 DRAFT

Round	Name	Pos.	Ht.	Wt.	College
1.	Carter, Russell	DB	6-2	185	Southern Methodist
1.	Faurot, Ron	DE	6-7	265	Arkansas
2.	Sweeney, Jim	C	6-3	255	Pittsburgh
2.	Dennison, Glenn	TE	6-2	219	Miami
3.	Clifton, Kyle	LB	6-2	230	Texas Christian
4.	Bell, Bobby Jr.	LB	6-2	218	Missouri
5.	Armstrong, Tron	WR	6-0	195	Eastern Kentucky
6.	Paige, Tony	RB	5-11	225	Virginia Tech.
7.	Hamilton, Harry	DB	5-11	190	Penn State
8.	Griggs, Billy	TE	6-2	228	Virginia
8.	Wright, Brett	P	6-4	205	S.E. Louisiana
9.	Baldwin, Tom	DT			Tulsa
10.	Cone, Ronny	RB	6-1	220	Georgia Tech.
11.	Martin, Dan	T	6-4	272	Iowa State
12.	Roberson, David	WR		184	Houston

1984 SCHEDULE

September
2	at Indianapolis	4:00
6	PITTSBURGH	9:00
16	CINCINNATI	1:00
23	at Buffalo	1:00
30	NEW ENGLAND	1:00

October
7	at Kansas City	12:00
14	at Cleveland	1:00
21	KANSAS CITY	4:00
28	at New England	1:00

November
4	MIAMI	4:00
11	INDIANAPOLIS	1:00
18	at Houston	3:00
26	at Miami	9:00

December
2	NEW YORK GIANTS	1:00
8	BUFFALO	12:30
16	at Tampa Bay	1:00

The 'Sack Exchange'

VETERAN ROSTER

No.	Name	Pos.	Ht.	Wt.	NFL Year	College
60	Alexander, Dan	G	6-4	260	8	Louisiana State
35	Augustyniak, Mike	FB	5-11	226	4	Purdue
31	Barber, Marion	RB	6-3	224	3	Minnesota
78	Bennett, Barry	DT	6-4	257	7	Concordia
64	Bingham, Guy	C-G-T	6-3	255	5	Montana
89	Brown, Preston	WR-KR	5-11	187	4	Vanderbilt
86	Bruckner, Nick	WR	5-11	185	2	Syracuse
51	Buttle, Greg	LB	6-3	232	9	Penn State
88	Coombs, Tom	TE	6-3	236	3	Idaho
50	Crable, Bob	LB	6-3	228	3	Notre Dame
52	Eliopulos, Jim	LB	6-3	231	2	Wyoming
65	Fields, Joe	C	6-2	253	10	Widener
38	Floyd, George	S	5-11	190	3	Eastern Kentucky
81	Gaffney, Derrick	WR	6-1	182	7	Florida
99	Gastineau, Mark	DE	6-5	269	6	East Central Oklahoma
94	Guilbeau, Rusty	DE	6-4	250	3	McNeese State
42	Harper, Bruce	RB	5-8	177	8	Kutztown State, Pa.
34	Hector, Johnny	RB	5-11	200	2	Texas A & M
40	Jackson, Bobby	CB	5-10	180	7	Florida State
80	Jones, Johnny 'Lam'	WR	5-11	180	4	Texas
73	Klecko, Joe	DT	6-3	269	8	Temple
30	Klever, Rocky	RB	6-3	225	2	Montana
5	Leahy, Pat	K	6-0	189	11	St Louis
22	Lewis, Kenny	RB	6-0	196	5	Virginia Tech.
59	Lilja, George	C	6-4	250	3	Michigan
29	Lynn, Johnny	CB-S	6-0	198	5	UCLA
93	Lyons, Marty	DT	6-5	269	6	Alabama
68	McElroy, Reggie	T	6-6	270	2	West Texas State
24	McNeil, Freeman	RB	5-11	216	4	UCLA
56	Mehl, Lance	LB	6-3	235	5	Penn State
20	Mullen, Davlin	CB-PR	6-1	175	2	Western Kentucky
16	O'Brien, Ken	QB	6-4	210	2	Cal-Davis
62	Pellegrini, Joe	G-C	6-4	252	3	Harvard
79	Powell, Marvin	T	6-5	271	8	USC
15	Ramsey, Chuck	P	6-2	189	8	Wake Forest
28	Ray, Darrol	S	6-1	206	5	Oklahoma
76	Rudolph, Ben	DT-DE	6-5	270	4	Long Beach State
10	Ryan, Pat	QB	6-3	210	7	Tennessee
48	Schroy, Ken	S	6-2	198	8	Maryland
82	Shuler, Mickey	TE	6-3	236	7	Penn State
21	Springs, Kirk	S-PR	6-0	192	4	Miami, Ohio
70	Waldemore, Stan	G-C-T	6-4	269	7	Nebraska
85	Walker, Wesley	WR	6-0	179	8	California
72	Ward, Chris	T	6-3	267	7	Ohio State
57	Woodring, John	LB	6-2	232	4	Brown

CINCINNATI BENGALS AFC Central

Address 200, Riverfront Stadium, Cincinnati, Ohio 45202.
Stadium Riverfront Stadium, Cincinnati.
  Capacity 59,754 *Playing Surface* AstroTurf.
Team Colours Black, Orange and White.
Head Coach Sam Wyche — first year.
Championships AFC 1981; Division 1970,'73.
History AFL 1968-69, AFC 1970—

Offense

Anthony Munoz, a four-time Pro Bowler, is outstanding at left tackle and, over on the right side, Max Montoya and Mike Wilson have been together for several years at guard and tackle respectively. Last year's first-round draft choice, center Dave Rimington, has moved ahead of Blake Moore, who may be tried at left guard following the departure of Dave Lapham for the USFL. A good line will be reinforced by the arrival of this year's first round pick, the 320-lb tackle, Brian Blados. In a significant player swap, the heavyweight running back, Pete Johnson, has been traded to the Chargers in exchange for the quicksilver James Brooks. Clearly, this brings about a shift in emphasis from power to speed and it remains to be seen how Charles Alexander, who played well in partnership with Johnson, will fit in. He could be displaced by the young Stanley Wilson who last year almost unnoticed, gained 267 yards at the excellent average of 4.8 yards per carry. At quarterback, Ken Anderson is a master and narrowly missed leading the entire NFL for the third successive year. Anderson holds NFL records for completion percentage over a season (70·3%) and most consecutive pass completions (20). Turk Schonert, too, is an accurate passer when playing in relief of the great man. Wide receiver Cris Collinsworth continues as a high class performer and went to the Pro Bowl for the third straight year. However, this is almost certainly his last season with the Bengals (he intends to go to the USFL) and, with Isaac Curtis perhaps losing a yard or two, approaching the end of a fine career, the

search for replacements will soon be a necessity. For the moment, Steve Kreider is a good reserve and may even assume a starting role. The Bengals have lost tight end Dan Ross to the USFL but M.L. Harris will be back after injury, supported by Rodney Holman.

Defense

Statistically, the Bengals have the best defense in the NFL and, by any measure, must be rated amongst the top half dozen. Both Eddie Edwards and Ross Browner are penetrative, playing at defensive end, and Jerry Boyarsky is solid at nose tackle. Browner's delayed start to the 1983 season enabled defensive end Glen Collins to make his mark (he had five sacks) and he is joined by the first-round draftee, Pete Koch, on standby duty. The linebacking quartet has beefed up, and played its full part in a defense which rated second in the NFL against the rush. Glenn Cameron led the team in tackles and dovetails well with the pass-rushing outside linebacker, Reggie Williams. Guy Frazier moved up to start at left outside linebacker but he will be without his partner, Jim LeClair, who occupied the inside position. Nonetheless, both Rick Razzano and Ron Simpkins are inside linebackers and either or both could fill the gap. The defensive secondary will be without the veteran experience of cornerback Ken Riley but his obvious replacement, Ray Horton, has learned the trade (he had five interceptions and returned one for a 55-yard touchdown). Louis Breeden also knows the way to the opposing end zone. An excellent group will be complete with the return of free safety Bryan Hicks playing alongside strong safety Bobby Kemp.

Special Teams

The special team has slipped a little from the high quality of 1981. However, both the kicker, Jim Breech, and the punter, Pat McInally, are sound players. John Simmons averaged a poor 6·9-yard average returning punts but could develop into a consistent kickoff returner, having been tried with some success last year. As a bonus, James Brooks is available should the need arise in the really important games.

1984 DRAFT

Round	Name	Pos.	Ht.	Wt.	College
1.	Hunley, Ricky	LB	6-1	235	Arizona
1.	Koch, Pete	DE	6-5	250	Maryland
1.	Blados, Brian	T	6-5	320	North Carolina
2.	Esiason, Boomer	QB	6-4	210	Maryland
3.	Jennings, Stanford	RB	6-0	198	Furman
4.	Farley, John	RB	5-10	190	Cal State Sacramento
5.	Bussey, Barney	DB	5-10	190	South Carolina State
6.	Kern, Don	TE	6-3	217	Arizona State
7.	Barker, Leo	LB	6-1	222	New Mexico State
8.	Reimers, Bruce	T	6-6	275	Iowa State
9.	Kozerski, Bruce	C	6-4	275	Holy Cross
10.	Jackson, Aaron	LB	6-4	235	North Carolina
10.	Ziegler, Brent	RB	5-11	230	Syracuse
11.	McKeaver, Steve	RB			Central State Oklahoma
12.	Raquet, Steve	LB	6-4	245	Holy Cross

1984 SCHEDULE

September
2	at Denver	2:00
9	KANSAS CITY	1:00
16	at New York Jets	1:00
23	LOS ANGELES RAMS	1:00

October
1	at Pittsburgh	9:00
7	HOUSTON	4:00
14	at New England	1:00
21	CLEVELAND	1:00
28	at Houston	12:00

November
4	at San Francisco	1:00
11	PITTSBURGH	1:00
18	SEATTLE	1:00
25	ATLANTA	1:00

December
2	at Cleveland	1:00
9	at New Orleans	12:00
16	BUFFALO	1:00

VETERAN ROSTER

No.	Name	Pos.	Ht.	Wt.	NFL Year	College
40	Alexander, Charles	HB	6-1	221	6	Louisiana State
14	Anderson, Ken	QB	6-3	212	14	Augustana, Ill.
61	Boyarsky, Jerry	NT	6-3	290	4	Pittsburgh
10	Breech, Jim	K	5-6	161	6	California
34	Breeden, Louis	CB	5-11	185	7	North Carolina Central
	Brooks, James	RB	5-9	177	4	Auburn
79	Browner, Ross	DE	6-3	261	7	Notre Dame
67	Burley, Gary	DE	6-3	274	9	Pittsburgh
50	Cameron, Glenn	LB	6-2	228	10	Florida
11	Christensen, Jeff	QB	6-3	202	2	Eastern Illinois
76	Collins, Glen	DE	6-6	260	3	Mississippi State
80	Collinsworth, Cris	WR	6-5	192	4	Florida
85	Curtis, Isaac	WR	6-1	192	12	San Diego State
73	Edwards, Eddie	DE	6-5	256	8	Miami
49	Frazier, Guy	LB	6-2	215	4	Wyoming
48	Gibler, Andy	TE	6-4	235	2	Missouri
22	Griffin, James	S	6-2	197	2	Middle Tennessee
44	Griffin, Ray	CB	5-10	186	7	Ohio State
66	Hannula, Jim	T	6-6	251	2	Northern Illinois
83	Harris, M.L.	TE	6-5	238	5	Kansas State
27	Hicks, Bryan	S	6-0	192	5	McNeese State
82	Holman, Rodney	TE	6-3	230	3	Tulane
20	Horton, Ray	CB	5-10	189	2	Washington
37	Jackson, Robert	S	5-10	184	3	Central Michigan
26	Kemp, Bobby	S	6-0	186	4	Cal State – Fullerton
28	Kinnebrew, Larry	RB	6-1	266	2	Tennessee State
86	Kreider, Steve	WR	6-3	192	6	Lehigh
69	Krumrie, Tim	NT	6-2	247	2	Wisconsin – Madison
47	Maidlow, Steve	LB	6-2	234	2	Michigan State
87	McInally, Pat	P-WR	6-6	212	9	Harvard
65	Montoya, Max	G	6-5	275	6	UCLA
60	Moore, Blake	C	6-5	267	5	Wooster
78	Munoz, Anthony	T	6-6	278	5	USC
68	Obrovac, Mike	T	6-6	275	4	Bowling Green
51	Razzano, Rick	LB	5-11	227	5	Virginia Tech.
64	Rimington, Dave	C	6-3	292	2	Nebraska
15	Schonert, Turk	QB	6-1	185	5	Stanford
59	Schuh, Jeff	LB	6-2	228	4	Minnesota
25	Simmons, John	CB-KR	5-11	192	4	Southern Methodist
56	Simpkins, Ron	LB	6-1	235	4	Michigan
23	Tate, Rodney	RB	5-11	190	3	Texas
35	Turner, Jimmy	CB	6-0	187	2	UCLA
81	Verser, David	WR	6-1	200	4	Kansas
70	Weaver, Emanuel	NT	6-4	260	3	South Carolina
57	Williams, Reggie	LB	6-0	228	9	Dartmouth
77	Wilson, Mike	T	6-5	271	7	Georgia
32	Wilson, Stanley	RB	5-10	209	2	Oklahoma

Anthony Munoz

CLEVELAND BROWNS AFC Central

Address Tower B, Cleveland Stadium, Cleveland, Ohio 44114.

Stadium Cleveland Stadium, Cleveland.
Capacity 80,322 *Playing Surface* Grass.

Team Colours Orange and White.

Head Coach Sam Rutigliano — seventh year.

Championships AAFC 1946,'47,'48'49; NFL 1950,'54,'55,'64; Division 1971,'80.

History AAFC 1946-49, NFL 1950-69, AFC 1970—

Offense

The Browns always seem to have a good offensive line and the tradition will be maintained by the experienced veterans, left tackle Doug Dieken, right guard Joe DeLamielleure and left guard Robert Jackson, who are entering their 14th, 12th and 10th years respectively. Cody Risien has become one of the NFL's best tackles and Mike Baab is an outstanding prospect at center, where he displaced another great Browns veteran, Tom DeLeone. Again, rushing has historically been a Cleveland strongpoint (Jim Brown, Leroy Kelly, Greg Pruitt, Marion Motley and the like) and another Pruitt, Mike, maintains the quality. A speedy fullback with four 1,000-yard seasons to his credit and more to come, he is supported by the exciting Boyce Green, who confounded the scouts (he was an eleventh round pick) with 497 yards at an average of 4·8 yards per carry in his rookie year. Charles White, a former Heisman Trophy winner, has never quite played up to his potential but remains as a dangerous option in reserve. There will be changes in the passing offense, which might take time to come together. Quarterback Brian Sipe has departed for the USFL, leaving Paul McDonald, who has been given previous opportunities, in the driving seat. The departure of wide receiver Dave Logan for Denver may be less felt by the arrival of Duriel Harris. Feeling somewhat aggrieved at being used only sparingly (so he felt) with the Dolphins, he has something to prove. Bobby Jones (formerly of the Jets) will continue to pressurize Willis Adams for the other starting role, with Ricky Feacher, a former starter, completing an experienced corps. Tight end Ozzie Newsome is terrific and, with 89 pass receptions, only narrowly missed winning the receiving title and a second trip to the Pro Bowl. Playing behind Newsome, rookie Harry Holt made an impressive start to his career.

Defense

Carl Hairston has been acquired from Philadelphia, hopefully to improve the pass rush and lend his considerable experience to a modest defensive line. Nose tackle Bob Golic, a former linebacker with the Patriots, rates about par but for rookie left end Reggie Camp 1983 was a learning year. A return to form by Keith Baldwin would be welcomed. This coming season, the linebacking quartet could well emerge as the NFL's best. The marauding Chip Banks made his second Pro Bowl appearance after only two years in the NFL and, even though Scott Nicolas was a good stand-in, he will give way to the returning Dick Ambrose, 'Mr Dependable'. Tom Cousineau has learned his way around the NFL after having played in Canada and Clay Matthews is fast becoming a feared pass rusher. The defensive secondary maintains good pass coverage, despite what has been overall a weak pass rush by the defensive line. Right cornerback Hanford Dixon is regarded as the best of the four whilst strong safety Clinton Burrell is secure. Left cornerback Lawrence Johnson continues to improve, backed up by the experienced Rod Perry. The conversion of the 1982 rookie, Mike Whitwell, to free safety was an inspired move (he was drafted as a receiver). He made three interceptions and is now the established starter. The Browns took safety Don Rogers and cornerback Chris Rockins with their first two options in the collegiate draft.

Special Teams

Kicker Matt Bahr was excellent all season and Jeff Gossett's respectable 40·8-yard gross punting average should be improved by Steve Cox, returning after injury. Cox is the long field goal specialist and kicked a 58-yarder against Denver. Punt returns were average at best and Dwight Walker may take over from Dino Hall. Equally, kickoff returner Boyce Green seems likely to be used exclusively at running back, leaving Walker in sole charge.

1984 DRAFT

Round	Name	Pos.	Ht.	Wt.	College
1.	Rogers, Don	DB	6-0	207	UCLA
2.	Rockins, Chris	DB	5-11	190	Oklahoma State
2.	Davis, Bruce	WR	5-8	170	Baylor
4.	Bolden, Rickey	TE	6-5	245	Southern Methodist
4.	Brennen, Brian	WR	5-9	180	Boston College
5.	Piepkorn, Dave	T	6-6	268	North Dakota State
6.	Nugent, Terry	QB	6-3	210	Colorado State
7.	Dumont, Jim	LB	6-1	225	Rutgers
9.	Jones, Don	WR	6-1	190	Texas A & M
10.	Byner, Earnest	RB	5-9	210	East Carolina

1984 SCHEDULE

September

2	at Seattle	1:00
9	at Los Angeles Rams	1:00
16	DENVER	9:00
23	PITTSBURGH	1:00
30	at Kansas City	12:00

October

7	NEW ENGLAND	1:00
14	NEW YORK JETS	1:00
21	at Cincinnati	1:00
28	NEW ORLEANS	1:00

November

4	at Buffalo	1:00
11	SAN FRANCISCO	1:00
18	at Atlanta	1:00
25	HOUSTON	1:00

December

2	CINCINNATI	1:00
9	at Pittsburgh	1:00
16	at Houston	12:00

Mike Pruitt

VETERAN ROSTER

No.	Name	Pos.	Ht.	Wt.	NFL Year	College
80	Adams, Willis	WR	6-2	194	5	Houston
52	Ambrose, Dick	LB	6-0	228	10	Virginia
61	Baab, Mike	C	6-4	270	3	Texas
9	Bahr, Matt	K	5-10	165	6	Penn State
99	Baldwin, Keith	DE	6-4	245	3	Texas A & M
56	Banks, Chip	LB	6-4	233	3	USC
88	Belk, Rocky	WR	6-0	187	2	Miami
47	Braziel, Larry	CB	6-0	184	6	USC
97	Brown, Thomas	DE	6-3	245	4	Baylor
49	Burrell, Clinton	S	6-1	192	5	Louisiana State
96	Camp, Reggie	DE	6-4	264	2	California
59	Carver, Dale	LB	6-2	225	2	Georgia
75	Contz, Bill	T	6-5	260	2	Penn State
50	Cousineau, Tom	LB	6-3	225	3	Ohio State
15	Cox, Steve	K-P	6-4	195	4	Arkansas
38	Davis, Johnny	RB	6-1	235	7	Alamaba
64	DeLamielleure, Joe	G	6-3	245	12	Michigan State
54	DeLeone, Tom	C	6-2	248	13	Ohio State
73	Dieken, Doug	T	6-5	252	14	Illinois
29	Dixon, Hanford	CB	5-11	182	4	Southern Mississippi
74	Farren, Paul	G-C	6-5	251	2	Boston University
83	Feacher, Ricky	WR	5-10	174	9	Mississippi Valley
	Flick, Tom	QB	6-1	190	4	Washington
94	Franks, Elvis	DE	6-4	238	5	Morgan State
79	Golic, Bob	NT	6-2	248	5	Notre Dame
30	Green, Boyce	HB	5-11	215	2	Carson-Newman
31	Gross, Al	S	6-3	190	2	Arizona
	Hairston, Carl	DE	6-3	260	9	Maryland — Eastern Shore
26	Hall, Dino	RB-PR	5-7	165	6	Glassboro State
	Harris, Duriel	WR	5-11	176	9	New Mexico State
81	Holt, Harry	TE	6-4	230	2	Arizona
78	Hopkins, Thomas	T	6-6	260	2	Alabama A & M
68	Jackson, Robert	G	6-5	260	10	Duke
51	Johnson, Eddie	LB	6-1	210	4	Louisville
48	Johnson, Lawrence	CB	5-11	204	5	Wisconsin
89	Jones, Bobby	WR	5-11	185	7	No College
57	Matthews, Clay	LB	6-2	230	7	USC
16	McDonald, Paul	QB	6-2	185	5	USC
82	Newsome, Ozzie	TE	6-2	232	7	Alabama
58	Nicolas, Scott	LB	6-3	226	3	Miami
40	Perry, Rod	CB	5-9	185	10	Colorado
43	Pruitt, Mike	RB	6-0	225	9	Purdue
72	Puzzuoli, Dave	NT	6-3	260	2	Pittsburgh
63	Risien, Cody	T	6-7	255	6	Texas A & M
22	Scott, Clarence	S	6-0	190	14	Kansas State
87	Stracka, Tim	TE	6-3	220	2	Wisconsin
12	Trocano, Rick	QB	6-0	188	4	Pittsburgh
42	Walker, Dwight	RB	5-10	185	3	Nicholls State
55	Weathers, Curtis	LB	6-5	220	6	Mississippi
25	White, Charles	RB	5-10	183	5	USC
21	Whitwell, Mike	S	6-0	175	3	Texas A & M

HOUSTON OILERS AFC Central

Address Box 1516, Houston, Texas 77001.
Stadium The Astrodome, Houston.
   Capacity 50,496 *Playing Surface* AstroTurf.
Team Colours Scarlet, Columbia Blue and White.
Head Coach Hugh Campbell — first year.
Championships AFL 1960,'61.
History AFL 1960-69, AFC 1970—

Offense

Both right guard Bruce Matthews and right tackle Harvey Salem (they were selected in the first and second rounds, respectively, of the 1983 collegiate draft) played up to expectations, as did second-year man Mike Munchak, who missed most of his rookie season. With sound reserve strength in the form of guard Pat Howell, Morris Towns, John Schuhmacher and the number one draft selection, Dean Steinkuhler, the Oilers need only one more good year from veteran Doug France, a former Pro Bowler with the Rams, to see them through what has been a difficult transitional period. Playing with renewed confidence in his maturing offensive line, Earl Campbell could easily regain his status as the NFL's best (he was the Leading Rusher in each of his first three seasons, 1978,'79 and '80, and led the AFC in 1981). However, reserve strength is shallow with only the inexperienced Larry Moriarty and Donnie Craft available if Campbell is injured. The Oilers could well be given a significant boost by the arrival of quarterback Warren Moon, who was wooed by several NFL teams before opting for Houston. Like Joe Theismann, Moon perfected his skills in the Canadian Football League. He joined the Edmonton Eskimos as a rookie in 1978, a year which marked the beginning of a sequence of five consecutive Grey Cup victories, and it is no coincidence that Edmonton's head coach during this period was none other than the new Oilers' head coach, Hugh Campbell. Moon will firstly have to see off the challenge from Oliver Luck but, assuming this, he will be presented with the most exciting set of wide receivers to don Oiler jerseys for some time. Butch Johnson, who is known to British fans not only for his 'California Quake' routine but also for spectacular receptions going back as far as Super Bowl XII, arrives from Dallas to team up with last year's revelation, Tim Smith. Between them, they should attract some of the attention away from Earl Campbell, and more.

Defense

Using the 3-4 formation in 1983, the defense gave up an alarming 4·8 rushing yards per attempt, 576 of which compute to a long season. Recognising this weakness, opposing offenses threw only 424 passes, conceding to the Oilers the flattering rank of second best of the AFC's pass defenses. Together with San Diego and Atlanta, they registered the fewest sacks in the NFL and only San Diego gave up more points. On the other hand, eight rookies, four of whom were starters, gathered the kind of experience which they might soon be putting to good use. Equally, a former starter, left end Ken Kennard, and the ex-Bengal, nose guard Wilson Whitley, will be rejoining right end Jesse Baker and linebackers Robert 'Dr Doom' Brazile and Gregg Bingham, to plug the holes at the battlefront. In addition, Pro Bowler Mike Reinfeldt, who started in every game from 1977 until his injury in 1983, returns to the defensive secondary alongside the established cornerback, Willie Tullis, and strong safety Keith Bostic. There will be competition at left corner-back, where Steve Brown faces the challenge of former Colts player Derick Hatchett.

Special Teams

Kicker Florian Kempf is reliable and can be expected to extend his form of 1983, when he failed on only four field goal attempts and missed one PAT, but punter John James, who previously played for Atlanta and, briefly, with Detroit, has still to find his feet, so to speak. Steve Brown and Carl Roaches share the kick return duties to good effect. In 1983, Brown maintained an excellent 25·6-yard average and his 93-yard touchdown return was bettered only by Zachary Dixon's 94-yarder and the 97-yard touchdown spectacular by his mate Roaches. The versatile Roaches has sole responsibility for returning punts and in this he has a career longest of 68 yards.

1984 DRAFT

Round	Name	Pos.	Ht.	Wt.	College
1.	Steinkuhler, Dean	T	6-3	270	Nebraska
2.	Smith, Doug	DE	6-3	280	Auburn
2.	Eason, Bo	DB	6-2	194	Cal — Davis
3.	Meads, Johnny	LB	6-0	222	Nicholls State
4.	Studaway, Mark	DE	6-3	250	Tennessee
4.	Allen, Patrick	DB	5-10	175	Utah State
5.	Lyles, Robert	LB			Texas Christian
6.	Grimsley, John	LB	6-1	225	Kentucky
6.	Mullins, Eric	WR	5-10	175	Stanford
7.	Joyner, Willie	RB	5-10	210	Maryland
8.	Baugh, Kevin	WR	5-8	173	Penn State
9.	Donaldson, Jeff	DB	5-11	195	Colorado
9.	Johnson, Mike	DE	6-4	235	Illinois
9.	Russell, Mike	LB	6-2	232	Toledo

Mike Munchak

1984 SCHEDULE

September
2	LOS ANGELES	
	RAIDERS	3:00
9	INDIANAPOLIS	3:00
16	at San Diego	1:00
23	at Atlanta	1:00
30	NEW ORLEANS	3:00

October
7	at Cincinnati	4:00
14	at Miami	1:00
21	SAN FRANCISCO	3:00
28	CINCINNATI	12:00

November
4	at Pittsburgh	1:00
11	at Kansas City	12:00
18	NEW YORK JETS	3:00
25	at Cleveland	1:00

December
2	PITTSBURGH	12:00
9	at Los Angeles Rams	1:00
16	CLEVELAND	12:00

VETERAN ROSTER

No.	Name	Pos.	Ht.	Wt.	NFL Year	College
56	Abraham, Robert	LB	6-1	217	3	North Carolina State
87	Arnold, Watt	TE	6-3	234	5	New Mexico
80	Bailey, Harold	WR	6-2	193	4	Oklahoma State
75	Baker, Jesse	DE	6-5	272	6	Jacksonville State
54	Bingham, Gregg	LB	6-1	225	12	Purdue
25	Bostic, Keith	S	6-1	209	2	Michigan
52	Brazile, Robert	LB	6-4	245	10	Jackson State
24	Brown, Steve	CB	5-11	178	2	Oregon
81	Bryant, Steve	WR	6-2	194	3	Purdue
34	Campbell, Earl	RB	5-11	240	7	Texas
58	Carter, David	C	6-2	262	8	Western Kentucky
40	Craft, Donnie	RB	6-0	209	3	Louisville
88	Dressel, Chris	TE	6-4	230	2	Stanford
35	Edwards, Stan	RB	6-0	215	3	Michigan
78	Foster, Jerome	DE	6-2	268	2	Ohio State
77	France, Doug	T	6-5	270	9	Ohio State
90	Hamm, Bob	DE	6-4	250	2	Nevada-Reno
36	Hartwig, Carter	S	6-0	205	6	USC
21	Hatchett, Derrick	CB	5-11	183	5	Texas
23	Hill, Greg	CB	6-1	194	2	Oklahoma State
84	Holston, Mike	WR	6-3	192	4	Morgan State
66	Howell, Pat	G	6-5	253	6	USC
50	Hunt, Daryl	LB	6-3	239	6	Oklahoma
6	James, John	P	6-3	196	13	Florida
	Johnson, Butch	WR	6-1	187	9	Cal-Riverside
57	Joiner, Tim	LB	6-4	230	2	Louisiana State
22	Kay, Bill	CB	6-1	190	4	Purdue
4	Kempf, Florian	K	5-9	170	3	Pennsylvania
71	Kennard, Ken	DE	6-2	258	8	Angelo State
10	Luck, Oliver	QB	6-2	198	3	West Virginia
74	Matthews, Bruce	G	6-4	276	2	USC
89	McCloskey, Mike	TE	6-5	244	2	Penn State
26	Meadows, Darryl	S	6-1	202	2	Toledo
	Moon, Warren	QB			R	Washington
30	Moriarty, Larry	RB	6-1	228	2	Notre Dame
63	Munchak, Mike	G	6-3	263	3	Penn State
12	Ramson, Brian	QB	6-3	205	2	Tennessee State
37	Reinfeldt, Mike	S	6-2	196	9	Wisconsin-Milwaukee
53	Riley, Avon	LB	6-3	219	4	UCLA
85	Roaches, Carl	PR-WR	5-8	170	5	Texas A & M
73	Salem, Harvey	T	6-6	274	2	California
62	Schuhmacher, John	T	6-3	269	5	USC
83	Smith, Tim	WR	6-2	202	5	Nebraska
72	Sochia, Brian	MG	6-3	252	2	Northwest Oklahoma
67	Stensrud, Mike	MG	6-5	290	6	Iowa State
68	Studdard, Les	C	6-4	260	3	Texas
51	Thompson, Ted	LB	6-1	229	10	Southern Methodist
76	Towns, Morris	T	6-4	261	8	Missouri
20	Tullis, Willie	CB	6-0	190	4	Troy State
	Turner, Kevin	LB	6-2	223	5	Pacific
86	Walls, Herkie	WR	5-8	160	2	Texas
79	Whitley, Wilson	MG	6-3	265	8	Houston
33	Wilson, J.C.	S	6-0	178	7	Pittsburgh

PITTSBURGH STEELERS AFC Central

Address Three Rivers Stadium, 300 Stadium Circle, Pittsburgh, Pa. 15212.
Stadium Three Rivers Stadium, Pittsburgh.
Capacity 59,000 *Playing Surface* AstroTurf.
Team Colours Gold and Black.
Head Coach Chuck Noll — fifteenth year.
Championships Super Bowl 1974,'75,'78,'79; Division 1972,'76,'77,'83.
History NFL 1933-69, AFC 1970—
(Until 1940, they were known as the Pittsburgh Pirates.)

Offense

Mike Webster extended his sequence of consecutive elections to the Pro Bowl to six, playing at center in an offensive line which had little difficulty clearing the way for the running backs (they rated fourth in the NFL) but yielded 52 quarterback sacks. Guards Craig Wolfley and Steve Courson are strong, right tackle Larry Brown is vastly experienced and left tackle Tunch Ilkin shows signs of greatness. But both Brown and Ilkin, together with tackle Ted Petersen, suffered injuries, and poor pass protection was the inevitable result. Playing in relief of the injured Terry Bradshaw, quarterback Cliff Stoudt was tentative and never brought his undoubted skills to bear — he has now departed for the USFL. To make matters worse, Bradshaw is to undergo further surgery on his right elbow and seems certain to miss the whole of 1984. Mark Malone and the former Miami quarterback, David Woodley, could well be in competition for the starting position throughout the season. Wide receiver John Stallworth, another veteran of four Super Bowls, was sadly missed and the responsibility fell to Calvin Sweeney, who did well under the circumstances. Stallworth returns to join Sweeney, Greg Hawthorne, Wayne Capers and Gregg Garrity, in a passing offense which, reinforced by draftee Louis Lipps, must surely improve. However, for the first few games, they may have to yield the spotlight to running back Franco Harris who, after a glittering career, lies only 362 yards adrift of Jim Brown's all time rushing record of 12,312 yards. Frank Pollard, whose reliability dimmed the potential brilliance of

Walter Abercrombie, has emerged as Harris's successor in an offensive backfield which made a useful 'bonus' contribution to the passing offense (between them, Harris, Abercrombie and Pollard caught 76 passes). Tight end Bennie Cunningham caught 36 passes but didn't quite make the impact expected of a player with his experience.

Defense

Despite the tragic loss of Gabe Rivera (he was paralysed in a road traffic accident), the defense will maintain a standard which earned the ranking of overall third best in the NFL. The young defensive ends, Keith Gary and Keith Willis, have an appetite for quarterbacks (they had 8 and 14 sacks respectively) when they substitute in anticipation of a passing play. The usual starters, ends John Goodman and Tom Beasley, and nose tackle Gary Dunn, excel against the run. In addition, reserve nose tackle Ed Nelson is considered to be a bright prospect. Jack Lambert remains as one of the NFL's most fearsome linebackers and, even when not in action, can be seen on the sidelines, growling over the chalkboard. Outside linebacker Mike Merriweather showed considerable promise in his second season, and David Little will be an adequate replacement for the retired veteran Loren Toews, playing the inside position with the underrated Robin Cole to his right. In 1983 the defense in total picked off 28 interceptions to lead the NFL in percentage terms (this relates the number off interceptions to passes attempted by the opposition). Free safety Rick Woods came through and equalled the five interceptions snared by the former All Pro, strong safety Donnie Shell. Left cornerback Dwayne Woodruff, who has blazing speed, continues to mature and Harvey Clayton, who returned his only interception for a 70-yard touchdown against Cincinnati, will attempt to fill in for the retired former Pro Bowler, Mel Blount.

Special Teams

Kicker Gary Anderson led the AFC with 119 points and went to the Pro Bowl in only his second NFL year. Punter Craig Colquitt came back from injury to average a good 41·9 yards gross. Kickoff returning is an unsolved problem but Paul Skansi's punt returns were at the average of 8·4 yards and included one for 57 yards.

1984 DRAFT

Round	Name	Pos.	Ht.	Wt.	College
1.	Lipps, Louis	WR	5-10	188	So. Mississippi
2.	Kolodziejski, Chris	TE	6-3	232	Wyoming
4.	Thompson, Weegie	WR	6-6	210	Florida State
4.	Long, Terry	G	5-11	280	East Carolina
5.	Hughes, Van	DT	6-3	270	S.W. Texas State
6.	Brown, Chris	DB	6-0	196	Notre Dame
7.	Campbell, Scott	QB	6-0	200	Purdue
8.	Rasmussen, Randy	C	6-1	260	Minnesota
9.	Erenberg, Rich	RB	5-10	197	Colgate
10.	McJunkin, Kirk	T	6-3	250	Texas
11.	Veals, Elton	RB	5-11	220	Tulane
12.	Gillespie, Fernanda	RB			William Jewell

1984 SCHEDULE

September
2	KANSAS CITY	1:00
6	at New York Jets	9:00
16	LOS ANGELES RAMS	4:00
23	at Cleveland	1:00

October
1	CINCINNATI	9:00
8	MIAMI	1:00
14	at San Francisco	1:00
21	at Indianapolis	1:00
28	ATLANTA	4:00

November
4	HOUSTON	1:00
11	at Cincinnati	1:00
19	at New Orleans	8:00
25	SAN DIEGO	1:00

December
2	at Houston	12:00
9	CLEVELAND	1:00
16	at Los Angeles Raiders	1:00

Walter Abercrombie

VETERAN ROSTER

No.	Name	Pos.	Ht.	Wt.	NFL Year	College
34	Abercrombie, Walter	RB	5-11	201	3	Baylor
1	Anderson, Gary	K	5-11	156	3	Syracuse
65	Beasley, Tom	DE-NT	6-5	248	7	Virginia Tech.
25	Best, Greg	S	5-10	185	2	Kansas City
54	Bingham, Craig	LB	6-2	211	3	Syracuse
71	Boures, Emil	C-G	6-1	252	3	Pittsburgh
12	Bradshaw, Terry	QB	6-3	210	15	Louisiana Tech.
79	Brown, Larry	T	6-4	270	14	Kansas
80	Capers, Wayne	WR	6-2	193	2	Kansas
33	Clayton, Harvey	CB	5-9	170	2	Florida State
56	Cole, Robin	LB	6-2	220	8	New Mexico
5	Colquitt, Craig	P	6-1	182	6	Tennessee
77	Courson, Steve	G	6-1	260	7	South Carolina
89	Cunningham, Bennie	TE	6-5	260	9	Clemson
45	Davis, Russell	FB	6-1	231	5	Michigan
55	Donnalley, Rick	C-G	6-2	257	3	North Carolina
84	Dunaway, Craig	TE	6-2	233	2	Michigan
67	Dunn, Gary	NT	6-3	260	8	Miami
86	Garrity, Gregg	WR	5-10	171	2	Penn State
92	Gary, Keith	DE	6-3	255	2	Oklahoma
95	Goodman, John	DE	6-6	250	4	Oklahoma
32	Harris, Franco	RB	6-2	225	13	Penn State
43	Harris, Tim	RB-KR	5-9	206	2	Washington State
27	Hawthorne, Greg	WR	6-2	225	6	Baylor
53	Hinkle, Bryan	LB	6-1	214	3	Oregon
62	Ilkin, Tunch	T	6-3	253	5	Indiana State
29	Johnson, Ron	S	5-10	200	7	Eastern Michigan
90	Kohrs, Bob	LB-DE	6-3	245	4	Arizona State
58	Lambert, Jack	LB	6-4	220	11	Kent State
50	Little, David	LB	6-1	220	4	Florida
16	Malone, Mark	QB	6-4	223	5	Arizona State
57	Merriweather, Mike	LB	6-2	215	3	Pacific
	Meyer, John	T	6-6	257	2	Arizona State
64	Nelson, Edmund	NT-DE	6-3	263	3	Auburn
44	Odum, Henry	RB-KR	5-10	200	2	South Carolina State
66	Petersen, Ted	T	6-5	256	7	Eastern Illinois
30	Pollard, Frank	RB	5-10	210	5	Baylor
87	Rodgers, John	TE	6-2	220	3	Louisiana Tech.
	Seabaugh, Todd	LB	6-4	220	1	San Diego State
31	Shell, Donnie	S	5-11	190	11	South Carolina State
81	Skansi, Paul	WR-PR	5-11	190	2	Washington
82	Stallworth, John	WR	6-2	191	11	Alabama A & M
85	Sweeney, Calvin	WR	6-2	190	5	USC
41	Washington, Sam	CB	5-8	180	3	Mississippi Valley State
52	Webster, Mike	C	6-1	255	11	Wisconsin
21	Williams, Eric	S	5-11	183	2	North Carolina State
93	Willis, Keith	DE	6-1	251	3	Northeastern
	Wilson, Frank	RB-TE	6-2	233	1	Rice
61	Wingle, Blake	G	6-2	267	2	UCLA
73	Wolfley, Craig	G	6-1	265	5	Syracuse
	Woodley, David	QB	6-2	204	5	Louisiana State
49	Woodruff, Dwayne	CB	5-11	198	6	Louisville
22	Woods, Rick	S-PR	6-0	196	3	Boise State

DENVER BRONCOS AFC West

Address 5700, Logan Street, Denver, Colorado 80216.
Stadium Denver Mile High Stadium.
Capacity 75,103 *Playing Surface* Grass (Prescription Athletic Turf).
Team Colours Orange, Royal Blue and White.
Head Coach Dan Reeves — fourth year.
Championships AFC 1977; Division 1978.
History AFL 1960-69, AFC 1970—

Offense

The line gave up a few too many quarterback sacks for comfort (only Philadelphia and St Louis yielded more than Denver's 55) and rarely established a platform for the strike players who, as a consequence, rated 20th and 23rd in passing and rushing yards respectively. Nonetheless, Dave Studdard, Keith Bishop, Bill Bryan, Paul Howard and Ken Lanier (going left to right), retain the confidence of coach Reeves, who was not panicked into using high draft options for improvement. The most heralded rookie quarterback for many years, John Elway, made all the headlines which, in the early going, were uncomplimentary. But he showed significant improvement later in the season and clearly will be a good one. Perhaps in recognition of this, the veteran Steve DeBerg, who certainly never let the Broncos down, left for Tampa Bay. With only Gary Kubiak, himself an eighth-round draft choice in 1983, in reserve, Scott Brunner was acquired from the Giants. Elway will have the targets in wide receivers Steve 'Scorched Earth' Watson and Dave Logan, the last-named acquired from the Cleveland Browns. Ever since being turned loose by Craig Morton in 1981, Watson has been a closely-marked man, despite which he gained 1,133 yards at the high average of 19·2 yards per reception in 1983. Logan, too, is a deep threat, giving Elway the choice of two big-play wide receivers and posing a problem for the opposing defenses, which cannot afford to ignore tight end Ron Egloff, probing the medium range. Eason Ramson, who was obtained from San Francisco, joins Egloff and five other tight ends in the scramble for a starting role. Running back Sammy Winder is sound without perhaps being the kind of player who can break a game open. The return of Gerald Willhite, who is a class performer, hopefully free from the injury which hampered him in 1983, will relegate Nathan Poole to the 'experienced reserve' category, along with Dave Preston.

Defense

The defensive line is no longer the feared 'Orange Crush'. Left end Barney Chavous is approaching retirement, as is the only experienced nose tackle, Rubin Carter. On the other hand, right end Rulon Jones, entering his fifth year, has developed into a good pass rusher and reinforcement arrives in the form of Andre Townsend, who was the Broncos' first draft selection overall (he was taken in round two). The linebackers continue to play well, although it is asking a lot of Stan Blinka (he was acquired from the Jets) to step in for the retired Denver 'great', Randy Gradishar. Outside linebacker Bob Swenson is another former outstanding player but has been plagued by injury of late and may have lost his starting spot to Jim Ryan for good. Tom Jackson is secure and his experience will be invaluable in providing stability whilst Ken Woodard eases into the lineup. The defensive secondary suffered for lack of a consistent pass rush up front and was challenged more than has been usual in the past. But the peerless Louis Wright and Steve Foley countered that, with six and five interceptions respectively. Steve Wilson grabbed five, coming on as the nickel back, and both Dennis Smith and Mike Harden snared four as part of valuable contributions.

Special Teams

Both the barefooted kicker, Rich Karlis, and the punter, Luke Prestridge, do everything required of them. Zack Thomas had an excellent year, returning punts at an average of 11·2 yards, including one for a 70-yard touchdown against the Raiders, but he has gone to the USFL. His kickoff returning was less spectacular but nonetheless adequate in partnership with Steve Wilson, who will have to shoulder the burden.

1984 DRAFT

Round	Name	Pos.	Ht.	Wt.	College
2.	Townsend, Andre	DE	6-3	260	Mississippi
3.	Lilly, Tony	DB	6-0	195	Florida
4.	Robbins, Randy	DB	6-1	185	Arizona
6.	Smith, Aaron	LB	6-2	220	Utah State
7.	Kay, Clarence	TE	6-2	236	Georgia
8.	Hood, Winford	T	6-3	255	Georgia
8.	Garnett, Scott	DT	6-2	265	Washington
9.	Brewer, Chris	RB	6-1	195	Arizona
10.	Micho, Bobby	TE	6-3	222	Texas
11.	Lang, Gene	RB	5-10	190	Louisiana State
12.	Jarmin, Murray	WR	6-5		Clemson

1984 SCHEDULE

September
2	CINCINNATI	2:00
9	at Chicago	12:00
16	at Cleveland	9:00
23	KANSAS CITY	2:00
30	LOS ANGELES RAIDERS	2:00

October
7	at Detroit	1:00
15	GREEN BAY	7:00
21	at Buffalo	1:00
28	at Los Angeles Raiders	1:00

November
4	NEW ENGLAND	2:00
11	at San Diego	1:00
18	MINNESOTA	2:00
25	SEATTLE	2:00

December
2	at Kansas City	12:00
9	SAN DIEGO	2:00
15	at Seattle	1:00

VETERAN ROSTER

No.	Name	Pos.	Ht.	Wt.	NFL Year	College
74	Baker, Jerry	T	6-2	294	2	Tulane
89	Barnett, Dean	TE				
54	Bishop, Keith	G-C	6-3	260	4	Baylor
	Blinka, Stan	LB	6-2	230	6	Sam Houston State
65	Bowyer, Walt	DE	6-4	245	2	Arizona State
	Brunner, Scott	QB	6-5	200	5	Delaware
64	Bryan, Bill	C	6-2	258	7	Duke
58	Busick, Steve	LB	6-4	227	4	USC
68	Carter, Rubin	NT	6-0	256	10	Miami
79	Chavous, Barney	DE	6-3	258	12	South Carolina State
59	Comeaux, Darren	LB	6-1	227	3	Arizona State
63	Cooper, Mark	G	6-5	267	2	Miami
21	Dupree, Myron	S	5-11	180	2	North Carolina Central
85	Egloff, Ron	TE	6-5	227	8	Wisconsin
7	Elway, John	QB	6-3	205	2	Stanford
43	Foley, Steve	S	6-2	190	8	Tulane
31	Harden, Mike	CB	6-1	192	5	Michigan
	Harris, George	LB	6-2	223	1	Houston
73	Hollingsworth, Shawn	G	6-2	260	2	Angelo State
60	Howard, Paul	G	6-3	260	11	Brigham Young
28	Jackson, Roger	CB-S	6-0	186	3	Bethune-Cookman
57	Jackson, Tom	LB	5-11	220	12	Louisville
75	Jones, Rulon	DE	6-6	260	5	Utah State
3	Karlis, Rich	K	6-0	180	3	Cincinnati
8	Kubiak, Gary	QB	6-0	192	2	Texas A & M
76	Lanier, Ken	T	6-3	269	4	Florida State
	Logan, Dave	WR	6-4	216	9	Colorado
41	Lytle, Rob	RB-TE	5-11	195	8	Michigan
66	Manor, Brison	DE	6-4	248	8	Arkansas
77	Mecklenburg, Karl	DE	6-3	250	2	Minnesota
29	Myers, Wilbur	CB	5-11	195	2	Delta State
39	Myles, Jesse	RB	5-10	210	2	Louisiana State
24	Parros, Rick	RB	5-11	200	4	Utah State
34	Poole, Nathan	RB	5-9	212	5	Louisville
11	Prestridge, Luke	P	6-4	235	6	Baylor
	Ramson, Eason	TE	6-2	234	6	Washington State
50	Ryan, Jim	LB	6-1	215	6	William & Mary
84	Sampson, Clinton	WR	5-11	183	2	San Diego State
83	Sawyer, John	TE	6-2	230	9	Southern Mississippi
49	Smith, Dennis	S	6-3	200	4	USC
78	Stachowski, Rich	NT	6-4	245	2	California
70	Studdard, Dave	T	6-4	260	6	Texas
51	Swenson, Bob	LB	6-3	225	9	California
67	Uecker, Keith	T	6-5	260	3	Auburn
81	Watson, Steve	WR	6-4	195	6	Temple
47	Willhite, Gerald	RB	5-10	200	3	San Jose State
45	Wilson, Steve	CB	5-10	195	6	Howard
23	Winder, Sammy	RB	5-11	203	3	Southern Mississippi
52	Woodard, Ken	LB	6-1	218	3	Tuskegee Institute
87	Wright, Jim	TE	6-3	240	5	Texas Christian
20	Wright, Louis	CB	6-2	200	10	San Jose State

Tom Jackson

KANSAS CITY CHIEFS AFC West

Address 1 Arrowhead Drive, Kansas City, Missouri 64129.

Stadium Arrowhead Stadium, Kansas City.
Capacity 78,067 *Playing Surface* Tartan Turf.

Team Colours Red, Gold and White.

Head Coach John Mackovic — second year.

Championships Super Bowl 1969; AFL 1962,'66,'69; Division 1971.

History AFL 1960-69, AFC 1970—
(Until 1963, they were known as the Dallas Texans.)

Offense

The offensive line rated fifth best in the AFC for fewest sacks allowed, which is good considering that they were protecting a quarterback who threw more passes than any other in the NFL. The pool of veteran talent allowed for the smooth introduction of rookie right tackle David Lutz and center Bob Rush, who replaced the retired Jack Rudnay. The departure of right guard Bob Simmons for the USFL will be felt less if the ten-year veteran Tom Condon can return from injury. Coach Mackovic resolved what had been uncertainty at quarterback by trading Steve Fuller to the Rams, and Bill Kenney responded by having his best year to earn a trip to the Pro Bowl (he replaced the injured Dan Marino). Kenney's favourite target very quickly emerged in the form of wide receiver Carlos Carson, whose 1,351 yards gained was the thirteenth best in NFL history. Together with Henry Marshall, he will form a formidable combination in 1984 and, with Anthony Hancock, J.T. Smith and Stephone Paige waiting in the wings, the scouts can afford to direct their attentions elsewhere. Tight end Willie Scott, a number one pick in 1981, is making steady progress albeit slower than expected, and shares time with Ed Beckman, who is used more as a blocker. The running backs, too, play their full part in the passing offense, with a combined 122 receptions for 971 yards in 1983. However, these same players, Billy Jackson, Theotis Brown and the Thomas brothers, Jewerl and Ken, were unable to generate any sort of rushing offense. With this in mind, Ken Lacy, who was the third leading rusher in the USFL in 1983, was signed in April.

Defense

As a whole, a defense which has its fair share of talent was inconsistent in 1983 and failed to put the arm-lock on anybody. On the other hand, only Seattle, Dallas and San Diego were able to run up the points. Defensive right end Mike Bell had his best year to date with a team-leading ten quarterback sacks. All Pro Art Still, at left end, was slowed by injuries and his return to full fitness will be welcomed. The linebacking quartet is solid at the inside positions, where Jerry Blanton led the team with 136 solo tackles to take over in this category from Gary Spani, who missed the first six games with injury. However, with both Charles Jackson and Thomas Howard (outside linebackers) no better than par, the search is on for a player who can both mount an effective blitz and maintain adequate pass coverage (this is no small order). The departure of Pro Bowler Gary Barbaro was a blow to what was becoming one of the better defensive secondaries in the NFL but his replacement at free safety, Deron Cherry, promptly picked off seven interceptions and earned his first trip to the Pro Bowl. In this, he was joined by cornerback Gary Green, who represented the AFC for the third successive year. However Green, too, has left (he has been traded to the Rams) and the Chiefs will be indeed fortunate to fill his shoes. Lucious Smith maintains a tenuous hold on the right cornerback position, though he may have to share increasing time with last year's rookie Albert Lewis.

Special Teams

Nick Lowery continues as one of the finest field goal kickers in the NFL. Successful with every attempt up to 40 yards he established a Chiefs record for field goal accuracy (80 per cent) and, with a 58-yarder against Washington, equalled the third longest in NFL history. Yet, ironically, his season will be remembered for the 48 and 43-yard attempts which he missed in separate close games which the Chiefs lost the the Raiders. Rookie Jim Arnold recovered after a hesitant start to punt for a gross average of 39.9 yards. Returning kicks was a problem all year, when both the speedy Anthony Hancock and the experienced Theotis Brown proved ineffective, but there is room for optimism with the return to full fitness of J.T. Smith, a former All Pro punt returner.

1984 DRAFT

John Mackovic

Round	Name	Pos.	Ht.	Wt.	College
1.	Maas, Bill	DT	6-4	270	Pittsburgh
1.	Alt, John	T	6-7	280	Iowa
2.	Radecic, Scott	LB	6-3	240	Penn State
3.	Heard, Herman	RB	5-10	182	Southern Colorado
4.	Robinson, Mark	DB	5-11	210	Penn State
5.	Holle, Eric	DE	6-4	245	Texas
5.	Paine, Jeff	LB			Texas A & M
6.	Stevens, Rufus	WR	6-1	184	Grambling
7.	Ross, Kevin	DB	5-9	176	Temple
8.	Clark, Randy	DB	6-0	195	Florida
9.	Auer, Scott	T	6-5	249	Michigan State
9.	Hestera, Dave	TE	6-3	227	Colorado
10.	Wenglikowski, Al	LB	6-0	215	Pittsburgh
11.	Johnson, Bobby	RB	6-0	190	San Jose State
12.	Lang, Mark	LB	6-2	235	Texas

1984 SCHEDULE

September

2	at Pittsburgh	1:00
9	at Cincinnati	1:00
16	LOS ANGELES RAIDERS	12:00
23	at Denver	2:00
30	CLEVELAND	12:00

October

7	NEW YORK JETS	12:00
14	SAN DIEGO	12:00
21	at New York Jets	4:00
28	TAMPA BAY	12:00

November

4	at Seattle	1:00
11	HOUSTON	12:00
18	at Los Angeles Raiders	1:00
25	at New York Giants	1:00

December

2	DENVER	12:00
9	SEATTLE	12:00
16	at San Diego	1:00

Nick Lowery

VETERAN ROSTER

No.	Name	Pos.	Ht.	Wt.	NFL Year	College
6	Arnold, Jim	P	6-2	212	2	Vanderbilt
77	Baldinger, Rich	T	6-4	270	3	Wake Forest
85	Beckman, Ed	TE	6-4	239	8	Florida State
99	Bell, Mike	DE	6-4	260	5	Colorado State
14	Blackledge, Todd	QB	6-3	225	2	Penn State
57	Blanton, Jerry	LB	6-1	236	6	Kentucky
27	Brown, Theotis	RB	6-2	225	6	UCLA
66	Budde, Brad	G	6-4	260	5	USC
34	Burruss, Lloyd	S	6-0	202	4	Maryland
88	Carson, Carlos	WR	5-11	174	5	Louisiana State
20	Cherry, Deron	S	5-11	190	4	Rutgers
65	Condon, Tom	G	6-3	275	11	Boston College
50	Daniels, Calvin	LB	6-3	236	3	North Carolina
75	Gardner, Ellis	T	6-4	263	2	Georgia Tech.
82	Hancock, Anthony	WR-KR	6-0	187	3	Tennessee
56	Haynes, Louis	LB	6-0	227	3	North Texas State
60	Herkenhoff, Matt	T	6-4	272	9	Minnesota
52	Howard, Thomas	LB	6-2	215	8	Texas Tech.
43	Jackson, Billy	FB	5-10	215	4	Alabama
51	Jackson, Charles	LB	6-2	222	7	Washington
22	Jakes, Van	CB-S	6-0	195	2	Kent State
9	Kenney, Bill	QB	6-4	211	6	Northern Colorado
64	Kirchner, Mark	G	6-3	261	2	Baylor
55	Klug, Dave	LB	6-4	230	4	Concordia, Minn.
91	Kremer, Ken	NT	6-4	252	6	Ball State
	Lacy, Ken*	RB	6-1	220	R	Tulsa
29	Lewis, Albert	CB	6-2	190	2	Grambling
71	Lindstrom, Dave	DE	6-6	255	7	Boston University
62	Lingner, Adam	C	6-4	240	2	Illinois
8	Lowery, Nick	K	6-4	189	5	Dartmouth
72	Lutz, Dave	T	6-5	280	2	Georgia Tech.
74	Mangiero, Dino	NT	6-2	264	5	Rutgers
89	Marshall, Henry	WR	6-2	220	9	Missouri
	McAlister, Ken	LB-S	6-5	210	3	San Francisco
	Metcalf, Isaac	S	6-2	193	2	Baylor
83	Paige, Stephone	WR	6-1	175	2	Fresno State
58	Potter, Steve	LB	6-3	235	4	Virginia
79	Prater, Dean	DE	6-5	245	2	Oklahoma State
42	Ricks, Lawrence	RB	5-9	194	2	Michigan
38	Roquemore, Durwood	S	6-1	180	3	Texas A & I
70	Rourke, Jim	T	6-5	263	5	Boston College
53	Rush, Bob	C	6-5	270	7	Memphis State
81	Scott, Willie	TE	6-4	245	4	South Carolina
86	Smith, J.T.	WR-PR	6-2	185	7	North Texas State
23	Smith, Lucious	CB	5-10	190	5	Cal State-Fullerton
59	Spani, Gary	LB	6-2	228	7	Kansas State
67	Still, Art	DE	6-7	252	7	Kentucky
35	Thomas, Ken	RB	5-9	211	2	San Jose State
54	Walker, James	LB	6-1	250	2	Kansas State
87	Wetzel, Ron	TE	6-5	242	2	Arizona State
	Yakavonis, Ray	NT	6-4	250	4	East Stroudsburg State
61	Zamberlin, John	LB	6-2	226	6	Pacific Lutheran

* has played one year in the USFL

LOS ANGELES RAIDERS AFC West

Address 332, Center Street, El Segundo, California 90245.
Stadium Los Angeles Memorial Coliseum.
  Capacity 92,498 *Playing Surface* Grass.
Team Colours Silver and Black.
Head Coach Tom Flores — sixth year.
Championships Super Bowl 1976,'80,'83; AFL 1967; Division
  1970,'72,'73,'74,'75.
History AFL 1960-69, AFC 1970—
  (Until 1982, they were known as the Oakland Raiders.)

Offense

It is difficult to avoid the conclusion that the Raiders could well be even more over-powering in 1984. A massive offensive line, which discards any consideration of frills, need go undisturbed, and yet, Curt Marsh, returning from injury, could be the best of the bunch. The possibility exists that, with Dave Dalby entering his thirteenth year, Marsh may be converted to step into the great man's shoes at center. Elsewhere, left guard Charley Hannah was an inspired acquisition from Tampa Bay and last year's number one draft choice, guard Don Mosebar, is said to be making sound (Raider style) progress. Quarterback Jim Plunkett gets better and better, stepping up into the pass pocket as he did in the playoffs, to dismiss any suggestion that he has lost the power in his arm. Marc Wilson must be the highest paid reserve quarterback in the league and will do a good job when eventually his chance comes, sometime before the year 2000. The evergreen Cliff Branch, at wide receiver, equalled the NFL record for the longest touchdown reception with a 99-yarder against Washington, before taking over from former Raider Fred Biletnikoff as the all time leading receiver (73 receptions) in playoff games. Malcolm Barnwell does enough and, with the nippy Dokie Williams and the smouldering Calvin Muhammad in reserve, what might well have been a problem seems to have been solved. Tight end Todd Christensen, meanwhile, happened to catch 92 passes to earn himself the reputation of being the best pass receiving tight end in the NFL. With players such as Kellen Winslow around, that's no small assertion, but any way you look at it, he's a good one. And then there is Marcus Allen. After a quiet regular season in which he had only one 100-yard game (even so he gained over 1,000 yards and caught 68 passes), in the playoffs he rushed for 466 yards at the staggering average of 8.03 yards per carry. Against Dallas in the regular season, he took a back seat watching Frank Hawkins rush for 118 yards on 17 carries. Kenny King, the big-play man of Super Bowl XV (he caught a record 80-yard touchdown pass) is a dangerous multi-purpose option and a more-than-useful blocker.

Defense

Playing nominally 3-4 defense, the Raiders use a variety of substitutions according to circumstances. Against the expected pass, linebackers Ted 'Mad Stork' Hendricks and the aggressive Matt Millen give way to the 1983 rookie discoveries, Greg Townsend and Bill Pickel, who registered 10½ and 6½ sacks respectively. Overall, the team came top of the AFC and second in the NFL with 57 quarterback collars. Outside linebacker Rod Martin, another hero of Super Bowl XV with three pass interceptions, finally made it to the Pro Bowl, and his partner playing the inside position, Bob Nelson, had another good year. After an illustrious career, Ted Hendricks may share time with Jack Squirek (remember his interception touchdown in Super Bowl XVIII?). Another veteran, Lyle Alzado, has reversed his decision to retire and, together with defensive end Howie Long and nose tackle Reggie Kinlaw, will form an unchanged line. The secondary is virtually impenetrable. Lester Hayes and Mike Haynes form the NFL's best combination at cornerback, free safety Vann McElroy went to the Pro Bowl and Mike Davis gives little away at strong safety. There is the expressive talent of James Davis in reserve.

Special Teams

Kicker Chris Bahr does everything expected of him, and if the punter, Ray Guy, may be losing a little of his distance, he retains the composure of a man who was selected All Pro for six consecutive seasons. Greg Pruitt combines with Cleo Montgomery to maintain a respectable standard returning kicks, but is in sole charge of punt returns and a 97-yarder against Washington boosted his average to 11.5 yards per attempt, which was good enough to gain election to the Pro Bowl.

1984 DRAFT

Round	Name	Pos.	Ht.	Wt.	College
2.	Jones, Sean	DE	6-7	265	Northeastern
3.	McCall, Joe	RB	5-10	190	Pittsburgh
5.	Parker, Andy	TE	6-4	230	Utah
6.	Toran, Stacey	DB	6-2	210	Notre Dame
7.	Willis, Mitch	DE	6-7	265	Southern Methodist
8.	Seale, Sam	WR			Western State, Colorado
11.	Williams, Gardner	DB			St. Mary's, California
12.	Essington, Randy	QB		210	Colorado

1984 SCHEDULE

September

2	at Houston	3:00
9	GREEN BAY	1:00
16	at Kansas City	12:00
24	SAN DIEGO	6:00
30	at Denver	2:00

October

7	SEATTLE	1:00
14	MINNESOTA	1:00
21	at San Diego	1:00
28	DENVER	1:00

November

4	at Chicago	12:00
12	at Seattle	6:00
18	KANSAS CITY	1:00
25	INDIANAPOLIS	1:00

December

2	at Miami	4:00
10	at Detroit	9:00
16	PITTSBURGH	1:00

Jim Plunkett

VETERAN ROSTER

No.	Name	Pos.	Ht.	Wt.	NFL Year	College
32	Allen, Marcus	RB	6-2	205	3	USC
77	Alzado, Lyle	DE	6-3	250	14	Yankton
10	Bahr, Chris	K	5-10	175	9	Penn State
56	Barnes, Jeff	LB	6-2	225	8	California
80	Barnwell, Malcolm	WR	5-11	185	4	Virginia Union
40	Berns, Rick	RB	6-2	205	5	Nebraska
21	Branch, Cliff	WR	5-11	170	13	Colorado
54	Byrd, Darryl	LB	6-1	220	2	Illinois
57	Caldwell, Tony	LB	6-1	225	2	Washington
46	Christensen, Todd	TE	6-3	230	6	Brigham Young
50	Dalby, Dave	C	6-3	250	13	UCLA
79	Davis, Bruce	T	6-6	280	6	UCLA
45	Davis, James	CB	6-0	190	3	Southern
36	Davis, Mike	S	6-3	205	7	Colorado
	Golsteyn, Jerry	QB	6-4	200	6	Northern Illinois
8	Guy, Ray	P	6-3	195	12	Southern Mississippi
73	Hannah, Charley	G	6-6	265	8	Alabama
87	Hasselbeck, Don	TE	6-7	245	8	Colorado
27	Hawkins, Frank	RB	5-9	210	4	Nevada-Reno
37	Hayes, Lester	CB	6-0	200	8	Texas A & M
22	Haynes, Mike	CB	6-2	202	9	Arizona State
83	Hendricks, Ted	LB	6-7	230	16	Miami
48	Hill, Kenny	S	6-0	195	4	Yale
11	Humm, David	QB	6-2	195	10	Nebraska
31	Jensen, Derrick	TE	6-1	220	6	Texas-Arlington
64	Jordan, Shelby	T	6-7	280	9	Washington, Mo.
33	King, Kenny	RB	5-11	205	6	Oklahoma
62	Kinlaw, Reggie	NT	6-2	245	5	Oklahoma
70	Lawrence, Henry	T	6-4	270	11	Florida A & M
75	Long, Howie	DE	6-5	265	4	Villanova
60	Marsh, Curt	G	6-5	270	4	Washington
53	Martin, Rod	LB	6-2	215	8	USC
65	Marvin, Mickey	G	6-4	270	8	Tennessee
26	McElroy, Vann	S	6-2	190	3	Baylor
23	McKinney, Odis	S	6-2	190	7	Colorado
55	Millen, Matt	LB	6-2	255	4	Penn State
28	Montgomery, Cleotha	WR	5-8	185	4	Abilene Christian
72	Mosebar, Don	T-G	6-6	270	2	USC
82	Muhammad, Calvin	WR	5-11	190	3	Texas Southern
76	Muransky, Ed	T	6-7	280	3	Michigan
51	Nelson, Bob	LB	6-4	235	8	Nebraska
71	Pickel, Bill	DE	6-5	260	2	Rutgers
16	Plunkett, Jim	QB	6-2	215	14	Stanford
34	Pruitt, Greg	RB-PR	5-10	190	12	Oklahoma
68	Robinson, Johnny	NT	6-2	260	4	Louisiana Tech.
52	Romano, Jim	C	6-3	260	3	Penn State
58	Squirek, Jack	LB	6-4	225	3	Illinois
66	Sylvester, Steve	C-G	6-4	260	10	Notre Dame
93	Townsend, Greg	DE	6-3	240	2	Texas Christian
20	Watts, Ted	CB	6-0	190	4	Texas Tech.
85	Williams, Dokie	WR	5-11	180	2	UCLA
38	Willis, Chester	RB	5-11	195	4	Auburn
6	Wilson, Marc	QB	6-6	205	5	Brigham Young

SAN DIEGO CHARGERS AFC West

Address San Diego Jack Murphy Stadium, P.O. Box 20666, San Diego, California 92120.

Stadium San Diego Jack Murphy Stadium.
Capacity 60,100 *Playing Surface* Grass.

Team Colours Royal Blue, Gold and White.

Head Coach Don Coryell — seventh year.

Championships AFL 1963; Division 1979,'80,'81.

History AFL 1960-69, AFC 1970—
(For 1960 only, they were known as the Los Angeles Chargers.)

Offense

An offensive line featuring the guards Ed White and Doug Wilkerson, who are entering their sixteenth and fifteenth seasons respectively, qualifies for the nickname 'Dad's Army' and really ought to be past its best. And yet, there is none better at protecting the quarterback and providing the base for a passing offense which seems certain to retain its status as the NFL's finest. Quarterback Dan Fouts, who missed six games and failed to finish two more in 1983, will be back and raring to go at the controls of the 'San Diego Air Force'. With such a galaxy of receivers available, Fouts is the best bet to become the first man to pass for over 5,000 yards in a season. Wes Chandler, an elusive runner who explodes for the big play, is considered by many to be the NFL's best pure receiver and, even though limping through the 1983 season hampered by niggling injuries, still caught 58 passes for 845 yards. Charlie Joiner will be 37 in 1984 but remains a dangerous target and, with 65 pass receptions in 1983, fell short of his career best (recorded in 1979) by only seven. Bobby Duckworth, a real burner, averaged 21·1 yards per reception but even at this level of performance will find difficulty breaking into the starting lineup. Running back Chuck Muncie is a short range threat and then there is the small matter of the NFL's premier tight end, Kellen Winslow, to keep the opposing defenses occupied. 'Mr Everything', as they say, established a Chargers record with 14 receptions, for 162

yards and 3 touchdowns, when terrorising the Chiefs on week 15. The rushing offense, however, has gone off the boil and coach Don Coryell readily snapped up Cincinnati's Pete Johnson in exchange for James Brooks, who considered himself under-used. Johnson is one of the NFL's great power runners and his arrival firmly places the Chargers in contention with the Raiders for the Western division title.

Defense

Defense continues to be a San Diego problem. Keith Ferguson, Richard Ackerman and Gary Johnson are on the small side for defensive linemen (Ackerman is the heaviest at 254 lb), and Johnson has slipped below the level of performance which earned Pro Bowl recognition for the four years 1980-83. They are helped enormously by the arrival of Abdul Salaam and Kenny Neil, both formerly with the Jets. At inside linebacker, Mike Green, a ninth-round pick in 1983, was a surprise starter who did well, but the more illustrious apprentice, Billy Ray Smith, found it hard going in the thick of things. Playing on the outsides, Woodrow Lowe has plenty of experience and Linden King, a hard tackler, led the team with eight sacks. Brian Kelley brings his veteran savvy from the Giants and the second-round draftee, Mike Guendling, represents a continuation of the youth programme. A serious back injury to rookie cornerback Gill Byrd was a bitter blow to a defensive secondary which, even though collectively registering only 13 interceptions, was firming up. Rookie cornerback Danny Walters was responsible for seven of these and will be joined by another exciting prospect, first round draftee Mossy Cade. Strong safety Andre Young (entering his third season) is now established alongside free safety Ken Greene, who has replaced Tim Fox.

Special Teams

Kicker Rolf Benirschke had an off season for the former Pro Bowler that he is, but punter Maury Buford finished third in the NFL, with a gross average of 43·9 yards. The multi-talented James Brooks turned in a surprisingly modest performance, returning both kickoffs and punts, and a specialist kickoff returner, Lionel James, was drafted in the fifth round as a replacement.

1984 DRAFT

Round	Name	Pos.	Ht.	Wt.	College
1.	Cade, Mossy	DB	5-11	175	Texas
2.	Guendling, Mike	LB	6-2	232	Northwestern
5.	James, Lionel	KR	5-7	167	Auburn
6.	Guthrie, Keith	DT	6-3	270	Texas A & M
7.	Bendross, Jesse	WR	6-0	190	Alabama
8.	Woodward, Raymond	DT	6-4	280	Texas
8.	Craighead, Bob	RB	6-0	205	N.E. Louisiana
9.	Barnes, Zack	DT	6-5	260	Alabama State
11.	McGee, Buford	RB	6-0	200	Mississippi
12.	Harper, Maurice	WR			La Verne

1984 SCHEDULE

September

2	at Minnesota	12:00
9	at Seattle	1:00
16	HOUSTON	1:00
24	at Los Angeles Raiders	6:00
30	DETROIT	1:00

October

7	at Green Bay	3:00
14	at Kansas City	12:00
21	LOS ANGELES RAIDERS	1:00
29	SEATTLE	6:00

November

4	at Indianapolis	1:00
11	DENVER	1:00
18	MIAMI	1:00
25	at Pittsburgh	1:00

December

3	CHICAGO	6:00
9	at Denver	2:00
16	KANSAS CITY	1:00

Kellen Winslow

VETERAN ROSTER

No.	Name	Pos.	Ht.	Wt.	NFL Year	College
91	Ackerman, Richard	NT	6-4	254	3	Memphis State
6	Benirschke, Rolf	K	6-1	179	8	Cal-Davis
50	Bradley, Carlos	LB	6-0	226	4	Wake Forest
61	Brown, Don	T	6-6	262	2	Santa Clara
7	Buford, Maury	P	6-0	185	3	Texas Tech.
22	Byrd, Gill	CB	5-11	191	2	San Jose State
89	Chandler, Wes	WR	6-0	183	7	Florida
77	Claphan, Sam	T	6-6	267	4	Oklahoma
	Downing, Walt	C-G	6-3	270	7	Michigan
82	Duckworth, Bobby	WR	6-3	197	3	Arkansas
78	Ehin, Chuck	DE	6-4	255	2	Brigham Young
68	Elko, Bill	G-NT	6-5	278	2	Louisiana State
56	Evans, Larry	LB	6-2	220	9	Mississippi College
76	Ferguson, Keith	DE	6-5	241	4	Ohio State
84	Fortune, Hosea	WR	6-0	174	2	Rice
14	Fouts, Dan	QB	6-3	205	12	Oregon
48	Fox, Tim	S	5-11	186	9	Ohio State
75	Gissinger, Andrew	T	6-5	279	3	Syracuse
69	Gofourth, Derrel	G-C	6-3	260	8	Oklahoma State
58	Green, Mike	LB	6-0	226	2	Oklahoma State
28	Greene, Ken	S	6-3	205	7	Washington State
43	Gregor, Bob	S	6-2	190	4	Washington State
20	Henderson, Reuben	CB	6-1	200	4	San Diego State
88	Holohan, Pete	TE	6-4	240	4	Notre Dame
41	Jackson, Earnest	RB	5-10	208	2	Texas A & M
40	Jodat, Jim	RB	5-11	208	8	Carthage
79	Johnson, Gary	DE	6-2	251	10	Grambling
	Johnson, Pete	RB	6-0	249	8	Ohio State
18	Joiner, Charlie	WR	5-11	180	16	Grambling
53	Kelley, Brian	LB	6-3	222	12	California Lutheran
57	King, Linden	LB	6-5	245	7	Colorado State
64	Loewen, Chuck	G-T	6-4	264	5	South Dakota
51	Lowe, Woodrow	LB	6-0	226	9	Alabama
11	Luther, Ed	QB	6-3	202	5	San Jose State
62	Macek, Don	C	6-2	260	9	Boston College
12	Mathison, Bruce	QB	6-3	210	2	Nebraska
60	McKnight, Dennis	C-G	6-3	253	3	Drake
24	McPherson, Miles	CB	6-0	175	3	New Haven
46	Muncie, Chuck	RB	6-2	228	9	California
72	Neil, Kenny	DE	6-4	244	4	Iowa State
55	Nelson, Derrie	LB	6-1	236	2	Nebraska
38	Pleasant, Mike	RB	6-1	195	1	Oklahoma
52	Preston, Ray	LB	6-0	220	9	Syracuse
74	Salaam, Abdul	NT	6-3	269	9	Kent State
66	Shields, Billy	T	6-8	284	10	Georgia
85	Sievers, Eric	TE	6-4	235	4	Maryland
54	Smith, Billy Ray	LB	6-3	242	2	Arkansas
47	Smith, Sherman	RB	6-4	225	9	Miami, Ohio
	Thomas, Jewerl	RB	5-10	228	5	San Jose State
59	Thrift, Cliff	LB	6-1	230	6	East Central Oklahoma
23	Walters, Danny	CB	6-1	186	2	Arkansas
67	White, Ed	G	6-2	279	16	California
63	Wilkerson, Doug	G	6-3	258	15	North Carolina Central
45	Williams, Henry	S	5-10	180	3	San Diego State
80	Winslow, Kellen	TE	6-5	251	6	Missouri
49	Young, Andre	S	6-0	203	3	Louisiana Tech.

SEATTLE SEAHAWKS AFC West

Address 5305 Lake Washington Boulevard, Kirkland, Washington 98033.
Stadium Kingdome, Seattle.
   Capacity 64,757 *Playing Surface* AstroTurf.
Team Colours Blue, Green and Silver.
Head Coach Chuck Knox — second year.
Championships None.
History NFC 1976, AFC 1977—

Offense

Center Blair Bush was acquired from Cincinnati and left guard Reggie McKenzie came with coach Knox from Buffalo, to provide leadership and veteran experience on an offensive line, in preparation for the arrival of rookie running back Curt Warner. McKenzie is no stranger to this role (he tended O.J. Simpson when both men were in their early days with Buffalo) and for him, it must have been rewarding to see his latest charge, Warner, win the AFC rushing title. Though an average of four quarterback sacks yielded per game is respectable, the line tended to crumble under the weight of the better teams — against Dallas, they gave up eight sacks — and is an aspect in which improvement will be necessary if the Seahawks are to maintain their challenge in the AFC West. Quarterback David Krieg was a sensation, displacing Jim Zorn, before establishing a passer rating of 95·0 to earn second place behind Dan Marino in the AFC. He showed surprising coolness under pressure against Miami and can be forgiven for making no impact in the subsequent AFC Championship Game loss to the Raiders. Wide receiver Steve Largent continued in prime form, with his fifth 1,000-yard season in a sequence interrupted only by the brevity of 1982, and we must hope that rumours of his premature retirement prove to be false. The other starter, Paul Johns, had by far his best season in a three-year career, with 34 receptions, and tight end Charle Young settled in well after the move from San Francisco (he caught 36 passes for 529 yards). The remarkable Curt Warner was Seattle's first ever 1,000-yard rusher, setting records all the way, in particular with six 100-yard games, including a 207-yard romp against Kansas City. David Hughes was a reliable partner in what, for the first time in the Seahawks' history, has become a bona fide rushing offense.

Defense

The emergence of the Seahawks as a great 'takeaway' defense was a startling revelation. With 54 'steals' they were second only to the ball-hawking Redskins in the NFL. Defensive left end Jacob Green was responsible for 16 of the team total of 43 quarterback sacks and right end Jeff Bryant had 8½ but, on a cautionary note, reserve strength is modest and, following the departure of Manu Tuiasosopo for San Francisco, there is no obvious backup to Joe Nash at nose tackle. At linebacker, both Shelton Robinson and Bruce Scholtz are solid, playing on the left side, although both Robinson and the other starter, Keith Butler, will be pushed by the veteran Jim Youngblood, who was acquired from the Los Angeles Rams. Michael Jackson is immensely talented and could well mature into a really great outside linebacker. Kenny Easley has already achieved this status, playing at strong safety in a defensive secondary which will be joined by the number one draftee, Terry Taylor. On the other hand, free safety John Harris had an off year, measured by his own high standards. Equally, the cornerbacks, Dave Brown and Kerry Justin, appeared vulnerable when attempting man-for-man coverage (but then, who wouldn't be in the modern NFL?). On the credit side, Brown had six pass interceptions (Easley led the team with seven). Justin has since departed for the USFL and will be replaced almost certainly by Terry Jackson, who was acquired from the Giants.

Special Teams

Kicker Norm Johnson is good, but Jeff West came bottom of the AFC with a gross average of 39·5 yards. Zachary Dixon included a kickoff return for a 94-yard touchdown in his average of 23·0, which helped raise the team performance to second best in the NFL. Paul Johns, too, was excellent, returning punts for an average of 11·3 yards, including one for a 75-yard touchdown against the Raiders.

1984 DRAFT

Round	Name	Pos.	Ht.	Wt.	College
1.	Taylor, Terry	DB	5-10	168	Southern Illinois
2.	Turner, Daryl	WR	6-3	190	Michigan State
3.	Young, Fred	LB	6-1	220	New Mexico State
4.	Hagood, Rickey	DT	6-1	285	South Carolina
6.	Kaiser, John	LB	6-3	220	Arizona
7.	Slater, Sam	T	6-8	275	Weber State
8.	Puzar, John	C	6-5	250	Cal State — Long Beach
9.	Schreiber, Adam	G	6-2	255	Texas
10.	Morris, Randall	RB	5-11	195	Tennessee
11.	Gemza, Steve	T	6-8	280	UCLA
12.	Windham, Theodis	DB			Utah State

1984 SCHEDULE

September
2	CLEVELAND	1:00
9	SAN DIEGO	1:00
16	at New England	1:00
23	CHICAGO	1:00
30	at Minnesota	12:00

October
7	at Los Angeles Raiders	1:00
14	BUFFALO	1:00
21	at Green Bay (Milwaukee)	12:00
29	at San Diego	6:00

November
4	KANSAS CITY	1:00
12	LOS ANGELES RAIDERS	6:00
18	at Cincinnati	1:00
25	at Denver	2:00

December
2	DETROIT	1:00
9	at Kansas City	12:00
15	DENVER	1:00

Paul Johns (85)

VETERAN ROSTER

No.	Name	Pos.	Ht.	Wt.	NFL Year	College
76	August, Steve	T	6-5	254	8	Tulsa
65	Bailey, Edwin	G-C	6-4	265	4	South Carolina State
22	Brown, Dave	CB	6-2	190	10	Michigan
32	Bryant, Cullen	RB	6-1	235	12	Colorado
77	Bryant, Jeff	DE	6-5	260	3	Clemson
59	Bush, Blair	C	6-3	252	7	Washington
53	Butler, Keith	LB	6-4	225	7	Memphis State
83	Castor, Chris	WR	6-0	170	2	Duke
31	Dixon, Zachary	RB-KR	6-1	204	6	Temple
33	Doornink, Dan	RB	6-3	210	7	Washington State
35	Dufek, Dan	S	6-0	195	8	Michigan
66	Dugan, Bill	G	6-4	271	4	Penn State
45	Easley, Kenny	S	6-3	206	4	UCLA
64	Essink, Ron	T	6-6	254	5	Grand Valley State
56	Gaines, Greg	LB	6-3	220	3	Tennessee
79	Green, Jacob	DE	6-3	247	5	Texas A & M
75	Hardy, Robert	NT	6-2	250	6	Jackson State
44	Harris, John	S	6-2	200	7	Arizona State
69	Hernandez, Matt	T	6-6	260	2	Purdue
63	Hicks, Mark	LB	6-2	225	2	Arizona State
46	Hughes, David	RB	6-0	220	4	Boise State
70	Irvin, Darrell	DE	6-4	255	5	Oklahoma
29	Jackson, Harold	WR	5-10	175	17	Jackson State
55	Jackson, Michael	LB	6-1	220	6	Washington
	Jackson, Terry	CB	5-11	197	7	San Diego State
85	Johns, Paul	WR-PR	5-11	170	4	Tulsa
9	Johnson, Norm	K	6-2	193	3	UCLA
26	Justin, Kerry	CB	5-11	175	7	Oregon State
62	Kauahi, Kani	C	6-2	260	3	Hawaii
17	Krieg, Dave	QB	6-1	185	5	Milton
37	Lane, Eric	RB	6-0	195	4	Brigham Young
80	Largent, Steve	WR	5-11	184	9	Tulsa
67	McKenzie, Reggie	G	6-5	242	13	Michigan
51	Merriman, Sam	LB	6-3	225	2	Idaho
88	Metzelaars, Pete	TE	6-7	240	3	Wabash
21	Moyer, Paul	S	6-1	201	2	Arizona State
72	Nash, Joe	NT	6-3	250	3	Boston College
52	Norman, Joe	LB	6-1	220	5	Indiana
61	Pratt, Robert	G	6-4	250	11	North Carolina
57	Robinson, Shelton	LB	6-2	233	3	North Carolina
58	Scholtz, Bruce	LB	6-6	240	3	Texas
42	Simpson, Keith	CB	6-1	195	7	Memphis State
86	Tice, Mike	TE	6-7	250	4	Maryland
89	Walker, Byron	WR	6-4	190	3	Citadel
28	Warner, Curt	RB	5-11	205	2	Penn State
8	West, Jeff	P	6-2	220	9	Cincinnati
54	Williams, Eugene	LB	6-1	220	3	Tulsa
87	Young, Charle	TE	6-4	234	12	USC
	Youngblood, Jim	LB	6-3	231	12	Tennessee Tech.
10	Zorn, Jim	QB	6-2	200	9	Cal Poly-Pomona

CHAPTER 7

NATIONAL FOOTBALL CONFERENCE

TEAM RANKINGS

| | OFFENSE | | | | | | DEFENSE | | | | | |
	Total Yds.	Rushing	Passing	Points For	% Intercepted	% Sacked	Total Yds.	Rushing	Passing	Points Against	% Interceptions	% Sacks
Atlanta	6	7	6	6	1	11	13	11	10	12	13	13
Chicago	5	1	11	11	11	13	4	7	5	3	9	4
Dallas	4	9	2	2	6	3	10	2	13	10	4	5
Detroit	10	8	12	8	8	9	6	10	4	1	10	11
Green Bay	1	11	1	4	14	6	14	13	12	14	12	12
L.A. Rams	7	6	7	7	10	1	8	4	11	7	11	14
Minnesota	11	10	8	10	5	5	12	12	3	9	3	6
New Orleans	12	3	14	9	13	7	1	8	1	6	7	2
N.Y. Giants	8	12	5	12	12	8	2	3	8	8	5	7
Philadelphia	13	13	10	14	4	12	11	14	2	4	14	10
St Louis	9	4	13	5	9	14	3	5	6	13	2	1
San Francisco	3	5	3	3	2	2	5	6	7	2	8	3
Tampa Bay	14	14	9	13	7	10	9	9	9	11	6	9
Washington	2	2	4	1	3	4	7	1	14	5	1	8

NFC PASSERS

	Att	Comp	% Comp	Yards	Ave Gain	TD	% TD	Long	Int	Pct Int	Rating Points
Bartkowski, Steve, *Atl.*	432	274	63.4	3167	7.33	22	5.1	t76	5	1.2	97.6
Theismann, Joe, *Wash.*	459	276	60.1	3714	8.09	29	6.3	84	11	2.4	97.0
Montana, Joe, *S.F.*	515	332	64.5	3910	7.59	26	5.0	t77	12	2,3	94.6
Lomax, Neil, *St. L.*	354	209	59.0	2636	7.45	24	6.8	t71	11	3.1	92.0
Dickey, Lynn, *G.B.*	484	289	59.7	4458	9.21	32	6.6	t75	29	6.0	87.3
White, Danny, *Dall.*	533	334	62.7	3980	7.47	29	5.4	t80	23	4.3	85.6
McMahon, Jim, *Chi.*	295	175	59.3	2184	7.40	12	4.1	t87	13	4.4	77.6
Ferragamo, Vince, *Rams*	464	274	59.1	3276	7.06	22	4.7	t61	23	5.0	75.9
Jaworski, Ron, *Phil.*	446	235	52.7	3315	7.43	20	4.5	t83	18	4.0	75.1
Thompson, Jack, *T.B.*	423	249	58.9	2906	6.87	18	4.3	80	21	5.0	73.3
Dils, Steve, *Minn.*	444	239	53.8	2840	6.40	11	2.5	68	16	3.6	66.8
Hipple, Eric, *Det.*	387	204	52.7	2577	6.66	12	3.1	t80	18	4.7	64.7
Stabler, Ken, *N.O.*	311	176	56.6	1988	6.39	9	2.9	48	18	5.8	61.4
Brunner, Scott, *Giants*	386	190	49.2	2516	6.52	9	2.3	62	22	5.7	54.3

NFC RECEIVERS

	No	Yards	Ave	Long	TD
Green, Roy, *St.L.*	78	1227	15.7	t71	14
Brown, Charlie, *Wash.*	78	1225	15.7	t75	8
Gray, Earnest, *Giants*	78	1139	14.6	62	5
Springs, Ron, *Dall.*	73	589	8.1	t80	1
Clark, Dwight. *S.F.*	70	840	12.0	t46	8
Quick, Mike, *Phil.*	69	1409	20.4	t83	13

	No	Yards	Ave	Long	TD
Johnson, Billy, *Atl.*	64	709	11,1	t47	4
Andrews, William, *Atl.*	59	609	10.3	40	4
Lofton, James, *G.B.*	58	1300	22.4	t74	8
Jefferson, John, *G.B.*	57	830	14.6	36	7
Wilder, James, *T.B.*	57	380	6.7	31	2
Bailey, Stacey, *Atl.*	55	881	16.0	53	6
Barber, Mike, *Rams.*	55	657	11.9	t42	3
Coffman, Paul, *G.B.*	54	814	15.1	74	11
Anderson, Ottis, *St.L.*	54	459	8.5	40	1
Payton, Walter, *Chi.*	53	607	11.5	t74	2
Ellis, Gerry, *G.B.*	52	603	11.6	56	2
Nelson, Darrin, *Minn.*	51	618	12.1	68	0
Dickerson, Eric, *Rams.*	51	404	7.9	t37	2
Hill, Tony, *Dall.*	49	801	16.3	t75	7
Groth, Jeff, *N.O.*	49	585	11.9	42	1
Suhey, Matt, *Chi.*	49	429	8.8	52	1
Oliver, Hubert, *Phil.*	49	421	8.6	25	2
Carter, Gerald, *T.B.*	48	694	14.5	t56	2
Craig, Roger, *S.F.*	48	427	8.9	23	4
House, Kevin, *T.B.*	47	769	16.4	t74	5
Monk, Art, *Wash.*	47	746	15.9	t43	5
Pearson, Drew, *Dall.*	47	545	11.6	32	5
Washington, Joe, *Wash.*	47	454	9.7	67	6
Cosbie, Doug, *Dall.*	46	588	12.8	t61	6
Jones, James, *Det.*	46	467	10.2	46	1
Mistler, John, *Giants.*	45	422	9.4	24	0
Galbreath, Tony, *Minn.*	45	348	7.7	23	2
Tilley, Pat, *St.L.*	44	690	15.7	t71	5
Moorehead, Emery, *Chi.*	42	597	14.2	36	3
Sims, Billy, *Det.*	42	419	10.0	54	0
Thompson, Leonard, *Det.*	41	752	18.3	t80	3
Brenner, Hoby, *N.O.*	41	574	14.0	t38	3
Johnson, Butch, *Dall.*	41	561	13.7	46	3
Goodlow, Eugene, *N.O.*	41	487	11.9	26	2
Brown, Ted, *Minn.*	41	357	8.7	25	1
Gault, Willie, *Chi.*	40	836	20.9	t87	8
Chadwick, Jeff, *Det.*	40	617	15.4	45	4
Farmer, George, *Rams*	40	556	13.9	t46	5
Dorsett, Tony, *Dall.*	40	287	7.2	24	1
Carmichael, Harold, *Phil.*	38	515	13.6	35	3
Jenkins, Alfred, *Atl.*	38	487	12.8	26	1
Guman, Mike, *Rams.*	34	347	10.2	60	4
Tyler, Wendell, *S.F.*	34	285	8.4	26	2
Dennard, Preston, *Rams.*	33	465	14.1	t61	5
Francis, Russ, *S.F.*	33	357	10.8	25	4
Marsh, Doug, *St.L.*	32	421	13.2	38	8
Carver, Mel, *T.B.*	32	262	8.2	20	1
Solomon, Freddie, *S.F.*	31	662	21.4	t77	4
Bruer, Bob, *Minn.*	31	315	10.2	26	2
Wilson, Mike, *S.F.*	30	433	14.4	49	0
Nichols, Mark, *Det.*	29	437	15.1	46	1
White, Sammy, *Minn.*	29	412	14.2	t43	4
Woolfolk, Butch, *Giants*	28	368	13.1	44	0
Hill, David, *Rams*	28	280	10.0	34	2
Giaquinto, Nick, *Wash.*	27	372	13.8	35	0
Norris, Ulysses, *Det.*	26	291	11.2	41	7
Carpenter, Rob, *Giants*	26	258	9.9	38	2
Bell, Theo, *T.B.*	25	410	16.4	52	2
Giles, Jimmie, *T.B.*	25	349	14.0	80	1
Garrett, Alvin, *Wash.*	25	332	13.3	84	1

	No	Yards	Ave	Long	TD
Hodge, Floyd, *Atl.*	25	280	11.2	t76	4
Scott, Lindsay, *N.O.*	24	274	11.4	35	0
Haddix, Michael, *Phil.*	23	254	11.0	34	0
Ring, Bill, *S.F.*	23	182	7.9	24	0
Margerum, Ken, *Chi.*	21	336	16.0	60	2
LeCount, Terry, *Minn.*	21	318	15.1	49	2

NFC RUSHERS

	Att	Yards	Ave	Long	TD
Dickerson, Eric, *Rams*	390	1808	4.6	t85	18
Andrews, William, *Atl.*	331	1567	4.7	27	7
Payton, Walter, *Chi.*	314	1421	4.5	t49	6
Riggins, John, *Wash.*	375	1347	3.6	44	24
Dorsett, Tony, *Dall.*	289	1321	4.6	77	8
Anderson, Ottis, *St.L.*	296	1270	4.3	43	5
Rogers, George, *N.O.*	256	1144	4.5	t76	5
Sims, Billy, *Det.*	220	1040	4.7	41	7
Woolfolk, Butch, *Giants*	246	857	3.5	22	4
Tyler, Wendell, *S.F.*	176	856	4.9	39	4
Wilson, Wayne, *N.O.*	199	787	4.0	29	9
Washington, Joe, *Wash.*	145	772	5.3	41	0
Craig, Roger, *S.F.*	176	725	4.1	71	8
Ellis, Gerry, *G.B.*	141	696	4.9	71	4
Suhey, Matt, *Chi.*	149	681	4.6	39	4
Nelson, Darrin, *Minn.*	154	642	4.2	t56	1
Wilder, James, *T.B.*	161	640	4.0	t75	4
Carpenter, Rob, *Giants*	170	624	3.7	37	4
Springs, Ron, *Dall.*	149	541	3.6	t19	7
Brown, Ted, *Minn.*	120	476	4.0	43	10
Jones, James, *Det.*	135	475	3.5	18	6
Galbreath, Tony, *Minn.*	113	474	4.2	t52	4
Riggs, Gerald, *Atl.*	100	437	4.4	t40	8
Oliver, Hubert, *Phil.*	121	434	3.6	24	1
Gajan, Hokie, *N.O.*	81	415	5.1	58	4
Williams, Mike, *Phil.*	103	385	3.7	32	0
Mitchell, Stump, *St.L.*	68	373	5.5	46	3
Redden, Barry, *Rams.*	75	372	5.0	t40	2
Carver, Mel, *T.B.*	114	348	3.1	16	0
Ivery, Eddie Lee, *G.B.*	86	340	4.0	21	2
Clark, Jessie, *G.B.*	71	328	4.6	42	0
McMahon, Jim, *Chi.*	55	307	5.6	32	2
Montana, Joe, *S.F.*	61	284	4.7	18	2
Owens, James, *T.B.*	96	266	2.8	15	5
Morris, Wayne, *St.L.*	75	257	3.4	17	2
Ring, Bill, *S.F.*	64	254	4.0	25	2
Bussey, Dexter, *Det.*	57	249	4.4	26	0
Theismann, Joe, *Wash.*	37	234	6.3	22	1
Haddix, Michael, *Phil.*	91	220	2.4	11	2
Meade, Mike, *G.B..*	55	201	3.7	15	1
Newsome, Tim, *Dall.*	44	185	4.2	20	2
Huckleby, Harlan, *G.B.*	50	182	3.6	20	4

Mark Murphy

	Att	Yards	Ave	Long	TD
Hipple, Eric, *Det.*	41	171	4.2	27	3
Morris, Joe, *Giants.*	35	145	4.1	16	0
Evans, Vince, *Chi.*	22	142	6.5	27	1
Montgomery, Wilbert, *Phil.*	29	139	4.8	32	0
Thompson, Vince, *Det.*	40	138	3.5	10	1
Jaworski, Ron, *Phil.*	25	129	5.2	29	1
Lomax, Neil, *St.L.*	27	127	4.7	35	2
Love, Randy, *St.L.*	35	103	2.9	16	2
Harrington, Perry, *Phil.*	23	98	4.3	35	1
Young, Rickey, *Minn.*	39	90	2.3	9	2
Wonsley, Otis, *Wash.*	25	88	3.5	9	0
Johnson, Billy, *Atl.*	15	83	5.5	36	0
Rogers, Jimmy, *N.O.*	26	80	3.1	13	0
Thompson, Leonard, *Det.*	4	72	18.0	t40	1
Gentry, Dennis, *Chi.*	16	65	4.1	17	0
Brunner, Scott, *Giants*	26	64	2.5	12	0
Cain, Lynn, *Atl.*	19	63	3.3	10	1
Hayes, Jeff, *Wash.*	2	63	31.5	48	0
Brown, Charlie, *Wash.*	4	53	13.3	17	0
Ferrell, Earl, *St.L.*	7	53	7.6	21	1
Giaquinto, Nick, *Wash.*	14	53	3.8	11	1
Green, Roy, *St.L.*	4	49	12.3	25	0
Tuggle, John, *Giants.*	17	49	2.9	t7	1
Redwine, Jarvis, *Minn.*	10	48	4.8	21	0
Moore, Jeff, *S.F.*	15	43	2.9	14	0
Guman, Mike, *Rams.*	7	42	6.0	11	0
LeCount, Terry, *Minn.*	2	42	21.0	40	0

NFC KICKERS

	XP	XPA	FG	FGA	PTS
Moseley, Mark, *Wash.*	62	63	33	47	161
Haji-Sheikh, Ali, *Giants*	22	23	35	42	127
Wersching, Ray, *S.F.*	51	51	25	30	126
Septien, Rafael, *Dall.*	57	59	22	27	123
Stenerud, Jan, *G.B.*	52	52	21	26	115
Murray, Ed, *Det.*	38	38	25	32	113
Ricardo, Benny, *Minn.*	33	34	25	33	108
Luckhurst, Mick, *Atl.*	43	45	17	22	94
Andersen, Morten, *N.O.*	37	38	18	23	91
O'Donoghue, Neil, *St.L.*	45	47	15	28	90
Thomas, Bob, *Chi.*	35	38	14	25	77
Franklin, Tony, *Phil.*	24	27	15	26	69
Capece, Bill, *T.B.*	23	26	10	20	53
Nelson, Chuck, *Rams.*	33	37	5	11	48
Lansford, Mike, *Rams*	9	9	6	9	27
Warnke, David, *T.B.*	1	2	0	1	1

NFC KICKOFF RETURNERS

	No	Yards	Ave	Long	TD
Nelson, Darrin, *Minn.*	18	445	24.7	50	0
Morton, Michael, *T.B.*	30	689	23.0	50	0
Nelms, Mike, *Wash.*	35	802	22.9	41	0
Bright, Leon, *Giants*	21	475	22.6	36	0
Redwine, Jarvis, *Minn.*	38	838	22.1	41	0
Duckett, Kenny, *N.O.*	33	719	21.8	61	0
Mitchell, Stump, *St.L.*	36	778	21.6	66	0
Hall, Alvin, *Det.*	23	492	21.4	32	0
Young, Glen, *Phil.*	26	547	21.0	52	0
Jenkins, Ken, *Det.*	22	459	20.9	30	0
Williams, Richard, *Atl.*	23	461	20.0	34	0
Fellows, Ron, *Dall.*	43	855	19.9	53	0
Riggs, Gerald, *Atl.*	17	330	19.4	35	0
McLemore, Dana, *S.F.*	30	576	19.2	39	0
Owens, James, *T.B.*	20	380	19.0	31	0
Redden, Barry, *Rams*	19	358	18.8	43	0
Huckleby, Harlan, *G.B.*	41	757	18.5	57	0
Lewis, Tim, *G.B.*	20	358	17.9	30	0
Hutchison, Anthony, *Chi.*	17	259	15.2	28	0
(Non-Qualifiers)					
Ellard, Henry, *Rams*	15	314	20.9	44	0
Everett, Major, *Phil.*	14	275	19.6	46	0
Morris, Joe, *Giants*	14	255	18.2	26	0
Hill, Rod, *Dall.*	14	243	17.4	40	0
Gault, Willie, *Chi.*	13	276	21.2	38	0
Ferrell, Earl, *St.L.*	13	257	19.8	28	0
Alexander, Robert, *Rams*	13	222	17.1	30	0
Johnson, Kenny, *Atl.*	11	224	20.4	28	0
Cain, Lynn, *Atl.*	11	200	18.2	24	0
Gray, Johnny, *G.B.*	11	178	16.2	26	0
Evans, Reggie, *Wash.*	10	141	14.1	28	0
Wilson, Wayne, *N.O.*	9	239	26.6	52	0
Seay, Virgil, *Wash.*	9	218	24.2	50	0
Bird, Steve, *St.L.*	9	194	21.6	33	0
Tuggle, John, *Giants*	9	156	17.3	28	0
Campfield, Billy, *Giants*	9	154	17.1	23	0
Allen, Gary, *Dall.*	8	178	22.3	31	0
Monroe, Carl, *S.F.*	8	152	19.0	32	0
Mauti, Rich, *N.O.*	8	147	18.4	35	0
Martin, Robbie, *Det.*	8	140	17.5	51	0
Smith, Johnny Ray, *T.B.*	8	136	17.0	43	0
Gentry, Dennis, *Chi.*	7	130	18.6	28	0
Ellis, Ray, *Phil.*	7	119	17.0	25	0
Moore, Jeff, *S.F.*	7	117	16.7	46	0
Austin, Cliff, *N.O.*	7	112	16.0	27	0
Rogers, Jimmy, *N.O.*	7	103	14.7	25	0
Pittman, Danny, *Giants*	6	107	17.8	24	0
Watts, Rickey, *Chi.*	5	79	15.8	21	0

Mark Moseley

	No	Yards	Ave	Long	TD
Heater, Larry, *Giants*	5	71	14.2	26	0
Harrington, Perry, *Phil.*	4	79	19.8	26	0
Caver, Jim, *Det.*	4	71	17.8	33	0
Ring, Bill, *S.F.*	4	68	17.0	18	0
Schmitt, George, *St.L.*	4	41	10.3	19	0
Love, Randy, *St.L.*	3	71	23.7	23	0
Duerson, Dave, *Chi.*	3	66	22.0	24	0
Harrell, Willard, *St.L.*	3	62	20.7	26	0
Williams, Mike, *Phil*	3	59	19.7	25	0
Haddix, Michael, *Phil.*	3	51	17.0	24	0
Cooper, Earl, *S.F.*	3	45	15.0	20	0
Baschnagel, Brian, *Chi.*	3	42	14.0	19	0
Huffman, Dave, *Minn.*	3	42	14.0	15	0
Spradlin, Danny, *T.B.*	3	35	11.7	24	0
Winters, Chet, *G.B.*	3	28	9.3	12	0
Young, Rickey, *Minn.*	3	27	9.0	15	0
Garrett, Alvin, *Wash.*	2	50	25.0	28	0
Bess, Rufus, *Minn.*	2	44	22.0	30	0
McKinnon, Dennis, *Chi.*	2	42	21.0	25	0
Wonsley, Otis, *Wash.*	2	36	18.0	20	0
Jones, Mike, *Minn.*	2	31	15.5	16	0
Miller, Mike, *Giants*	2	31	15.5	26	0
Guman, Mike, *Rams*	2	30	15.0	21	0
O'Steen, Dwayne, *T.B.*	2	30	15.0	16	0

NFC PUNTERS

	No	Yards	Long	Ave	Total Punts	TB	Blk	Opp Ret	Ret Yds	In 20	Net Ave
Garcia, Frank, *T.B.*	95	4008	64	42.2	96	12	1	59	603	15	33.0
Runager, Max, *Phil.*	59	2459	55	41.7	59	5	0	37	339	12	34.2
Scribner, Bucky, *G.B.*	69	2869	70	41.6	70	7	1	43	384	11	33.5
Coleman, Greg, *Minn.*	91	3780	65	41.5	91	8	0	40	297	28	36.5
Birdsong, Carl, *St.L.*	85	3529	59	41.5	85	7	0	47	307	14	36.3
Black, Mike, *Det.*	71	2911	60	41.0	72	9	1	39	302	17	33.7
Erxleben, Russell, *N.O.*	74	3034	60	41.0	74	9	0	49	571	10	30.9
Giacomarro, Ralph, *Atl.*	70	2823	57	40.3	71	8	1	34	179	18	35.0
Jennings, Dave, *Giants*	84	3386	66	40.3	85	5	1	47	283	29	35.3
Misko, John, *Rams*	82	3301	67	40.3	83	12	1	39	251	18	33.9
Orosz, Tom, *S.F.*	65	2552	61	39.3	66	6	1	38	278	16	32.6
Hayes, Jeff, *Wash.*	72	2796	56	38.8	72	2	0	41	407	29	32.6
Parsons, Bob, *Chi.*	79	2916	54	36.9	79	5	0	37	261	21	32.3

NFC PUNT RETURNERS

	No	FC	Yards	Ave	Long	TD
Ellard, Henry, *Rams*	16	4	217	13.6	t72	1
McLemore, Dana, *S.F.*	31	6	331	10.7	t56	1
Johnson, Billy, *Atl.*	46	4	489	10.6	t71	1
Jenkins, Ken, *Det.*	23	1	230	10.0	43	0
McKinnon, Dennis, *Chi.*	34	3	316	9.3	t59	1
Epps, Phillip, *G.B.*	36	13	324	9.0	t90	1
Mitchell, Stump, *St.L.*	38	1	337	8.9	34	0
Irvin, LeRoy, *Rams*	25	3	212	8.5	20	0
Shaw, Pete, *Giants*	29	4	234	8.1	27	0
Hill, Rod, *Dall.*	30	2	232	7.7	37	0
Tyler, Andre, *T.B.*	27	5	208	7.7	16	0
Nelms, Mike, *Wash.*	38	0	289	7.6	35	0
Bess, Rufus, *Minn.*	21	10	158	7.5	17	0
Groth, Jeff, *N.O.*	39	15	275	7.1	30	0
Bright, Leon, *Giants*	17	0	117	6.9	20	0
Sciarra, John, *Phil.*	22	3	115	5.2	14	0

NFC INTERCEPTORS

	No	Yards	Ave	Long	TD
Murphy, Mark, *Wash.*	9	127	14.1	48	0
Reece, Beasley, *Giants–T.B.*	8	103	12.9	29	0
Washington, Lionel, *St.L.*	8	92	11.5	26	0
Wright, Eric, *S.F.*	7	164	23.4	t60	2
Poe, Johnnie, *N.O.*	7	146	20.9	t31	1
Frazier, Leslie, *Chi.*	7	135	19.3	58	1
McNorton, Bruce, *Det.*	7	30	4.3	15	0
Thurman, Dennis, *Dall.*	6	49	8.2	34	0
Turner, John, *Minn.*	6	37	6.2	14	0
Jackson, Terry, *Giants*	6	20	3.3	17	0
Swain, John, *Minn.*	6	12	2.0	11	0
Fellows, Ron, *Dall.*	5	139	27.8	t58	1
Collins, Kirk, *Rams*	5	113	22.6	58	0
Lewis, Tim, *G.B.*	5	111	22.2	46	0
Anderson, John, *G.B.*	5	54	10.8	t27	1
Dean, Vernon, *Wash.*	5	54	10.8	26	0
Schmidt, Terry, *Chi.*	5	31	6.2	t32	1
Richardson, Mike, *Chi.*	5	9	1.8	6	0
Johnson, Johnnie, *Rams*	4	115	28.8	t60	2
Harris, Eric, *Rams*	4	100	25.0	45	0
Downs, Mike, *Dall.*	4	80	20.0	28	0
Brown, Cedric, *T.B.*	4	78	19.5	36	0
Walls, Everson, *Dall.*	4	70	17.5	37	0
Coffey, Ken, *Wash.*	4	62	15.5	29	0
Pridemore, Tom, *Atl.*	4	56	14.0	25	0
Williamson, Carlton, *S.F.*	4	51	12.8	26	0
Perrin, Benny, *St.L.*	4	50	12.5	30	0
Watkins, Bobby, *Det.*	4	48	12.0	31	0
Irvin, LeRoy, *Rams*	4	42	10.5	22	0
Lee, Mark, *G.B.*	4	23	5.8	15	0
Lott, Ronnie, *S.F.*	4	22	5.5	22	0
Cobb, Garry, *Det.*	4	19	4.8	13	0
Washington, A. *Wash.*	4	12	3.0	8	0
Butler, Bobby, *Atl.*	4	12	3.0	12	0
Cromwell, Nolan, *Rams*	3	76	25.3	t43	1

Gary Fencik

	No	Yards	Ave	Long	TD
Gary, Russell, *N.O.*	3	70	23.3	26	0
Griggs, Anthony, *Phil.*	3	61	20.3	32	0
Kinard, Terry, *Giants*	3	49	16.3	25	0
Holt, John, *T.B.*	3	43	14.3	25	0
Bess, Rufus, *Minn.*	3	38	12.7	19	0
Collier, Tim, *S.F.*	3	32	10.7	t32	1
Glazebrook, Bob, *Atl.*	3	30	10.0	25	0
Junior, E.J., *St.L.*	3	27	9.0	19	0
Teal, Willie, *Minn.*	3	26	8.7	12	0
Mack, Cedric, *St.L.*	3	25	8.3	13	0
Winston, Dennis, *N.O.*	3	21	7.0	15	0
Haynes, Mark, *Giants*	3	18	6.0	23	0
Harris, Bob, *St.L.*	3	10	3.3	10	0
Hicks, Dwight, *S.F.*	2	102	51.0	t62	2
Kaufman, Mel, *Wash.*	2	93	46.5	t70	1
Johnson, Bobby, *N.O.*	2	80	40.0	t70	1
Barnes, Roosevelt, *Det.*	2	70	35.0	70	0
Clinkscale, Dextor, *Dall.*	2	68	34.0	t68	1
Johnson, Kenny, *Atl.*	2	57	28.5	t31	2
Green, Hugh, *T.B.*	2	54	27.0	t33	2
Collins, Jim, *Rams*	2	46	23.0	29	0
Washington, Mike, *T.B.*	2	41	20.5	25	0
Currier, Bill, *Giants*	2	37	18.5	t30	1
Fencik, Gary, *Chi.*	2	34	17.0	20	0
Wattelet, Frank, *N.O.*	2	33	16.5	24	0
Williams, Greg, *Wash.*	2	25	12.5	25	0
Baker, Al, *St.L.*	2	24	12.0	19	0
Milot, Rich, *Wash.*	2	20	10.0	20	0
Hall, Alvin, *Det.*	2	18	9.0	18	0
Leopold, Bobby, *S.F.*	2	13	6.5	9	0
Hill, Rod, *Dall.*	2	12	6.0	12	0
Reese, Booker, *T.B.*	2	11	5.5	11	0
Taylor, Lawrence, *Giants*	2	10	5.0	10	0
Green, Darrell, *Wash.*	2	7	3.5	7	0
Van Pelt, Brad, *Giants*	2	7	3.5	6	0
Gray, Johnny, *G.B.*	2	5	2.5	5	0
Paul, Whitney, *N.O.*	2	3	1.5	3	0

DALLAS COWBOYS NFC East

Address 6116 North Central Expressway, Dallas, Texas 75206
Stadium Texas Stadium, Irving.
  Capacity 65,101 *Playing Surface* Texas Turf.
Team Colours Royal Blue, Metallic Silver Blue and White.
Head Coach Tom Landry — twenty-fifth year.
Championships Super Bowl 1971,'77; NFC 1970,'75,'78; Division 1973,'76,'79,'81.
History NFL 1960-69, NFC 1970—

Offense

There has been criticism levelled at an offensive line which went into a late-season slump, but it should not be forgotten that the same line was an integral part of a Dallas team which went 12-4 for the season. On the left side, guard Herb Scott is a former Pro Bowler who maintains that standard. Center Tom Rafferty has settled into his relatively new role, whilst to his right, guard Kurt Petersen forced his way in, flanked by the reliable tackle, Jim Cooper. Howard Richards, a former number one draft choice, is the most likely candidate to replace the retired Pro Bowler, Pat Donovan, at left tackle. Running back Tony Dorsett had another outstanding year, notwithstanding a modest closing spell, and could well be granted his wish for more carries in 1984. Dorsett's co-running back, Ron Springs, was marginally down on his career average (3·6 compared with 3·7) but excelled at pass receiving in which he caught more passes (73) than any other backfield player in the NFL. Timmy Newsome is being groomed as the successor to Dorsett but a serious knee injury to another bright young prospect, James Jones, may lead the veteran Robert Newhouse to defer his impending retirement. There will be healthy competition at quarterback — even so, Danny White, who ranks second in the list of all time leading passers (as measured by the passer rating formula), is likely to hold off the challenge of Gary Hogeboom for another year. On the face of it, the departure of wide receiver Butch Johnson for Houston, together with the

probable loss of Drew Pearson (he was injured in a road traffic accident), leaves the Cowboys a little thin. But Tony Hill will be back to full fitness and Doug Donley, a real burner, was set to move ahead of Johnson anyway. Furthermore, Mike Renfro has been acquired via the trade with Houston and will not be left simply to decorate the sideline. Doug Cosbie, at tight end, made his first Pro Bowl appearance but beyond him there was little depth before the Cowboys took Fred Cornwell in the third round of the 1984 collegiate draft.

Defense

The defensive line boasts three current or former All Pros. Defensive right tackle Randy White had a vintage season which included 12½ sacks, and defensive left end Ed 'Too Tall' Jones has lost little of his overpowering presence. The third All Pro, defensive left tackle John Dutton, remains solid but shares increasing time with Don Smerek. Sadly, Harvey Martin (he too was an All Pro) has announced his retirement, making way for Jim Jeffcoat or perhaps Smerek, who is too good to be kept out of the action. Bob Breunig and Mike Hegman are seasoned veterans in a linebacking unit which has been less effective during a period of transition. Anthony Dickerson, an aggressive tackler who recorded 10½ sacks, will be challenged by the number one draftee, Billy Cannon, with Angelo King and Jeff Rohrer as versatile reserves. There could be wholesale positional changes in the defensive secondary, except at left cornerback, where the outstanding Everson Walls is unchallenged. Dennis Thurman is likely to return to his former position of free safety at the expense of Michael Downs, who could in turn displace Dextor Clinkscale at strong safety. Either Ron Fellows or Rod Hill would then play the right cornerback position.

Special Teams

Rafael Septien is a consistently good kicker but there have been problems with the punting where coach Landry may well (reluctantly) have to re-install quarterback Danny White. Gary Allen, who made a late impact as a return specialist, will take over for punts and probably on kickoffs, replacing the combination of Fellows and Hill.

1984 Draft

Round	Name	Pos.	Ht.	Wt.	College
1.	Cannon, Billy,	LB	6-3	229	Texas A & M
2.	Scott, Victor	DB	5-10	190	Colorado
3.	Cornwell, Fred	TE	6-3	235	Southern California
4.	DeOssie, Steve	LB	6-1	235	Boston College
5.	Pelluer, Steve	QB	6-3	205	Washington
5.	Granger, Norm	RB	5-9	217	Iowa
6.	Lockhart, Eugene	LB	6-1	236	Houston
6.	Levelis, Joe	G	6-3	270	Iowa
7.	Martin, Ed	LB	6-3	227	Indiana State
8.	Revell, Mike	RB	5-10	190	Bethune — Cookman
9.	Hunt, John	G	6-3	265	Florida
9.	Maune, Neil	G	6-4	260	Notre Dame
10.	Salonen, Brian	TE	6-2	233	Montana
11.	Aughtman, Dowe	DT		269	Auburn
12.	Lewis, Carl	WR			Houston

1984 SCHEDULE

September
3	at Los Angeles Rams	6:00
9	at New York Giants	1:00
16	PHILADELPHIA	3:00
23	GREEN BAY	3:00
30	at Chicago	12:00

October
7	ST LOUIS	12:00
14	at Washington	4:00
21	NEW ORLEANS	9:00
28	INDIANAPOLIS	12:00

November
4	NEW YORK GIANTS	12:00
11	at St Louis	12:00
18	at Buffalo	1:00
22	NEW ENGLAND	3:00

December
2	at Philadelphia	1:00
9	WASHINGTON	3:00
17	at Miami	9:00

Dennis Thurman

VETERAN ROSTER

No.	Name	Pos.	Ht.	Wt.	NFL Year	College
31	Allen, Gary	RB-PR	5-10	183	3	Hawaii
62	Baldinger, Brian	G-C	6-4	253	3	Duke
40	Bates, Bill	S	6-0	194	2	Tennessee
53	Breunig, Bob	MLB	6-2	225	10	Arizona State
92	Caldwell, Bryan	DE	6-4	248	1	Arizona State
47	Clinkscale, Dextor	S	5-11	190	4	South Carolina State
61	Cooper, Jim	T	6-5	263	8	Temple
84	Cosbie, Doug	TE	6-6	232	6	Santa Clara
51	Dickerson, Anthony	LB	6-2	222	5	Southern Methodist
83	Donley, Doug	WR	6-0	173	4	Ohio State
33	Dorsett, Tony	RB	5-11	192	8	Pittsburgh
26	Downs, Michael	S	6-3	203	4	Rice
78	Dutton, John	DT	6-7	275	11	Nebraska
27	Fellows, Ron	CB-KR	6-0	174	4	Missouri
58	Hegman, Mike	LB	6-1	228	9	Tennessee State
25	Hill, Rod	CB	6-0	182	3	Kentucky State
80	Hill, Tony	WR	6-2	198	8	Stanford
14	Hogeboom, Gary	QB	6-4	199	5	Central Michigan
77	Jeffcoat, Jim	E	6-5	260	2	Arizona State
72	Jones, Ed	DE	6-9	272	10	Tennessee State
23	Jones, James	RB	5-10	202	5	Mississippi State
57	King, Angelo	LB	6-1	230	4	South Carolina State
52	McLean, Scott	LB	6-4	231	2	Florida State
35	McSwain, Chuck	RB	6-0	190	2	Clemson
3	Miller, Jim	P	5-11	183	4	Mississippi
44	Newhouse, Robert	RB	5-10	219	13	Houston
30	Newsome, Timmy	RB	6-1	231	5	Winston-Salem State
88	Pearson, Drew	WR	6-0	193	12	Tulsa
65	Petersen, Kurt	G	6-4	268	5	Missouri
75	Pozderac, Phil	T	6-9	270	3	Notre Dame
64	Rafferty, Tom	C	6-3	259	9	Penn State
	Renfro, Mike	WR	6-0	184	7	Texas Christian
70	Richards, Howard	G-T	6-6	258	4	Missouri
50	Rohrer, Jeff	LB	6-3	232	3	Yale
66	Schultz, Chris	T	6-8	259	2	Arizona
68	Scott, Herbert	G	6-2	260	10	Virginia Union
1	Septien, Rafael	K	5-10	180	8	Southwest Louisiana
82	Simmons, Cleo	TE	6-2	233	2	Jackson State
60	Smerek, Don	DT	6-7	257	4	Nevada-Reno
20	Springs, Ron	RB	6-1	210	6	Ohio State
32	Thurman, Dennis	CB	5-11	183	7	USC
63	Titensor, Glen	C	6-4	260	4	Brigham Young
71	Tuinei, Mark	DT	6-5	265	2	Hawaii
24	Walls, Everson	CB	6-1	194	4	Grambling
59	Walter, Mike	LB	6-3	230	2	Oregon
5	Warren, John	P	5-11	198	2	Tennessee
11	White, Danny	QB-P	6-2	196	9	Arizona State
54	White, Randy	DT	6-4	268	10	Maryland

NEW YORK GIANTS NFC East

Address Giants Stadium, East Rutherford, New Jersey 07073.
Stadium Giants Stadium, East Rutherford.
  Capacity 76,891 *Playing Surface* AstroTurf.
Team Colours Blue, Red and White.
Head Coach Bill Parcells — second year.
Championships NFL 1927,'34,'38,'56.
History NFL 1925-69, NFC 1970—

Offense

With 49 quarterback sacks yielded last season, the line clearly had trouble warding off the opposition. Offensive left tackle Brad Benson emerged as the most dependable player and John Tautolo, a second-year man, showed promise in displacing a former number one pick, Gordon King. Running back Rob Carpenter was going well with 624 yards after ten games, but his injury forced the main responsibility onto Butch Woolfolk, who went on to gain 857 yards over the season, though at the low average of 3·5 yards per carry. A gutsy player, Woolfolk rushed an NFL record 43 times when gaining 159 yards against Philadelphia. Joe Morris has his nuisance value but is on the small side and a great deal depends on the return of a healthy Carpenter to do the heavy work. Quarterback Scott Brunner (he is now a Denver player) had a poor season, throwing only nine touchdown passes and 22 interceptions, for figures which were reflected in his passer rating of an NFC low 54·3 per cent. Jeff Rutledge was not much better, playing in relief of Brunner, and there seems little doubt that Phil Simms, returning after injury, will resume at the controls. Given any kind of consistency from Simms, the prospects are really attractive. A faltering 1983 performance by wide receiver Floyd Eddings is the only bad news for, by contrast, wide receiver Earnest Gray caught 78 passes to tie for first place in the NFC. Rookie Byron Williams was a late-season acquisition, after being discarded by Green Bay and a short stay with Philadelphia. But in three of his four starts he caught passes for 119, 103 and 124 yards respectively — and that's All Pro stuff. Furthermore, a former starter, Johnny Perkins, will return after being out with injury all last year and another Green Bay reject, Mike Miller, could be a 'sleeper' — he is the fastest man in the NFL. There is an absence of quality at tight end, where rookies Zeke Mowatt and Malcolm Scott, together with Tom Mullady, combined for a total of only 51 receptions.

Defense

The defense as a whole improved during the latter half of 1983 — indeed, they held off the mighty Redskins for three quarters of the final game. The loss through injury of nose tackle Bill Neill and his backup, Jim Burt, was a blow. But they are fit to rejoin a squad which did well in restricting the opposition to 3·5 yards per rushing attempt. Defensive left end George Martin registered ten of the team's 44 quarterback sacks. At linebacker, the Giants are strong. Lawrence Taylor would be the popular choice as the best player (any position) in the NFL and Harry Carson, whose loss for five games was a devastating blow, dominates in the middle. Brad Van Pelt is still a good one but will be challenged by rookie Carl Banks, whilst last year's rookie, Andy Headen, who had five sacks, is the obvious replacement for the departed Brian Kelley. Again, the defensive secondary is strong enough to accomodate the trading of cornerback Terry Jackson to Seattle. Mark Haynes has been selected to the Pro Bowl for the past two years and free safety Terry Kinard lived up to his pedigree as last year's number one draft choice. Bill Currier is a respected strong safety.

Special Teams

Rookie kicker Ali Haji-Sheikh went nap, earning Pro Bowl and All Pro honours. He was successful with 35 out of 42 field goal attempts and two of those he missed were from beyond 60 yards. Punter Dave Jennings is a four-time Pro Bowler and plays like it. Leon Bright did everything required of him, returning kicks for an average of 22·6 yards, to rank fourth in the NFC, and Pete Shaw earned a par rating returning punts.

1984 DRAFT

Round	Name	Pos.	Ht.	Wt.	College
1.	Banks, Carl	LB	6-3	230	Michigan State
1.	Roberts, Bill	T	6-5	272	Ohio State
3.	Hostetler, Jeff	QB	6-2	215	West Virginia
4.	Goode, Conrad	T	6-5	268	Missouri
4.	Reasons, Gary	LB	6-4	235	North West Louisiana
5.	Harris, Clint	DB	5-10	205	East Carolina
6.	Scott, Jim	DE	6-4	250	Clemson
7.	Manuel, Lionel	WR	5-10	175	Pacific
10.	Jordan, David	G	6-4	270	Auburn
10.	Golden, Heyward	DB			South Carolina State
11.	Cephous, Frank	RB	5-10	205	UCLA
12.	Green, Lawrence	LB	6-1	235	Tennessee — Chattanooga

Lawrence Taylor

1984 SCHEDULE

September

2	PHILADELPHIA	1:00
9	DALLAS	1:00
16	at Washington	4:00
23	TAMPA BAY	4:00
30	at Los Angeles Rams	1:00

October

8	SAN FRANCISCO	9:00
14	at Atlanta	1:00
21	at Philadelphia	1:00
28	WASHINGTON	4:00

November

4	at Dallas	12:00
11	at Tampa Bay	4:00
18	ST LOUIS	1:00
25	KANSAS CITY	1:00

December

2	at New York Jets	1:00
9	at St Louis	12:00
15	NEW ORLEANS	12:30

VETERAN ROSTER

No.	Name	Pos.	Ht.	Wt.	NFL Year	College
67	Ard, Billy	G	6-3	250	4	Wake Forest
73	Belcher, Kevin	G	6-3	255	2	Texas-El Paso
60	Benson, Brad	T	6-3	258	7	Penn State
45	Bright, Leon	RB-PR	5-9	192	4	Florida State
64	Burt, Jim	NT	6-1	255	4	Miami
26	Carpenter, Rob	RB	6-1	230	8	Miami, Ohio
53	Carson, Harry	LB	6-2	235	9	South Carolina State
74	Cook, Charles	NT	6-3	255	2	Miami
29	Currier, Bill	S	6-0	202	8	South Carolina
46	Dennis, Mike	CB	5-10	190	5	Wyoming
88	Eddings, Floyd	WR	5-11	177	3	California
37	Flowers, Larry	S	6-1	190	4	Texas Tech.
83	Gray, Earnest	WR	6-3	195	6	Memphis State
6	Haji-Sheikh, Ali	K	6-0	172	2	Michigan
79	Hardison, Dee	DE	6-4	269	7	North Carolina
36	Haynes, Mark	CB	5-11	198	5	Colorado
54	Headen, Andy	LB	6-5	230	2	Clemson
27	Heater, Larry	RB	5-11	205	4	Arizona
61	Hughes, Ernie	C	6-3	265	6	Notre Dame
57	Hunt, Byron	LB	6-5	230	4	Southern Methodist
13	Jennings, Dave	P	6-4	205	11	St. Lawrence
43	Kinard, Terry	S	6-1	190	2	Clemson
72	King, Gordon	T	6-6	275	7	Stanford
51	Marion, Frank	LB	6-3	223	8	Florida A & M
70	Marshall, Leonard	DE	6-3	285	2	Louisiana State
75	Martin, George	DE	6-4	245	10	Oregon
39	Mayock, Mike	S	6-2	195	3	Boston College
	McDaniel, LeCharls	S-CB	5-9	169	4	Cal Poly — SLO
76	McGriff, Curtis	DE	6-5	265	5	Alabama
52	McLaughlin, Joe	LB	6-1	235	6	Massachusetts
71	Merrill, Casey	DE	6-4	255	6	Cal — Davis
89	Miller, Mike	WR	5-11	182	2	Tennessee
85	Mistler, John	WR	6-2	186	4	Arizona State
20	Morris, Joe	RB	5-7	190	3	Syracuse
84	Mowatt, Zeke	TE	6-3	238	2	Florida State
81	Mullady, Tom	TE	6-3	232	6	S'west'n at Memphis
77	Neill, Bill	NT	6-4	255	4	Pittsburgh
	Nelson, Karl	T	6-6	272	1	Iowa State
9	Owen, Tom	QB	6-1	194	11	Wichita State
86	Perkins, Johnny	WR	6-2	205	8	Abilene Christian
17	Rutledge, Jeff	QB	6-1	190	6	Alabama
78	Sally, Jerome	NT	6-3	260	3	Missouri
80	Scott, Malcolm	TE	6-4	240	2	Louisiana State
44	Shaw, Pete	S	5-10	183	8	Northwestern
11	Simms, Phil	QB	6-3	216	5	Morehead State
	Steinfeld, Al	C	6-4	256	3	C.W. Post
65	Tautolo, John	T	6-3	260	3	UCLA
56	Taylor, Lawrence	LB	6-3	237	4	North Carolina
38	Tuggle, John	RB	6-1	210	2	California
68	Turner, J.T.	G	6-3	250	8	Duke
59	Umphrey, Rich	C	6-3	255	3	Colorado
10	Van Pelt, Brad	LB	6-5	235	12	Michigan State
58	Whittington, Mike	LB	6-2	220	5	Notre Dame
87	Williams, Byron	WR	6-1	177	2	Texas-Arlington
25	Woolfolk, Butch	RB	6-1	207	3	Michigan

PHILADELPHIA EAGLES NFC East

Address Philadelphia Veterans Stadium, Broad St. and Pattison Ave., Philadelphia, Pa. 19148.

Stadium Philadelphia Veterans Stadium, Philadelphia. *Capacity 72,204 Playing Surface* AstroTurf.

Team Colours Kelly Green, White and Silver.

Head Coach Marion Campbell — second year.

Championships NFL 1948,'49,'60; NFC 1980.

History NFL 1933-69, NFC 1970–

Offense

The Eagles are coming off a disappointing year in which they gained only 3·5 yards per rushing attempt (joint third worst in the NFL) and gave up 57 quarterback sacks (second worst in the NFL). On the other hand, right tackle Jerry Sisemore was troubled by injuries and they will be strengthened by the arrival of former Miami center Mark Dennard to replace Guy Morriss who, together with his backup, Mark Slater, have been released. Dennard will be flanked by two respectable guards, Steve Kenney and Ron Baker. An injury to the all-purpose running back, Wilbert Montgomery, who is an integral part of the offense, meant that Hubert Oliver had to shoulder the burden of the rushing offense. Of the two rookie running backs, Mike Williams was the more productive, rushing for 385 yards at an average of 3·7, compared with 220 yards at 2·4 by Michael Haddix, who was surprisingly ineffective. Montgomery, in addition to being a fine pass receiver, is without doubt one of the NFL's best rushers, and his return must surely revitalise the Eagles backfield. The great Harold Carmichael has been released when on the verge of what could have been a record-breaking season. Currently lying fifth in the list of all time receivers, with 589 receptions he trails Charley Taylor by 60 and, of the active receivers, only Charlie Joiner, by 7. Last year, however, he yielded the spotlight to Mike Quick, who was a sensation with 69 receptions for a total of 1,409 yards, the latter being the NFL's best. Included in his receptions was one covering 83 yards for a touchdown against Dallas. Of the reserves, both Tony Woodruff and rookie Glen Young were a little green but Young showed his big play potential with a 71-yard touchdown against the Cowboys and could well emerge from obscurity, as did Quick last year. They are joined by the first round draftee, Kenny Jackson. The Eagles are a little thin at tight end, and the return of the five-year veteran, John Spagnola, who missed the whole of the 1983 season, will be welcomed.

Defense

It was a long hard year for the defense which conceded more rushing yards per game (165·9) than any other NFC team. Furthermore, with a low 36 quarterback sacks, they were better than only two conference rivals. Defensive left end Dennis Harrison led with 11½ sacks and Greg Brown, who took over from Carl Hairston at left end, had 8½. Defensive captain Carl Hairston has been traded to the Cleveland Browns, leaving two of last year's rookies, Byron Darby and Thomas Strauthers, as the best of the reserve strength. Left inside line-backer Jerry Robinson is by far the best defensive player of the quartet, perhaps even of the whole squad, and represents the hard core of a unit in transition. Many future hopes rest with last year's rookie, Jody Schulz, who had started before being injured. He will challenge Reggie Wilkes on the left outside. Anthony Griggs will continue at right inside linebacker, though more will be expected of Joel Williams, who was acquired from the Falcons for his ability to blitz and yet registered only 1½ sacks. Cornerback Roynell Young continues to play well and free safety Wes Hopkins is a brave tackler, but the secondary is some way short of the quality which, until very recently, was an Eagles tradition.

Special Teams

Kicker Tony Franklin has been traded to New England after a modest season in which he missed three PATs and kicked only 15 of 26 field goal attempts. Max Runager was reinstated after having been replaced by Tom Skladany, and celebrated by coming second in the NFC with a gross average of 41·7 yards. Glen Young was the best of the kick returners with a 21·0 average but no-one enjoyed much success returning punts.

1984 DRAFT

Wilbert Montgomery

Round	Name	Pos.	Ht.	Wt.	College
1.	Jackson, Kenny	WR	5-11	170	Penn State
3.	Russell, Rusty	T	6-5	278	South Carolina
4.	Cooper, Evan	DB	6-0	170	Michigan
5.	Hardy, Andre	RB	6-1	225	St. Mary's, California
6.	Raridon, Scott	T	6-3	295	Nebraska
7.	Hayes, Joe	RB	5-9	183	Central State, Oklahoma
8.	Matsakis, Manny	K			Capital
10.	Thomas, John	DB	6-0	200	Texas Christian
11.	Robertson, John	T	6-5	250	East Carolina
12.	McFadden, Paul	K	5-10	155	Youngstown

1984 SCHEDULE

September

2	at New York Giants	1:00
9	MINNESOTA	1:00
16	at Dallas	3:00
23	SAN FRANCISCO	1:00
30	at Washington	4:00

October

7	at Buffalo	1:00
14	INDIANAPOLIS	1:00
21	NEW YORK GIANTS	1:00
28	ST LOUIS	1:00

November

4	at Detroit	1:00
11	at Miami	1:00
18	WASHINGTON	1:00
25	at St Louis	12:00

December

2	DALLAS	1:00
9	NEW ENGLAND	1:00
16	at Atlanta	4:00

VETERAN ROSTER

No.	Name	Pos.	Ht.	Wt.	NFL Year	College
96	Armstrong, Harvey	NT	6-2	255	3	Southern Methodist
63	Baker, Ron	G	6-4	250	7	Oklahoma State
98	Brown, Greg	DE	6-5	240	4	Kansas State
71	Clarke, Ken	NT	6-2	255	7	Syracuse
57	Cowher, Bill	LB	6-3	225	4	North Carolina State
94	Darby, Byron	DE	6-4	250	2	USC
	Dennard, Mark	C	6-1	252	6	Texas A & M
25	DeVaughn, Dennis	CB	5-10	175	3	Bishop
46	Edwards, Herman	CB	6-0	190	8	San Diego State
24	Ellis, Ray	S	6-1	192	4	Ohio State
39	Everett, Major	RB-KR	5-10	207	2	Mississippi
67	Feehery, Gerry	C	6-2	268	2	Syracuse
29	Foules, Elbert	CB	5-11	185	2	Alcorn State
72	Fritzsche, Jim	G-T	6-8	265	2	Purdue
58	Griggs, Anthony	LB	6-3	220	3	Ohio State
26	Haddix, Michael	RB	6-2	225	2	Mississippi State
35	Harrington, Perry	RB	5-11	210	5	Jackson State
68	Harrison, Dennis	DE	6-8	275	7	Vanderbilt
85	Hoover, Melvin	WR	6-0	185	3	Arizona State
48	Hopkins, Wes	S	6-1	205	2	Southern Methodist
7	Jaworski, Ron	QB	6-2	196	11	Youngstown State
	Jelesky, Tom	T				
84	Kab, Vyto	TE	6-5	255	3	Penn State
73	Kenney, Steve	G	6-4	262	5	Clemson
52	Kraynak, Rich	LB	6-1	221	2	Pittsburgh
41	Logan, Randy	S	6-1	195	12	Michigan
64	Miraldi, Dean	T	6-5	254	2	Utah
74	Mitchell, Leonard	T	6-7	272	4	Houston
31	Montgomery, Wilbert	RB	5-10	195	8	Abilene Christian
34	Oliver, Hubie	RB	5-10	212	3	Arizona
62	Perot, Petey	G	6-2	261	6	Northwestern Louisiana
9	Pisarcik, Joe	QB	6-4	220	8	New Mexico State
82	Quick, Mike	WR	6-2	190	3	North Carolina State
56	Robinson, Jerry	LB	6-2	218	6	UCLA
5	Runager, Max	P	6-1	189	6	South Carolina
87	Sampleton, Lawrence	TE	6-5	233	3	Texas
53	Schulz, Jody	LB	6-4	235	2	East Carolina
76	Sisemore, Jerry	T	6-4	265	12	Texas
88	Spagnola, John	TE	6-4	240	6	Yale
93	Strauthers, Thomas	DE	6-4	255	2	Jackson State
51	Wilkes, Reggie	LB	6-4	230	7	Georgia Tech.
59	Williams, Joel	LB	6-0	215	6	Wisconsin-LaCrosse
32	Williams, Michael	RB	6-2	217	2	Mississippi
22	Wilson, Brenard	S	6-0	175	6	Vanderbilt
83	Woodruff, Tony	WR	6-0	175	3	Fresno State
89	Young, Glen	WR	6-2	205	2	Mississippi State
43	Young, Roynell	CB	6-1	181	5	Alcorn State

ST LOUIS CARDINALS NFC East

Address Busch Stadium, Box 888, St Louis, Missouri 63188.
Stadium Busch Memorial Stadium, St Louis.
 Capacity 51,392 *Playing Surface* AstroTurf.
Team Colours Cardinal Red, White and Black.
Head Coach Jim Hanifan — fifth year.
Championships NFL 1925,'47; Division 1974,'75.
History NFL 1920-69, NFC 1970—
 (Until 1960 they were known as the Chicago Cardinals.)

Offense

The monster tackles, James 'Tootie' Robbins and Luis Sharpe, improved significantly, blocking for the running backs, but the experience of retired center Dan Dierdorf will be missed on a line which was repeatedly penetrated by the blitz and yielded 59 quarterback sacks (worst in the NFL). Left guard Terry Stieve will be challenged by Ramsey Dardar, drafted last year as a defensive lineman, who will be tried on offense. Star running back Ottis Anderson made a slow start but recovered to rush for over 100 yards in five of the last eight games, to finish as the eighth leading NFL rusher. Wayne Morris made hard work of gaining 257 yards on 75 carries and it seems likely that Lyvonia 'Stump' Mitchell will be given more game-time after his 373 yards at the excellent average of 5·5 yards per carry. Neil Lomax, who started ahead of Jim Hart at quarterback, missed three early games with injury and took some time before clicking into gear with 24 touchdown passes and only 11 interceptions, to end with a good passer rating of 92.0. He should be even better in 1984, but the departure of the veteran Hart leaves only Rusty Lisch in reserve. Roy 'Jet Stream' Green completed the transition from defensive back to wide receiver, taking the Cardinals well and truly into the 'big-play' club. With 78 pass receptions, he shared the lead in the NFC and of his 14 touchdowns, four were in one half against Seattle. The elusive Pat Tilley, himself a former Pro Bowler, is the perfect foil for Green and, together with Ottis Anderson (he caught 54 passes), presents 'flame-thrower' Lomax with an attractive set of options. Tight end Doug Marsh had his best season to date with 32 receptions and eight touchdowns, but the Cardinals will need a greater output from this source if they are to be serious contenders in the tough NFC East.

Defense

This is rapidly becoming a Cardinals strength. Perhaps inspired by the arrival of Al 'Bubba' Baker, the unit was at times awesome, logging an NFL best 59 sacks, most of which were by the four-man defensive line. Defensive right end Curtis Greer led with 16, followed by Baker's 13½ (he also had two interceptions) and David Galloway, with 12. Elois Grooms was outstanding against the rush. Behind them, at outside and inside linebacker, E.J. Junior was described as 'sensational' and better, and rookie Bob Harris eased into a starting role on the outside, before a season-ending knee injury. The acquisition of just one more quality linebacker will give the Cardinals arguably the best front seven in the conference. Rookie cornerback Lionel Washington, who was drafted in the fourth round, was a major surprise with eight pass interceptions, in contrast to the number one pick, Leonard Smith, who progressed slowly and could not displace the former Detroit player, Wayne Smith. Strong safety Lee Nelson led the team with 119 solo tackles, ahead of the free safety, Benny Perrin, who had 96, but also grabbed four interceptions. They don't really need help but it will arrive in the shape of cornerback Jeff Griffin, who returns after injury.

Special Teams

Punter Carl Birdsong averaged 41·5 yards and fully deserved his first Pro Bowl appearance. Kicker Neil O'Donoghue (he was born in Dublin) does have his off days but, with two field goals from 52 yards out, retains coach Hanifan's confidence. Stump Mitchell, a hardworking lad, returned both kicks and punts at a respectable level, averaging 21·6 yards (with a longest of 66 yards) and 8·9 yards respectively.

E.J. Junior

1984 Draft

1984 DRAFT		Pos.	Ht.	Wt.	College
1.	Duncan, Clyde	WR	6-1	190	Tennessee
2.	Dawson, Doug	G	6-2	260	Texas
3.	McIvor, Rick	QB	6-3	205	Texas
4.	Bayless, Martin	DB	6-1	208	Bowling Green
5.	Leiding, Jeff	LB	6-3	245	Texas
5.	Goode, John	TE	6-2	220	Youngstown
6.	Clark, Rod	LB		207	Southwest Texas State
7.	Walker, Quentin	RB	6-0	200	Virginia
8.	Noga, Falaniko	LB	6-0	235	Hawaii
8.	Paulling, Bob	K	6-2	190	Clemson
9.	Walker, John	RB	6-0	205	Texas
10.	Smythe, Mark	DT	6-2	260	Indiana
11.	Mackey, Kyle	QB	6-2	210	East Texas State
12.	Parker, Paul	G	6-2	285	Oklahoma

1984 SCHEDULE

September

2	at Green Bay	12:00
9	BUFFALO	12:00
16	at Indianapolis	1:00
23	at New Orleans	12:00
30	MIAMI	12:00

October

7	at Dallas	12:00
14	CHICAGO	12:00
21	WASHINGTON	12:00
28	at Philadelphia	1:00

November

4	LOS ANGELES RAMS	3:00
11	DALLAS	12:00
18	at New York Giants	1:00
25	PHILADELPHIA	12:00

December

2	at New England	1.00
9	NEW YORK GIANTS	12.00
16	at Washington	1.00

VETERAN ROSTER

No.	Name	Pos.	Ht.	Wt.	NFL Year	College
58	Ahrens, Dave	LB	6-3	228	4	Wisconsin
51	Allerman, Kurt	LB	6-2	222	8	Penn State
32	Anderson, Ottis	HB	6-2	220	6	Miami
61	Audick, Dan	G	6-3	253	7	Hawaii
60	Baker, Al	DE	6-6	260	7	Colorado State
52	Baker, Charlie	LB	6-2	217	5	New Mexico
41	Bedford, Vance	CB	5-11	170	1	Texas
82	Bird, Steve	WR	5-11	171	2	Eastern Kentucky
18	Birdsong, Carl	P	6-0	192	4	S'West Oklahoma State
71	Bostic, Joe	G	6-3	265	6	Clemson
64	Clark, Randy	C-G	6-3	254	5	Northern Illinois
66	Dardar, Ramsey	G-DT	6-2	264	1	Louisiana State
59	Davis, Paul	LB	6-1	215	4	North Carolina
73	Duda, Mark	DT	6-3	263	2	Maryland
31	Ferrell, Earl	RB	6-0	215	3	East Tennessee State
65	Galloway, David	DT	6-3	277	3	Florida
81	Green, Roy	WR	6-0	195	6	Henderson State
75	Greer, Curtis	DE	6-4	252	5	Michigan
35	Griffin, Jeff	CB	6-0	185	4	Utah
78	Grooms, Elois	DT	6-4	250	9	Tennessee Tech.
39	Harrell, Willard	RB	5-8	182	10	Pacific
50	Harris, Bob	LB	6-2	205	2	Auburn
46	Heflin, Victor	CB	6-0	184	2	Delaware State
54	Junior, E.J.	LB	6-3	235	4	Alabama
89	LaFleur, Greg	TE	6-4	236	4	Louisiana State
16	Lisch, Rusty	QB	6-3	213	5	Notre Dame
15	Lomax, Neil	QB	6-3	215	4	Portland State
40	Love, Randy	RB	6-1	205	6	Houston
47	Mack, Cedric	CB	6-0	190	2	Baylor
80	Marsh, Doug	TE	6-3	240	5	Michigan
76	Mays, Stafford	DE	6-2	250	5	Washington
87	McGill, Eddie	TE	6-6	225	3	Western Carolina
30	Mitchell, Stump	RB-PR	5-9	188	4	Citadel
24	Morris, Wayne	FB	6-0	210	9	Southern Methodist
38	Nelson, Lee	S	5-10	185	9	Florida State
11	O'Donoghue, Neil	K	6-6	210	8	Auburn
57	Parlavecchio, Chet	LB	6-2	225	2	Penn State
23	Perrin, Benny	S	6-2	178	3	Alabama
	Pittman, Danny	WR	6-2	205	5	Wyoming
70	Plunkett, Art	T	6-7	270	4	Nevada-Las Vegas
	Puki, Craig	LB	6-1	231	5	Tennessee
63	Robbins, Tootie	T	6-4	278	3	East Carolina
26	Schmitt, George	S	5-11	193	2	Delaware
56	Scott, Carlos	C-G	6-4	300	2	Texas — El Paso
53	Shaffer, Craig	LB	6-0	230	3	Indiana State
67	Sharpe, Luis	T	6-4	260	3	UCLA
84	Shumann, Mike	WR	6-1	185	7	Florida State
45	Smith, Leonard	CB-S	5-11	190	2	McNeese State
44	Smith, Wayne	CB	6-0	175	5	Purdue
68	Stieve, Terry	G	6-2	265	8	Wisconsin
83	Tilley, Pat	WR	5-10	178	9	Louisiana Tech.
48	Washington, Lionel	CB	6-0	184	2	Tulane
55	Whitaker, Bill	LB	6-0	182	4	Missouri

WASHINGTON REDSKINS NFC East

Address Redskin Park, P.O. Box 17247, Dulles International Airport, Washington, D.C., 20041.
Stadium Robert F. Kennedy Stadium, Washington.
Capacity 55,045 *Playing Surface* Grass (Prescription Athletic Turf).
Team Colours Burgundy and Gold.
Head Coach Joe Gibbs — fourth year.
Championships Super Bowl 1982; NFL 1937,'42; NFC 1972; Division 1972,'83.
History NFL 1932-69, NFC 1970—
(Unitl 1937 they were known as the Boston Redskins.)

Offense

There can be little wrong with an offensive unit which established an NFL record of 541 regular season points in 1983. The outstanding offensive line is particularly strong on the left side where guard Russ Grimm and the 295-lb tackle, Joe Jacoby, clear the way for the running backs and, overall, they have little trouble protecting quarterback Joe Theismann (they gave up 35 sacks to come joint third in the NFC). Theismann was only 0·6 rating points behind the NFL leader, Steve Bartkowski, and, statistics apart, is now the most feared quarterback in the league, not only for his audacious passing but also for his composure and team leadership. Reserve strength has been modest but the veteran, Jim Hart, has arrived from St Louis to be on call in case of emergencies. 'Downtown' Charlie Brown caught 78 passes to tie for first place in the NFC and, with numerous big gains including a longest of 75 yards for a touchdown, represents the deep threat. Art Monk, the other starting wide receiver, is less prolific, but maintained a slightly better average gain with 15·9 yards compared with Brown's 15·7. Reserve Alvin Garrett, the hero of the 1982 playoffs, had the longest single gain of all (84 yards) and would surely start with many other clubs. Running back John Riggins is coming off his best-ever season, in which he established a touchdown — scoring record for all categories, and his were all by the hard route, namely rushing. Indeed, that has been his style throughout a career which has brought him to fifth place in the list of all time leading rushers. However, there were signs in the playoffs that this hitherto seemingly indestructable man might be feeling the effects of a career 2,413 rushing attempts — he was getting up a little more slowly. But the slippery Joe Washington, who rushed for 772 yards at an average of 5·3 per carry, would take up the slack. Furthermore, Washington is by far the better receiver. Outside of these two though, there is no sign of emerging talent. Three respectable tight ends, Rick Walker, Don Warren and Clint Didier, complete the strike force.

Defense

Using a four-man defensive line, the Redskins are miserly against the run and in 1983 allowed an average of only 80·6 rushing yards per game (this is by far the best in the NFL). On the other hand, the opposition had little difficulty passing and in this category no other NFL team conceded more than their average of 248·4 yards per game. Defense against the rush could even be improved by the re-introduction of defensive left end Mat Mendenhall, who missed the whole of 1983 for reasons unrelated to football. He would be rejoining his mates, Dave Butz, Darryl Grant and Dexter Manley, of the victorious 1982 Super Bowl team, providing of course he can displace Todd Liebenstein in training camp. The linebacking trio of Mel Kaufman, Neal Olkewicz and Rich Milot is reliable and effective, particularly against the rush. However, several quarterbacks exposed the weaknesses in a secondary which was disturbed by the departures of safety Tony Peters (he returns from suspension) and cornerback Jeris White. Free safety Mark Murphy had his best season with a league-leading nine interceptions, earning a first trip to the Pro Bowl, and rookie Darrell Green showed that he had the hands to go with his pure speed. However, cornerback Anthony Washington had trouble covering the more cunning wide receivers and will be challenged by Vernon Dean.

Special Teams

Mark Moseley established a regular season record for points scoring (kicking only) with 161, but Jeff Hayes was well down the list of punters. Mike Nelms is considered to be one of the best dual kick and punt returners, always likely to break one open.

1984 DRAFT

Round	Name	Pos.	Ht.	Wt.	College
2.	Slater, Bob	DT	6-5	255	Oklahoma
2.	Hamilton, Steve	DE	6-4	250	East Carolina
3.	Schroeder, Jay	QB	6-4	215	UCLA
4.	Smith, Jimmy	RB	5-10	195	Elon
5.	Pegues, Jeff	LB	6-1	235	East Carolina
6.	Singer, Curt	T	6-4	265	Tennessee
7.	Smith, Mark	WR	5-10	180	North Carolina
8.	Smith, Jeff	DB	5-11	185	Missouri
10.	Griffin, Keith	RB	5-7	185	Miami
11.	Jones, Anthony	TE	6-3	245	Wichita State
12.	Thomas, Curtland	WR	5-11	185	Missouri

1984 SCHEDULE

September

2	MIAMI	1:00
10	at San Francisco	6:00
16	NEW YORK GIANTS	4:00
23	at New England	1:00
30	PHILADELPHIA	4:00

October

7	at Indianapolis	1:00
14	DALLAS	4:00
21	at St Louis	12:00
28	at New York Giants	4:00

November

5	ATLANTA	9:00
11	DETROIT	1:00
18	at Philadelphia	1:00
25	BUFFALO	1:00
29	at Minnesota	9:00

December

| 9 | at Dallas | 3:00 |
| 16 | ST LOUIS | 1:00 |

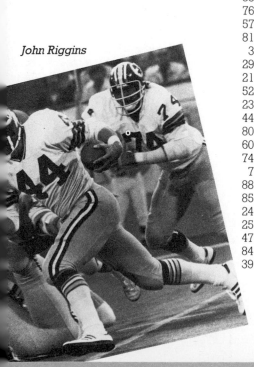

John Riggins

VETERAN ROSTER

No.	Name	Pos.	Ht.	Wt.	NFL Year	College
58	Anderson, Stuart	LB	6-1	247	2	Virginia
53	Bostic, Jeff	C	6-2	245	5	Clemson
69	Brooks, Perry	DT	6-3	265	7	Southern
87	Brown, Charlie	WR	5-10	179	3	South Carolina State
65	Butz, Dave	DT	6-7	295	11	Purdue
41	Carpenter, Brian	CB	5-10	167	3	Michigan
48	Coffey, Ken	S	6-0	190	2	S.W. Texas State
51	Coleman, Monte	LB	6-2	235	6	Central Arkansas
54	Cronan, Peter	LB	6-2	238	7	Boston College
32	Dean, Vernon	CB-S	5-11	178	3	San Diego State
86	Didier, Clint	TE	6-5	240	3	Portland State
26	Evans, Reggie	RB	5-11	201	2	Richmond
89	Garrett, Alvin	WR-KR	5-7	178	5	Angelo State
77	Grant, Darryl	DT	6-1	265	4	Rice
28	Green, Darrell	CB	5-8	170	2	Texas A & I
68	Grimm, Russ	G	6-3	273	4	Pittsburgh
	Hart, Jim	QB	6-1	210	19	Southern Illinois
5	Hayes, Jeff	P	5-11	175	3	North Carolina
8	Holly, Bob	QB	6-2	205	3	Princeton
61	Huff, Ken	G	6-4	259	10	North Carolina
66	Jacoby, Joe	T	6-7	295	4	Louisville
22	Jordan, Curtis	S	6-2	205	8	Texas Tech.
55	Kaufman, Mel	LB	6-2	218	4	Cal Poly — SLO
67	Kimball, Bruce	G	6-2	260	2	Massachusetts
50	Kubin, Larry	LB	6-2	234	3	Penn State
62	Laster, Donald	T	6-5	285	3	Tennessee State
12	Laufenberg, Babe	QB	6-2	195	2	Indiana
79	Liebenstein, Todd	DE	6-6	245	3	Nevada — Las Vegas
72	Manley, Dexter	DE	6-3	253	4	Oklahoma State
71	Mann, Charles	DE	6-6	250	2	Nevada — Reno
73	May, Mark	G	6-6	288	4	Pittsburgh
78	McGee, Tony	DE	6-4	250	14	Bishop
83	McGrath, Mark	WR	5-11	175	4	Montana State
76	Mendenhall, Mat	DE	6-6	255	4	Brigham Young
57	Milot, Rich	LB	6-4	237	6	Penn State
81	Monk, Art	WR	6-3	209	5	Syracuse
3	Moseley, Mark	K	6-0	205	13	Stephen F. Austin
29	Murphy, Mark	S	6-4	210	8	Colgate
21	Nelms, Mike	WR-PR	6-1	185	5	Baylor
52	Olkewicz, Neal	LB	6-0	227	6	Maryland
23	Peters, Tony	S	6-1	190	9	Oklahoma
44	Riggins, John	RB	6-2	235	13	Kansas
80	Seay, Virgil	WR	5-8	175	4	Troy State
60	Simmons, Roy	G	6-3	264	5	Georgia Tech.
74	Starke, George	T	6-5	260	12	Columbia
7	Theismann, Joe	QB	6-0	195	11	Notre Dame
88	Walker, Rick	TE	6-4	235	8	UCLA
85	Warren, Don	TE	6-4	242	6	San Diego State
24	Washington, Anthony	CB	6-1	204	4	Fresno State
25	Washington, Joe	RB	5-10	179	9	Oklahoma
47	Williams, Greg	S	5-11	185	3	Mississippi State
84	Williams, Mike	TE	6-4	245	3	Alabama A & M
39	Wonsley, Otis	RB	5-10	214	4	Alcorn State

CHICAGO BEARS NFC Central

Address 250 N. Washington, Lake Forest, Illinois 60045.
Stadium Soldier Field, Chicago.
  Capacity 65,793 *Playing Surface* AstroTurf.
Team Colours Navy Blue, Orange and White.
Head Coach Mike Ditka — third year.
Championships NFL 1921,'32,'33,'40,'41,'43,'46,'63.
History NFL 1920-69, NFC 1970—
  (Until 1922, they were known as the Chicago Staleys.)

Offense

The offensive line co-ordinated surprisingly well to block for what became the NFL's most productive rushing offense. Rookie left tackle Jimbo Covert started all year and formed a good partnership with the veteran left guard, Noah Jackson. Another young player, second-year man Kurt Becker, made good progress at guard, playing inside right tackle Keith Van Horne, whilst the third-year player, Jay Hilgenberg, took over from Dan Neal with no loss of performance. Their pass protection was, however, poor and led to 53 quarterback sacks. Accordingly, the passing offense was less productive than the rushing alternative and rated seventeenth in the NFL. At least now though, quarterback Jim McMahon can go about his work without having to look over his shoulder for Vince Evans, who has departed for the USFL. Evans has been replaced by Steve Fuller who was acquired from the Rams. Rookie Willie Gault, the 'Tennessee Tornado', came with all the qualities of a thoroughbred athlete and, of the pure wide receivers, led the team with 40 receptions, for 836 yards and eight touchdowns, one of which covered 87 yards. At the other end of the scale, Dennis McKinnon chipped in with 20 receptions at the average of 16·3 yards, in relief of the injured Rickey Watts, who didn't catch a pass all season, and Brian Baschnagel, who caught only five. They will be back in an improved passing offense which can rely on the supplementary contributions of both Walter Payton and Matt Suhey, who had 53 and 49 receptions respectively in 1983. The rushing game is outstanding and will surely see the great Walter Payton pass Jim Brown's

career 12,312 yards, and much more by the end of the season. Payton is the complete footballer, able to rush, block for a colleague, catch passes and throw them (he threw three touchdown passes in 1983). A modest, retiring man, he is the epitomy of everything about the NFL that is noble, and fully deserves a crack at pro football's greatest prize. Matt Suhey is no slouch and, with 681 yards at the average of 4·6 yards per carry, has just completed his best season. At tight end, Jay Saldi proved to be a valuable acquisition from the Cowboys, playing behind Emery Moorehead, who turned in a useful performance.

Defense

Steve McMichael was an exciting discovery and Mike Hartenstine had his best year (he had 11 quarterback sacks) in a four-man offensive line which will be even stronger with the return of defensive tackle Dan Hampton. Completing the lineup, right end Al Harris kept up good pressure on the quarterbacks. Hampton's return will be felt also at linebacker, where Mike Singletary was kept busy defending against the rush (he earned a first trip to the Pro Bowl). Otis Wilson should be approaching his prime at outside linebacker, but elsewhere there are questions to be asked, and coach Ditka used his first two draft options to take Wilber Marshall and Ron Rivera to strengthen the unit. In the defensive secondary, left corner — back Terry Schmidt grabbed five interceptions but had to give way to the rapidly improving rookie, Mike Richardson, who, too, picked off five. On the right side, Leslie Frazier went even better with seven interceptions. However, the pick of a good crew is Gary Fencik, whose season was marred by injury. He will be back to line up alongside strong safety Todd Bell, with Dave Duerson and Jeff Fisher in reserve.

Special Teams

Punters Bob Parsons and Ray Stachowicz met with little success in an area which needs some attention. Bob Thomas rated around par for his kicking duties. On the other hand, Dennis McKinnon did well returning punts and whilst Willie Gault was adequate returning kickoffs, his responsibilities at wide receiver will probably take preference and leave Anthony Hutchison in sole charge.

1984 DRAFT

Round	Name	Pos.	Ht.	Wt.	College
1.	Marshall, Wilber	LB	6-0	220	Florida
2.	Rivera, Ron	LB	6-2	230	California
3.	Humphries, Stefan	G	6-3	258	Michigan
4.	Andrews, Tom	G	6-3	250	Louisville
7.	Robertson, Nakita	RB	5-10	205	Central Arkansas
8.	Anderson, Brad	WR	6-2	205	Arizona
9.	Casale, Mark	QB	6-2	215	Montclair State
10.	Vestman, Kurt	TE	6-2	232	Idaho
10.	Gayle, Shaun	DB			Ohio State
11.	Butkus, Mark	DT	6-4	260	Illinois
12.	Jordan, Donald	RB	5-11	210	Houston

1984 SCHEDULE

September

2	TAMPA BAY	12:00
9	DENVER	12:00
16	at Green Bay	12:00
23	at Seattle	1:00
30	DALLAS	12:00

October

7	NEW ORLEANS	12:00
14	at St Louis	12:00
21	at Tampa Bay	1:00
28	MINNESOTA	12:00

November

4	LOS ANGELES RAIDERS	12:00
11	at Los Angeles Rams	1:00
18	DETROIT	12:00
25	at Minnesota	3:00

December

3	at San Diego	6:00
9	GREEN BAY	12:00
16	at Detroit	1:00

Dan Hampton (99)

VETERAN ROSTER

No.	Name	Pos.	Ht.	Wt.	NFL Year	College
51	Atkins, Kel	LB	6-4	240	2	Illinois
7	Avellini, Bob	QB	6-2	210	10	Maryland
84	Baschnagel, Brian	WR	6-0	184	9	Ohio State
79	Becker, Kurt	G	6-5	251	3	Michigan
25	Bell, Todd	S	6-0	207	4	Ohio State
62	Bortz, Mark	G	6-5	267	2	Iowa
54	Cabral, Brian	LB	6-1	224	6	Colorado
74	Covert, Jimbo	T	6-4	271	2	Pittsburgh
95	Dent, Richard	DE	6-2	240	2	Tennessee State
22	Duerson, Dave	S	6-0	202	2	Notre Dame
88	Dunsmore, Pat	TE	6-2	230	2	Drake
64	Fada, Rob	G-C	6-2	258	2	Pittsburgh
45	Fencik, Gary	S	6-1	197	9	Yale
24	Fisher, Jeff	S	5-10	188	4	USC
21	Frazier, Leslie	CB	6-0	189	4	Alcorn State
71	Frederick, Andy	T	6-6	265	8	New Mexico
	Fuller, Steve	QB	6-4	198	6	Clemson
83	Gault, Willie	WR	6-0	178	2	Tennessee
29	Gentry, Dennis	RB	5-8	173	3	Baylor
99	Hampton, Dan	DT	6-5	255	6	Arkansas
90	Harris, Al	DE-LB	6-5	250	6	Arizona State
73	Hartenstine, Mike	DE	6-3	243	10	Penn State
63	Hilgenberg, Jay	C	6-3	250	4	Iowa
31	Hutchison, Anthony	RB	5-10	180	2	Texas Tech.
65	Jackson, Noah	G	6-2	265	10	Tampa
72	Janata, John	T	6-7	255	2	Illinois
98	Keys, Tyrone	DE	6-7	260	2	Mississippi
82	Margerum, Ken	WR	5-10	170	4	Stanford
85	McKinnon, Dennis	WR	6-2	185	2	Florida State
9	McMahon, Jim	QB	6-0	187	3	Brigham Young
76	McMichael, Steve	DT	6-1	245	5	Texas
87	Moorehead, Emery	TE	6-2	220	8	Colorado
	Norman, Tim	G			2	
68	Osborne, Jim	DT	6-3	245	13	Southern
34	Payton, Walter	RB	5-10	202	10	Jackson State
20	Potter, Kevin	S	5-10	188	2	Missouri
53	Rains, Dan	LB	6-1	220	2	Cincinnati
	Renner, Bill	P	6-0	190	1	Virginia Tech.
27	Richardson, Mike	CB	5-11	197	2	Arizona State
81	Saldi, Jay	TE	6-3	230	9	South Carolina
44	Schmidt, Terry	CB	6-0	177	11	Ball State
57	Simmons, Dave	LB	6-5	219	4	North Carolina
50	Singletary, Mike	LB	5-11	230	4	Baylor
15	Stachowicz, Ray	P	5-11	185	4	Michigan State
26	Suhey, Matt	RB	5-11	217	5	Penn State
16	Thomas, Bob	K	5-10	175	9	Notre Dame
33	Thomas, Calvin	RB	5-11	220	3	Illinois
78	Van Horne, Keith	T	6-6	265	4	USC
80	Watts, Rickey	WR	6-1	203	6	Tulsa
43	Williams, Walt	CB	6-1	185	8	New Mexico State
55	Wilson, Otis	LB	6-2	222	5	Louisville

DETROIT LIONS NFC Central

Address Pontiac Silverdome, 1200 Featherstone Road, Box 4200, Pontiac, Mich. 48057.
Stadium Pontiac Silverdome.
   Capacity 80,638 *Playing Surface* AstroTurf.
Team Colours Honolulu Blue and Silver.
Head Coach Monte Clark — seventh year.
Championships NFL 1935,'52,'53,'57; Division 1983.
History NFL 1930-69, NFC 1970—
   (Until 1934, they were known as the Portsmouth Spartans.)

Offense

The offensive line lost two starters before the 1983 season (Baldischwiler to the Colts and Bolinger to the Rams) but continued to protect the quarterback and maintained excellent blocking for the running backs. Left tackle Chris Dieterich, left guard Homer Elias, right guard Don Greco and right tackle Keith Dorney, are all relatively young (for NFL linemen that is), and the emergence of center Steve Mott in his rookie year gives good reason for optimism. At quarterback, there is little to choose between Eric Hipple and Gary Danielson and though Hipple seems likely to be given the nod, it would be no surprise to see the two still locked in close competition by the end of the season. Wide receiver Leonard Thompson confirmed his big-play reputation, catching passes at an average of 18·3 yards, including one covering 80 yards for a touchdown, and last year's rookie, Jeff Chadwick, gave notice of joining him in this category. Starting in relief of the injured Thompson, Mark Nichols caught 29 passes and will be joined in the reserve depth by the second-round draftee, Pete Mandley. Running back Billy Sims is a great one and logged his third 1,000-yard season despite missing three games. James Jones supported the Lions' claim that he was the best 'pure fullback' in the 1983 collegiate draft (49ers fans could make a similar assertion about Roger Craig) by bashing his way for 475 yards, and the veteran Dexter Bussey showed that he still had a part to play with 249

yards at an average of 4·4 yards per carry. The departure of David Hill for the Rams left a gap at tight end which the Lions sought to fill by taking David Lewis in the first round of the draft. Lewis was widely considered to be the best available, and will provide instant competition for the incumbent, Ulysses Norris.

Defense

The four-man defensive line could well be the NFL's best. Tackles Doug English and Bill Gay are Pro Bowlers (they had 13 and 13½ sacks respectively) and yet coach Monte Clark thought enough of rookie Mike Cofer to rearrange the line (he shifted Gay from right end to left tackle) to give the 235-pounder his chance. Defensive left end Curtis Green will not be underrated for much longer and both Mike Dawson and Martin Moss represent good reserve strength. Again, the linebacking trio is young and very promising. Ken Fantetti and Garry Cobb are approaching their best and Jimmy Williams is rapidly improving. Steve Doig and Roosevelt Barnes will be joined by the returning August Curley to form adequate support for the starters. Right cornerback Bruce McNorton led the defensive secondary with seven interceptions and, over on the other corner, Bobby Watkins is beginning to settle down entering his third season. Both William Graham and Alvin Hall lack physical presence but are typical of a group which relies more on speed of reaction. Cornerback Al Latimer is a former starter who is returning after injury to a unit which seems certain to become less generous.

Special Teams

Kicker Eddie Murray had another good season which, sadly for him, will be remembered more for his last-second field goal miss which would have taken Detroit to victory over San Francisco and into the NFC Championship Game. Rookie punter Mike Black did well (he averaged 41·0 gross yards) maintaining the Lions' tradition. The combination of Alvin Hall and Ken Jenkins secured fifth place in the NFC for kickoff returns and whilst Robbie Martin returned a punt 81 yards for a touchdown against Pittsburgh, again it was Ken Jenkins who did most of the work, at the good average of 10·0 yards per attempt.

1984 DRAFT

Round	Name	Pos.	Ht.	Wt.	College
1.	Lewis, David	TE	6-2	230	California
2.	Mandley, Pete	WR	5-9	185	Northern Arizona
3.	Williams, Eric	DT	6-4	260	Washington State
3.	Anderson, Ernest	RB	5-8	186	Oklahoma State
3.	Baack, Steve	DE	6-3	240	Oregon
4.	D'Addio, Dave	RB	6-2	235	Maryland
6.	Witkowski, John	QB	6-1	205	Columbia
7.	Carter, Jimmie	LB	6-1	219	New Mexico
7.	Atkins, Renwick	T	6-3	265	Kansas
8.	Jones, David	C	6-2	255	Texas
9.	Hollins, Rich	WR			West Virginia
10.	Frizzell, William	DB			North Carolina Central
10.	Thaxton, James	DB			Louisiana Tech.
11.	Saxon, Mike	P	6-2	180	San Diego State
12.	Streno, Glenn	C		248	Tennessee

1984 SCHEDULE

September
2	SAN FRANCISCO	1:00
9	at Atlanta	1:00
16	at Tampa Bay	4:00
23	MINNESOTA	1:00
30	at San Diego	1:00

October
7	DENVER	1:00
14	TAMPA BAY	1:00
21	at Minnesota	12:00
28	at Green Bay	12:00

November
4	PHILADELPHIA	1:00
11	at Washington	1:00
18	at Chicago	12:00
22	GREEN BAY	12:30

December
2	at Seattle	1:00
10	LOS ANGELES RAIDERS	9:00
16	CHICAGO	1:00

Keith Dorney

VETERAN ROSTER

No.	Name	Pos.	Ht.	Wt.	NFL Year	College
54	Barnes, Roosevelt	LB	6-2	220	3	Purdue
11	Black, Mike	P	6-1	205	2	Arizona State
24	Bussey, Dexter	RB	6-1	210	11	Texas — Arlington
41	Caver, James	WR	5-9	175	1	Missouri
89	Chadwick, Jeff	WR	6-3	180	2	Grand Valley State
53	Cobb, Garry	LB	6-2	227	6	USC
66	Cofer, Mike	DE	6-5	235	2	Tennessee
50	Curley, August	LB	6-3	232	2	USC
16	Danielson, Gary	QB	6-2	196	8	Purdue
73	Dawson, Mike	DT	6-4	270	9	Arizona
72	Dieterich, Chris	T	6-3	255	5	North Carolina State
58	Doig, Steve	LB	6-2	240	3	New Hampshire
70	Dorney, Keith	T	6-5	260	6	Penn State
61	Elias, Homer	G	6-2	255	7	Tennessee State
78	English, Doug	DT	6-5	258	8	Texas
57	Fantetti, Ken	LB	6-2	227	6	Wyoming
65	Fowler, Amos	C-G	6-3	253	7	Southern Mississippi
79	Gay, William	DT-DE	6-5	255	7	USC
33	Graham, William	S	5-11	191	3	Texas
67	Greco, Don	G	6-3	255	3	Western Illinois
62	Green, Curtis	DE	6-3	252	4	Alabama State
35	Hall, Alvin	S-KR	5-10	184	4	Miami, Ohio
51	Harrell, James	LB	6-1	220	6	Florida
23	Harvey, Maurice	S	5-10	190	6	Ball State
17	Hipple, Eric	QB	6-2	196	5	Utah State
31	Jenkins, Ken	RB-PR	5-9	183	2	Bucknell
21	Johnson, Demetrious	S	5-11	186	2	Missouri
30	Jones, James	FB	6-3	235	2	Florida
32	Kane, Rick	RB	6-0	200	8	San Jose State
25	King, Horace	RB	5-11	205	10	Georgia
43	Latimer, Al	CB	5-11	177	5	Clemson
64	Lee, Larry	G	6-2	260	4	UCLA
14	Machurek, Mike	QB	6-1	205	3	Idaho State
83	Martin, Robbie	WR-PR	5-8	177	4	Cal Poly — SLO
81	McCall, Reese	TE	6-6	238	7	Auburn
29	McNorton, Bruce	CB	5-11	175	3	Georgetown, Ky.
63	Moss, Martin	DE	6-4	252	3	UCLA
52	Mott, Steve	C	6-3	259	2	Alabama
3	Murray, Ed	K	5-10	170	5	Tulane
86	Nichols, Mark	WR	6-2	213	4	San Jose State
80	Norris, Ulysses	TE	6-4	232	6	Georgia
84	Rubick, Rob	TE	6-2	228	3	Grand Valley State
20	Sims, Billy	RB	6-0	212	5	Oklahoma
71	Strenger, Rich	T	6-7	280	2	Michigan
39	Thompson, Leonard	WR	5-11	192	10	Oklahoma State
38	Thompson, Vince	RB	6-0	230	3	Villanova
55	Turnure, Tom	C	6-4	250	5	Washington
34	Wagoner, Danny	CB	5-10	177	2	Kansas
27	Watkins, Bobby	CB	5-10	184	3	Southwest Texas State
59	Williams, Jimmy	LB	6-3	221	3	Nebraska

GREEN BAY PACKERS NFC Central

Address 1265, Lombardi Avenue, Green Bay, Wisconsin 54303.

Stadium Lambeau Field, Green Bay and Milwaukee County Stadium, Milwaukee.
  Capacity (Lambeau Field) 56,189, (Milwaukee County Stadium) 55,958 *Playing Surface* Grass, both stadia.

Team Colours Dark Green, Gold and White.

Head Coach Forrest Gregg — first year.

Championships Super Bowl 1966,'67; NFL 1929,'30,'31,'44,'61,'62,'65,'66,'67; Division 1972.

History NFL 1921-69, NFC 1970—

Offense

New head coach Forrest Gregg, himself an offensive tackle with the Packers throughout the glorious Lombardi years, takes over a team which for some time now has hovered on the edge of greatness but has fallen short when it mattered most. Pro Bowl center Larry McCarren anchors an offensive line which features the veteran experience of right tackle Greg Koch and last year's talented rookie, David Drechsler, at left guard. Both left tackle Karl Swanke and right guard Syd Kitson are noted more for their pass protection than blocking for the running backs and it is the latter which is likely to receive Gregg's closest attention. Rushing used to be a Packers strength but, last year, a backfield depleted by the loss of Eddie Lee Ivery rated only 21st in the NFL. Gerry Ellis, who shifted from fullback to halfback, led the team with 696 yards at the good average of 4·9 yards per carry, followed by Ivery and rookie Jessie Clark, who averaged 4·6 gaining 328 yards. With Ivery's return and both Mike Meade and Harlan Huckleby providing depth, they must surely improve. There are no problems with a passing offense which led the NFC by some way and was second only to San Diego in the NFL. Having his best season, quarterback Lynn Dickey set club records for attempts (484), completions (289) and touchdowns (32), and his 4,458 yards was the third highest regular season total in NFL history. Hunting as a pair, wide receivers James Lofton and John Jefferson are unrivalled. Lofton has emerged as the big play specialist, but Jefferson is no less dangerous probing for weaknesses in the medium range. They are but two of half a dozen players who can strike from long range with unforgiving venom. Tight end Paul Coffman and Gerry Ellis caught 54 and 52 passes respectively, the former with a longest gain of 74 yards to equal Lofton's best. But the biggest single gain came from Jessie Clark, who latched on to a Lynn Dickey bullet for a 75-yarder against Tampa Bay.

Defense

There is a problem on defense, which is weak against both rushing and passing, and rated last in the NFL in yardage conceded. Defensive right end Ezra Johnson had 15½ sacks and left end Byron Braggs is strong against the rush, but neither Charles Johnson nor Daryle Skaugstad solved the problem raised by injuries to Terry Jones and Richard Turner at nose tackle. They will return perhaps in competition with some new players. The all-veteran group of linebackers is the strongest unit in the defensive squad. Outside linebackers Mike Douglass and John Anderson are particularly impressive, and last year had 127 and 120 unassisted tackles respectively. An injury to Randy Scott allowed Rich Wingo to regain his inside line-backer position alongside George Cumby. The probability is that with Scott's return, Wingo will rejoin Guy Prather, Cliff Lewis and Jim Laughlin, giving the Packers more than ample reserve depth. A club record of 3,762 yards passing conceded in 1983 reflects rather badly on the defensive secondary, and yet it is more likely the result of an inconsistent pass rush by the defensive line. Mark Lee and last year's number one draft choice, Tim Lewis, played well enough at corner-back, and new secondary coach Ken Riley is considering the experiment of trying Mike McCoy at safety, where he will play alongside Johnnie Gray or Mark Murphy.

Special Teams

Jan Stenerud, the NFL's most efficient field goal kicker over the last three years, may retire, allowing Eddie Garcia to take his chance. At the other end of the scale, rookie punter Bucky Scribner was a pleasant surprise, averaging 41·6 yards. Punt returner Phil Epps raised his average to a respectable 9·0 with a 90-yard touchdown, but several players had a bash at kickoff returns without much success.

1984 DRAFT

Round	Name	Pos.	Ht.	Wt.	College
1.	Carreker, Alphonso	DE	6-6	255	Florida State
3.	Humphrey, Donnie	DT	6-2	280	Auburn
4.	Dorsey, John	LB	6-2	242	Connecticut
5.	Flynn, Tom	DB	5-11	190	Pittsburgh
6.	Wright, Randy	QB	6-1	197	Wisconsin
7.	Jones, Daryll	DB	5-11	189	Georgia
10.	Hoffman, Gary	T	6-7	275	Santa Clara
11.	Cannon, Mark	C	6-3	260	Texas — Arlington
12.	Taylor, Lenny	WR	5-11	175	Tennessee
12.	Emans, Mark	LB			Bowling Green

1984 SCHEDULE

September
2	ST LOUIS	12:00
9	at Los Angeles Raiders	1:00
16	CHICAGO	12:00
23	at Dallas	3:00
30	at Tampa Bay	4:00

October
7	SAN DIEGO	3:00
15	at Denver	7:00
21	SEATTLE (Milwaukee)	12:00
28	DETROIT	12:00

November
4	at New Orleans	12:00
11	MINNESOTA (Milwaukee)	12:00
18	LOS ANGELES RAMS (Milwaukee)	12:00
22	at Detroit	12:30

December
2	TAMPA BAY	12:00
9	at Chicago	12:00
16	at Minnesota	12:00

VETERAN ROSTER

No.	Name	Pos.	Ht.	Wt.	NFL Year	College
59	Anderson, John	LB	6-3	221	7	Michigan
72	Boyd, Greg	DE	6-6	280	7	San Diego State
73	Braggs, Byron	DE	6-4	290	4	Alabama
93	Brown, Robert	DE	6-2	238	3	Virginia Tech.
19	Campbell, Rich	QB	6-4	224	4	California
88	Cassidy, Ron	WR	6-0	185	5	Utah State
33	Clark, Jessie	RB	6-0	226	2	Arkansas
82	Coffman, Paul	TE	6-3	218	7	Kansas State
52	Cumby, George	LB	6-0	215	5	Oklahoma
12	Dickey, Lynn	QB	6-4	220	12	Kansas State
53	Douglass, Mike	LB	6-0	224	7	San Diego State
61	Drechsler, Dave	G	6-3	250	2	North Carolina
31	Ellis, Gerry	RB	5-11	216	5	Missouri
85	Epps, Phillip	WR-PR	5-10	165	3	Texas Christian
11	Garcia, Eddie	K	5-8	188	2	Southern Methodist
24	Gray, Johnnie	S	5-11	185	10	Cal State – Fullerton
65	Hallstrom, Ron	T-G	6-6	286	3	Iowa
69	Harris, Leotis	G	6-1	267	7	Arkansas
38	Hood, Estus	CB	5-11	180	7	Illinois State
25	Huckleby, Harlan	RB	6-1	199	5	Michigan
74	Huffman, Dave	G	6-5	277	4	Notre Dame
40	Ivery, Eddie Lee	RB	6-0	210	5	Georgia Tech.
83	Jefferson, John	WR	6-1	198	7	Arizona State
99	Johnson, Charles	NT	6-1	262	4	Maryland
90	Johnson, Ezra	DE	6-4	240	8	Morris Brown
63	Jones, Terry	NT	6-2	259	7	Alabama
64	Kitson, Syd	G	6-4	252	4	Wake Forest
68	Koch, Greg	T	6-4	265	8	Arkansas
	Lapka, Myron	NT	6-4	260	4	USC
62	Laughlin, Jim	LB	6-0	212	5	Ohio State
22	Lee, Mark	CB	5-11	187	5	Washington
56	Lewis, Cliff	LB	6-1	226	4	Southern Mississippi
26	Lewis, Tim	CB	5-11	194	2	Pittsburgh
80	Lofton, James	WR	6-3	187	7	Stanford
54	McCarren, Larry	C	6-3	238	12	Illinois
29	McCoy, Mike	CB	5-11	183	9	Colorado
39	Meade, Mike	FB	5-10	228	3	Penn State
37	Murphy, Mark	S	6-2	199	4	West Liberty State
44	O'Steen, Dwayne	CB	6-1	195	7	San Jose State
51	Prather, Guy	LB	6-2	230	4	Grambling
35	Rogers, Del	RB	5-10	197	3	Utah
58	Rubens, Larry	C	6-1	253	3	Montana State
55	Scott, Randy	LB	6-1	220	4	Alabama
28	Scribner, Bucky,	P	6-0	203	2	Kansas
91	Skaugstad, Daryle	NT	6-5	268	4	California
79	Spears, Ron	DE	6-6	255	3	San Diego State
10	Stenerud, Jan	K	6-2	190	18	Montana State
67	Swanke, Karl	T	6-6	251	5	Boston College
75	Turner, Rich	NT	6-2	260	4	Oklahoma
17	Whitehurst, David	QB	6-2	204	8	Furman
50	Wingo, Rich	LB	6-1	230	5	Alabama
20	Winters, Chet	RB	6-0	205	2	Oklahoma

James Lofton (80) and John Jefferson (83)

MINNESOTA VIKINGS NFC Central

Address 9520, Viking Drive, Eden Prairie, Minnesota 55344.
Stadium Hubert H. Humphrey Metrodome, Minneapolis. *Capacity* 62,212 *Playing Surface* Super Turf.
Team Colours Purple, White and Gold.
Head Coach Les Steckel — first year.
Championships NFL 1969, NFC 1973,'74,'76, Division 1970,'71,'73,'74,'75,'76,'77,'78,'80.
History NFL 1961-69, NFC 1970—

Offense

There could be some positional changes on this offensive line which rates around the average in the NFC. Center Dennis Swilley may swap places with offensive left guard Jim Hough who, being the stronger of the two, might be more effective in handling the many forceful nose tackles around the conference. Equally, there could be an injection of youth with Curtis Rouse stepping in for veteran Steve Riley, who is considering retirement. With Tommy Kramer's injury likely to keep him out for some time yet, Steve Dils, Archie Manning and Wade Wilson will be competing for the starting quarterback position. Dils has the advantage of last season's good experience and yet, when given his chance on week sixteen, Wilson showed a great deal of poise, directing the Vikings to a 20-14 victory over the Bengals. Equally, the wily veteran, Archie Manning, would not let the team down. Curiously, running backs Darrin Nelson, Ted Brown and Tony Galbreath, led the team in both rushing yardage and passes caught, though not in the same order. Darrin Nelson is maturing into a top class multi-purpose running back and is always likely to repeat his 1983 performance against Green Bay, when he did the 'double' with 119 yards rushing and 137 yards receiving. Tony Galbreath often appears to be dragging a milk float but gained over 100 yards, rushing against Chicago and receiving against Tampa Bay. Ted Brown makes pass receiving look easy and rushed for 179 yards against Green Bay. Added to these, Rickey Young has caught more passes than any active running back in the NFL. The disappointing loss of form by wide receiver Sammy White is more than offset by the return of tight end Joe Senser, who teams up with the former All Pro, Dave Casper, in an exciting offensive unit which possesses a bewildering array of options.

Defense

Playing in the 3-4 formation, the front seven have the talent to be respectable and yet they gave up an average of 4·5 yards per rushing attempt to rate third worst in the NFL. Certainly, left end Doug Martin was a shade less awesome with 13½ sacks but then, right end Neil Elshire came on well, nailing the quarterback 9½ times. One hesitates to suggest that nose tackle Charlie Johnson may be slowing down (he has been a great one) but age is a factor both here and elsewhere. Johnson is replaced, in the face of obvious passing downs, by Randy Holloway, who clearly thrives in the role of pass rusher. At left outside linebacker, Matt Blair missed going to the Pro Bowl for the first time in seven years and will be 34 this season. Fred McNeill, on the right side, will be 32. With Dennis Johnson and Scott Studwell playing no better than par, rookie Walker Lee Ashley saw more action than the cautious Bud Grant would have wished. The defensive secondary is promising. Right cornerback Willie Teal maintains excellent pass coverage and both left cornerback John Swain and the safety, John Turner, netted six interceptions. Last year's number one pick, Joey Browner, lived up to his reputation playing as a versatile reserve and, with safety Keith Nord returning after injury, there is ample depth.

Special Teams

Benny Ricardo adequately filled in for the injured Rick Danmeier and kept his nerve when attempting the game-deciders. Greg Coleman averaged 41·5 gross yards to rate fourth equal in the NFC. The punt returners, led by Rufus Bess (remember the Wembley Bowl?), didn't exactly break any records, but Jarvis Redwine and Darrin Nelson combined to average 21·6 yards returning kicks, lifting the Vikings to the top of the NFC and to third position in the NFL.

1984 DRAFT

Round	Name	Pos.	Ht.	Wt.	College
1.	Millard, Keith	DE	6-4	252	Washington State
3.	Anderson, Alfred	RB	6-1	220	Baylor
5.	Rice, Allen	RB	5-10	198	Baylor
6.	Collins, Dwight	WR	6-1	205	Pittsburgh
7.	Haines, John	DT	6-5	260	Texas
7.	Lewis, Loyd	G	6-3	245	Texas A & I
8.	Sverchek, Paul	DT			Cal Poly — Obispo
9.	Kidd, Keith	WR	6-1	190	Arkansas
10.	Spencer, James	LB	6-3	230	Oklahoma State
11.	Pickett, Edgar	LB	6-1	235	Clemson
11.	Thompson, Lawrence	WR			Miami
12.	Jones, Mike	RB			North Carolina A & T

Doug Martin (79)

1984 SCHEDULE

September

2	SAN DIEGO	12:00
9	at Philadelphia	1:00
16	ATLANTA	12:00
23	at Detroit	1:00
30	SEATTLE	12:00

October

7	at Tampa Bay	1:00
14	at Los Angeles Raiders	1:00
21	DETROIT	12:00
28	at Chicago	12:00

November

4	TAMPA BAY	12:00
11	at Green Bay (Milwaukee)	12:00
18	at Denver	2:00
25	CHICAGO	3:00
29	WASHINGTON	9:00

December

8	at San Francisco	1:00
16	GREEN BAY	12:00

VETERAN ROSTER

No.	Name	Pos.	Ht.	Wt.	NFL Year	College
58	Ashley, Walker Lee	LB	6-0	234	2	Penn State
33	Bell, Rick	RB	6-0	205	2	St. Johns, Minn.
21	Bess, Rufus	CB-PR	5-9	185	6	South Carolina State
59	Blair, Matt	LB	6-5	234	11	Iowa State
62	Boyd, Brent	G	6-3	260	5	UCLA
23	Brown, Ted	RB	5-10	210	6	North Carolina State
47	Browner, Joey	S	6-2	202	2	USC
82	Bruer, Bob	TE	6-5	235	6	Mankato State
44	Casper, Dave	TE	6-4	241	11	Notre Dame
8	Coleman, Greg	P	6-0	185	8	Florida A & M
7	Danmeier, Rick	K	6-0	200	7	Sioux Falls
12	Dils, Steve	QB	6-1	190	5	Stanford
73	Elshire, Neil	DE	6-6	260	4	Oregon
50	Fowlkes, Dennis	LB	6-2	230	2	West Virginia
32	Galbreath, Tony	RB	6-0	228	9	Missouri
61	Hamilton, Wes	G	6-3	268	9	Tulsa
45	Hannon, Tom	S	5-11	190	8	Michigan State
75	Holloway, Randy	DE	6-5	250	7	Pittsburgh
51	Hough, Jim	G	6-2	267	7	Utah State
76	Irwin, Tim	T	6-6	275	4	Tennessee
65	Johnson, Charlie	NT	6-3	265	8	Colorado
52	Johnson, Dennis	LB	6-3	230	5	USC
89	Jones, Mike	WR	5-11	175	2	Tennessee State
83	Jordan, Steve	TE	6-3	230	3	Brown
9	Kramer, Tommy	QB	6-2	200	8	Rice
80	LeCount, Terry	WR	5-10	180	7	Florida
39	Lee, Carl	CB	5-11	176	2	Marshall
87	Lewis, Leo	WR	5-8	170	4	Missouri
4	Manning, Archie	QB	6-3	211	14	Mississippi
79	Martin, Doug	DE	6-3	255	5	Washington
84	McCullum, Sam	WR	6-2	190	11	Montana State
88	McDole, Mardye	WR	5-11	195	3	Mississippi State
54	McNeill, Fred	LB	6-2	230	11	UCLA
86	Mularkey, Mike	TE	6-4	235	2	Florida
77	Mullaney, Mark	DE	6-6	245	10	Colorado State
20	Nelson, Darrin	RB	5-9	180	3	Stanford
49	Nord, Keith	S	6-0	195	6	St. Cloud State
22	Redwine, Jarvis	RB	5-10	205	4	Nebraska
1	Ricardo, Benny	K	5-10	170	7	San Diego State
78	Riley, Steve	T	6-6	255	11	USC
68	Rouse, Curtis	T-G	6-3	290	3	Tennessee-Chattanooga
57	Sendlein, Robin	LB	6-3	225	4	Texas
81	Senser, Joe	TE	6-4	235	5	West Chester State
55	Studwell, Scott	LB	6-2	225	8	Illinois
29	Swain, John	CB	6-1	195	4	Miami
66	Tausch, Terry	T	6-5	275	3	Texas
37	Teal, Willie	CB	5-10	195	5	Louisiana State
27	Turner, John	S	6-0	199	7	Miami
72	White, James	NT	6-3	270	9	Oklahoma State
85	White, Sammy	WR	5-11	190	9	Grambling
11	Wilson, Wade	QB	6-3	210	4	East Texas State
34	Young, Rickey	RB	6-2	200	10	Jackson State

TAMPA BAY BUCCANEERS NFC Central

Address One Buccaneer Place, Tampa, Florida 33607.
Stadium Tampa Stadium, Tampa
   Capacity 72,812 *Playing Surface* Grass.
Team Colours Florida Orange, White and Red.
Head Coach John McKay — ninth year.
Championships Division 1979,'81.
History AFC 1976, NFC 1977—

Offense

The season started badly against Detroit, got worse and didn't get better. In that Detroit game, all three offensive tackles were lost through injury and, just by way of variation later in the season, tackles Kelly Thomas and Gene Sanders were sidelined by muscle injuries incurred during pre-game warm-ups. Sean Farrell, a former number one pick, was out for six games and even when present was shifted around (he played every position except center) as a temporary solution to a very immediate problem. Happily, however, all will be back, fit and well, with the exception of George Yarno and Jim Leonard, both of whom are USFL-bound. Third-year running back James Wilder was in tremendous form, rushing for 219 yards in the Bucs' first victory, over Minnesota, before (you guessed it) his season came to a premature end, the following week against Cleveland. He too will return to team up with Melvin Carver, who finished the season well after a slow start. Beyond these two, though, there is no sign of emerging talent. Quarterback Jack Thompson, 'The Throwin' Samoan', arrived from Cincinnati, with the difficult job of emulating the departed local favourite, Doug Williams. Again, after a hesitant start, he asserted his dominance over Jerry Golsteyn to claim the starting role, and rounded off his first season as an undisputed leader with 11 touchdowns in the last four games. He now faces the challenge from former Denver quarterback Steve DeBerg. The versatile James Wilder topped the club with 57 receptions, followed by the 48 of wide receiver Gerald Carter. But the real threat lies in the burning speed of Kevin House, whose productivity graph showed a sharp upturn in the late season and included a 74-yard touchdown against the 49ers. Tight end Jimmie Giles suffered a loss of form and, apparently, enthusiasm after being involved in pre-season contractual difficulties. If he regains his appetite, this offensive unit will be more than a handful for anybody.

Defense

Nose tackle Dave Logan and defensive right end Lee Roy Selmon are outstanding in a three-man front where Booker Reese and John Cannon share the left end position. A former All Pro and current Pro Bowler, Selmon registered eleven sacks even though invariably being manhandled by two opponents (double-teamed). Logan played his part in a powerful pass rush with 8½ sacks. Right outside linebacker Hugh Green is the complete player and has few equals in the NFL. Blitzing the quarterback, closing down on the running play and in defense against the pass, he is the jewel of a young, aggressive linebacking quartet which played its full part in restricting opponents to only 3·7 yards per rushing attempt (joint third in the NFC). Scot Brantley is highly rated and, in the absence of the injured Cecil Johnson, Jeff Davis and Danny Spradlin performed well. Even though the defensive secondary was devastated by injuries, the Buccaneers allowed only fifteen touchdown passes through the net and can expect to be even less charitable with the return of cornerback Mike Washington and the safeties, Neal Colzie and Cedric Brown. Even so, Beasley Reece, who had eight interceptions on the year (two were with the Giants), will be difficult to dislodge.

Special Teams

Frank Garcia, who replaced Larry Swider as punter, was a pleasant surprise, averaging a gross 42·2 yards per attempt. However, there could be changes in the kicking department, where Bill Capece was successful with only 10 out of 20 field goal attempts. Kick returner Michael Morton averaged 23·0 yards to rank fifth in the NFL, but the combination of Andre Tyler, Theo Bell and John Holt, made little impact returning punts.

1984 DRAFT

Round	Name	Pos.	Ht.	Wt.	College
2.	Browner, Keith	LB	6-5	228	Southern California
3.	Acorn, Fred	DB	5-9	185	Texas
4.	Gunter, Michael	RB	5-10	196	Tulsa
4.	Heller, Ron	T	6-5	260	Penn State
6.	Washington, Chris	LB	6-2	222	Iowa State
7.	Carroll, Jay	TE	6-4	223	Minnesota
8.	Robinson, Fred	DE	6-5	237	Miami
9.	Mallory, Rick	G	6-1	260	Washington
10.	Gallery, Jim	K	6-0	200	Minnesota
11.	Kiel, Blair	QB	5-11	200	Notre Dame
12.	Jemison, Thad	WR	6-1	190	Ohio State

1984 SCHEDULE

September
2	at Chicago	12:00
9	at New Orleans	12:00
16	DETROIT	4:00
23	at New York Giants	4:00
30	GREEN BAY	4:00

October
7	MINNESOTA	1:00
14	at Detroit	1:00
21	CHICAGO	1:00
28	at Kansas City	12:00

November
4	at Minnesota	12:00
11	NEW YORK GIANTS	4:00
18	at San Francisco	1:00
25	LOS ANGELES RAMS	1:00

December
2	at Green Bay	12:00
9	ATLANTA	1:00
16	NEW YORK JETS	1:00

Theo Bell

VETERAN ROSTER

No.	Name	Pos.	Ht.	Wt.	NFL Year	College
69	Arbubakrr, Hasson	DE	6-4	250	2	Texas Tech.
46	Armstrong, Adger	FB	6-0	225	5	Texas A & M
82	Bell, Jerry	TE	6-5	230	3	Arizona State
83	Bell, Theo	WR-PR	6-0	190	8	Arizona
52	Brantley, Scot	LB	6-1	230	5	Florida
80	Branton, Rheugene	WR	6-4	210	2	Texas Southern
34	Brown, Cedric	S	6-2	200	8	Kent State
77	Bujnoch, Glenn	G	6-6	265	9	Texas A & M
78	Cannon, John	DE	6-5	260	3	William & Mary
3	Capece, Bill	K	5-7	170	4	Florida State
87	Carter, Gerald	WR	6-1	190	5	Texas A & M
28	Carver, Melvin	RB	5-11	215	3	Nevada – Las Vegas
23	Castille, Jeremiah	CB	5-10	180	2	Alabama
20	Colzie, Neal	S	6-2	200	10	Ohio State
33	Cotney, Mark	S	6-0	200	9	Cameron State
58	Davis, Jeff	LB	6-0	225	3	Clemson
	DeBerg, Steve	QB	6-3	205	8	San Jose State
	Dierking, Scott	RB	5-10	220	8	Purdue
62	Farrell, Sean	G	6-3	260	3	Penn State
5	Garcia, Frank	P	6-1	190	2	Arizona
88	Giles, Jimmie	TE	6-3	245	8	Alcorn State
53	Green, Hugh	LB	6-2	225	4	Pittsburgh
60	Grimes, Randy	C	6-4	280	2	Baylor
8	Hewko, Bob	QB	6-3	195	2	Florida
21	Holt, John	CB	5-11	180	4	West Texas State
89	House, Kevin	WR	6-1	180	5	Southern Illinois
56	Johnson, Cecil	LB	6-2	235	8	Pittsburgh
51	Judie, Ed	LB	6-2	231	3	Northern Arizona
7	Komlo, Jeff	QB	6-2	200	6	Delaware
29	LaBeaux, Sandy	CB	6-3	205	2	Cal State – Hayward
76	Logan, Dave	NT	6-2	255	6	Pittsburgh
64	Lowry, Quentin	LB	6-2	225	4	Youngstown State
24	Morris, Thomas	CB	5-11	175	3	Michigan State
1	Morton, Michael	RB-KR	5-8	180	3	Nevada – Las Vegas
86	Obradovich, Jim	TE	6-2	225	10	USC
26	Owens, James	HB	5-11	195	6	UCLA
	Phillips, Irvin	CB	6-1	190	3	Arkansas Tech.
75	Reavis, Dave	T	6-5	265	10	Arkansas
43	Reece, Beasley	S	6-1	195	9	North Texas State
66	Reese, Booker	DE	6-6	260	3	Bethune-Cookman
74	Sanders, Gene	T	6-3	270	6	Texas A & M
63	Selmon, Lee Roy	DE	6-3	250	9	Oklahoma
22	Smith, Johnny Ray	CB-S	5-9	180	3	Lamar
72	Snell, Ray	G	6-4	265	5	Wisconsin
55	Spradlin, Danny	LB	6-1	241	4	Tennessee
70	Thomas, Kelly	T	6-6	270	2	USC
41	Thomas, Norris	CB	6-0	185	8	Southern Mississippi
14	Thompson, Jack	QB	6-3	217	6	Washington State
56	Thompson, Robert	LB	6-3	221	2	Michigan
81	Tyler, Andre	WR	6-0	180	3	Stanford
	Warnke, David	K	5-9	165	2	Augsburg
40	Washington, Mike	CB	6-2	200	9	Alabama
90	White, Brad	NT	6-2	250	4	Tennessee
32	Wilder, James	RB	6-3	225	4	Missouri
50	Wilson, Steve	C	6-4	265	9	Georgia
85	Witte, Mark	TE	6-3	230	2	North Texas State
54	Wood, Richard	LB	6-2	230	10	USC

ATLANTA FALCONS NFC West

Address Suwanee Road at I-85, Suwanee, Georgia 30174.
Stadium Atlanta-Fulton County Stadium.
  Capacity 60,748 *Playing Surface* Grass.
Team Colours Red, Black, White and Silver.
Head Coach Dan Henning — second year.
Championships Division 1980.
History NFL 1966-69, NFC 1970—

Offense

The power of the offensive line lies with its established trio of left tackle Mike Kenn, left guard R.C. Thielemann and center Jeff Van Note, but there could be some shuffling of players as the first stage in the search for a suitable replacement for Van Note, who will be 38 in 1984. The starting right guard, John Scully, who was drafted as a center, is an obvious candidate but his move would amplify a weakness on the right side where Warren Bryant had a sub-par year and may be under pressure from Eric Sanders. Collectively, they gave up a few too many sacks (55 — ranking 22nd in the NFL) but, in fairness, quarterback Steve Bartkowski is not the most mobile in the game. Even so, Bartkowski had an outstanding year and, as the top rated NFL passer, was unlucky not to be selected to the Pro Bowl. Adjusting to coach Henning's more conservative passing offense, he threw only five interceptions, compared with 30 in 1981 and 11 in the nine-game 1982 season. Reserve quarterback Mike Moroski, entering his sixth NFL year, has a strong arm, good mobility and proved his worth when, in relief of the injured Bartkowski, he completed 64·3 per cent of his passes for 575 yards and two touchdowns, one of which covered 50 yards. With veteran wide receivers Alfred Jenkins and Alfred Jackson injured, Stacey Bailey stepped in to take his chance in fine style and, together with Floyd Hodge, clearly represents Atlanta's future hopes. Both third-year men, they have good hands and burning speed, and will be difficult to displace by the returning veterans. Operating as the single running back in Atlanta's H-Back formation (this is the name for their variety of the offensive set, popular with many teams and known usually as the 'Ace Set'), William Andrews now ranks amongst the NFL's elite running backs — indeed he needs only 334 more yards to enter the list of top twenty all-time leading rushers. A powerful runner who virtually guarantees almost five yards every time he is handed the ball, he is ably supported by Gerald Riggs, whose slashing runs give the opposing defense little respite. There will be competition for roster spots in the positions known conventially as tight end, where seven players, including running back Bo Robinson and the versatile Billy 'White Shoes' Johnson, all saw action in 1983. Playing in the role of H-Back (this is the second tight end who, typically, might go 'in motion'), Johnson is secure but Junior Miller, a former rookie sensation, will be under pressure from last year's rookies, Arthur Cox and Ben Young, to start in the formal tight end position.

Defense

Even using a four-man defensive line (the majority of teams use three in the so-called 3-4 defense), the Falcons registered only 31 quarterback sacks, placing their secondary under pressure all season. They were not helped by an injury to their best lineman, defensive right tackle Don Smith, and the loss of left tackle Mike Zele was similarly felt. In their absence, rookie Andrew Provence logged a good deal of starting time. On the brighter side, rookie defensive end Mike Pitts revealed an appetite for quarterbacks, registering almost one quarter of the team total of sacks. Defensive tackle Rick Bryan arrives as the number one pick. Both Buddy Curry and Fulton Kuykendall are solid at linebacker, but again the injured Al Richardson was sorely missed. However, once more his absence gave the opportunity to blood another rookie, John Rade, who started after week seven. Behind them, the defensive secondary had been unchanged for essentially four years until rookie safety James Britt displaced Bob Glazebrook and yet, even allowing for the steady improvement of cornerback Bobby Butler, the unit as a whole remains modest.

Special Teams

Kicker Mick Luckhurst missed only five field goal attempts all year and keeps the flag flying. Punter Ralph Giacomarro maintains a respectable 40·3-yard average. Returning punts, Billy 'White Shoes' Johnson is always capable of putting on a one-man show, as he did when bringing the Falcons back from a 21-0 deficit to beat the Jets, 27-21, during the regular season. However, there is a need for elusive speed returning kicks, where a combination of Gerald Riggs and Richard Williams was barely average.

1984 DRAFT

Round	Name	Pos.	Ht.	Wt.	College
1.	Bryan, Rick	DT	6-3	260	Oklahoma
2.	Case, Scott	DB	6-0	175	Oklahoma
2.	Benson, Thomas	LB	6-2	235	Oklahoma
3.	McSwain, Rod	DB	6-0	195	Clemson
4.	Malancon, Rydell	LB	6-0	217	Louisiana State
5.	Benson, Cliff	TE	6-3	232	Purdue
6.	Bennett, Ben	QB	6-1	200	Duke
6.	Ralph, Dan	DT	6-4	265	Oregon
7.	Dodge, Kirk	LB	6-1	232	Nevada — Las Vegas
8.	Jackson, Jeff	LB	6-0	225	Auburn
9.	Howe, Glen	T	6-5	275	So. Mississippi
10.	Franklin, Derrick	DB	5-10	180	Fresno State
11.	Norman, Tommy	WR	5-11	185	Jackson State
12.	Holmes, Don	WR	6-5		Mesa, Colorado

1984 SCHEDULE

September

2	at New Orleans	12:00
9	DETROIT	1:00
16	at Minnesota	12:00
23	HOUSTON	1:00
30	at San Francisco	1:00

October

7	at Los Angeles Rams	1:00
14	NEW YORK GIANTS	1:00
22	LOS ANGELES RAMS	9:00
28	at Pittsburgh	4:00

November

5	at Washington	9:00
11	NEW ORLEANS	1:00
18	CLEVELAND	1:00
25	at Cincinnati	1:00

December

2	SAN FRANCISCO	1:00
9	at Tampa Bay	1:00
16	PHILADELPHIA	4:00

William Andrews

VETERAN ROSTER

No.	Name	Pos.	Ht.	Wt.	NFL Year	College
31	Andrews, William	RB	6-0	200	6	Auburn
82	Bailey, Stacey	WR	6-0	162	3	San Jose State
10	Bartkowski, Steve	QB	6-4	213	10	California
69	Benish, Dan	DT	6-5	259	2	Clemson
26	Britt, James	S	6-0	185	2	Louisiana State
66	Bryant, Warren	T	6-6	270	8	Kentucky
23	Butler, Bobby	CB	5-11	170	4	Florida State
21	Cain, Lynn	RB	6-1	205	6	USC
88	Cox, Arthur	TE	6-3	245	2	Texas Southern
89	Curran, Willie	WR	5-10	175	3	UCLA
50	Curry, Buddy	LB	6-3	221	5	North Carolina
51	Dixon, Rich	LB	6-2	225	2	California
71	Dufour, Dan	G	6-5	287	2	UCLA
58	Frye, David	LB	6-2	200	2	Purdue
34	Gaison, Blane	S	6-0	185	4	Hawaii
1	Giacomarro, Ralph	P	6-0	190	2	Penn State
36	Glazebrook, Bob	S	6-1	200	7	Fresno State
52	Harper, John	LB	6-3	234	2	Southern Illinois
30	Haworth, Steve	CB	5-11	189	2	Oklahoma
83	Hodge, Floyd	WR	6-0	195	3	Utah
85	Jackson, Alfred	WR	5-11	176	7	Texas
81	Johnson, Billy	WR-PR	5-9	170	9	Widener
37	Johnson, Kenny	CB	5-10	176	5	Mississippi State
20	Jones, Earl	CB	6-0	178	5	Norfolk State
78	Kenn, Mike	T	6-6	257	7	Michigan
54	Kuykendall, Fulton	LB	6-5	225	10	UCLA
70	Lee, Ronnie	G	6-3	236	6	Baylor
55	Levenick, Dave	LB	6-2	222	2	Wisconsin
18	Luckhurst, Mick	K	6-0	180	4	California
49	Matthews, Allama	H-B	6-3	230	2	Vanderbilt
87	Mikeska, Russ	TE	6-4	225	6	Nebraska
62	Miller, Brett	T	6-7	290	2	Iowa
80	Miller, Junior	TE	6-4	235	5	Nebraska
15	Moroski, Mike	QB	6-4	200	6	Cal – Davis
53	Musser, Neal	LB	6-2	218	4	Nth. Carolina State
74	Pitts, Mike	DE	6-5	260	2	Alabama
27	Pridemore, Tom	S	5-10	186	7	West Virginia
72	Provence, Andrew	DT	6-3	265	2	South Carolina
59	Rade, John	LB	6-1	214	2	Boise State
56	Richardson, Al	LB	6-2	206	5	Georgia Tech.
42	Riggs, Gerald	RB	6-1	230	3	Arizona State
33	Robinson, Bo	H-B	6-2	225	6	West Texas State
67	Sanders, Eric	T	6-6	255	4	Nevada – Reno
61	Scully, John	G	6-5	255	4	Notre Dame
	Simeta, Mike	DT	6-4	267	1	Kansas State
65	Smith, Don	DT	6-5	248	6	Miami
68	Thielemann, R.C.	G	6-4	247	8	Arkansas
43	Tutson, Thomas	CB	6-1	182	3	Sth. Carolina State
57	Van Note, Jeff	C	6-2	247	16	Kentucky
	White, Lyman	LB	6-0	217	3	Louisiana State
22	Williams, Richard	RB	6-0	205	2	Memphis State
79	Yeates, Jeff	DE	6-3	248	11	Boston College
86	Young, Ben	TE	6-4	235	2	Texas – Arlington
63	Zele, Mike	DT	6-3	236	6	Kent State

LOS ANGELES RAMS NFC West

Address 2327, West Lincoln Avenue, Anaheim, California 92801.

Stadium Anaheim Stadium, Anaheim.
Capacity 69,007 *Playing Surface* Grass.

Team Colours Royal Blue, Gold and White.

Head Coach John Robinson — second year.

Championships NFL 1945,'51; NFC 1979; Division 1973,'74,'75,' 76,'77,'78,'79.

History NFL 1937-69, NFC 1970—
(Until 1946, they were known as the Cleveland Rams.)

Offense

The Rams have a terrific offensive line featuring Pro Bowlers left guard Kent Hill, right tackle Jackie Slater and right guard Dennis Harrah. Another former starter, Irv Pankey, returns from injury and will probably replace the dependable Bill Bain, who would join the former Detroit player, Russ Bolinger, in the rich bank of reserve strength. In 1983, they restricted the opposing defenses to a meagre 23 quarterback sacks to equal Miami as the best in the NFL. But they will be remembered more for having prised open the gaps to release the big man, rookie running back Eric Dickerson, who, amongst other things, was the NFL leading rusher. With an average NFL experience of just over six years, they could dominate until the end of the decade. Dickerson's astonishing impact in his first NFL season has already earned him a place in the treasured annals of the game. It should not go unmentioned that he owes a great deal to Mike Guman, who sacrificed personal 'gain' (he had only seven rushing attempts) to help clear the way. Analysis of game tapes shows quite clearly that "wherever Guman goes, Dickerson is sure to follow". Should the unthinkable happen, Barry Redden, who averaged five yards per carry, would be a more than adequate substitute. Vince Ferragamo uses his pure wide receivers sparingly — Preston Dennard and George Farmer caught only 73 passes between them. Tight end Mike Barber led the club with 55 receptions and has settled down well after the frustrations of the latter part of his time with the Oilers. Dickerson was the next best with 51. The other tight end David Hill (a former Detroit player) was acquired for his blocking skills, but remains a potentially dangerous surprise receiver and has a longest touchdown reception of 61 yards.

Defense

Defensive right end Reggie Doss had another good year in a front three which was good against the rush, giving up an average of only 3·6 yards to rate equal third best in the NFL. But they were less efficient against the pass, with which they were challenged many times, and mounted a modest pass rush which generated just 33 quarterback sacks by the defense as a whole. Veteran left end Jack Youngblood came top of the class with 10½ sacks but had little support from the outside linebackers, Mel Owens and George Andrews, neither of whom is the penetrating type. Inside linebacker Jim Collins made good progress and had displaced Jim Youngblood, who joined Seattle in the close season. The defensive secondary, traditionally a Rams strength, would be well nigh impenetrable following the close-season acquisition of cornerback Gary Green from the Chiefs. Eric Harris settled in well (he too is a former Kansas City player) and, not unexpectedly, safety Nolan Cromwell made his fourth consecutive trip to the Pro Bowl. His safety partner, Johnnie Johnson, was unlucky not to be with him. In his first full year as a starter, LeRoy Irvin intercepted four passes and, in the playoffs against Dallas, was stopped five yards short of the end zone after returning a fifth 94 yards.

Special Teams

Kicker Chuck Nelson did not live up to his college reputation (statistically, his field goal percentage of 81·9 is the best in college football history) and gave way to Mike Lansford late in the season. Punter John Misko just about made par. There is abundant speed returning kicks and, particularly, punts in which Henry Ellard led the NFL with a 13·6-yard average and included one of 72 yards for a touchdown. His deep partner, LeRoy Irvin, had touchdown returns of 84 and 75 yards *in one game* (against Atlanta) in 1981. Kick returner Barry Redden can point to an 85-yard return against the Raiders in 1982.

1984 DRAFT

Round	Name	Pos.	Ht.	Wt.	College
5.	Stephens, Hal	DE	6-3	232	East Carolina
7.	Radachowsky, George	DB	5-10	188	Boston College
8.	Brady, Ed	LB	6-1	230	Illinois
9.	Reynolds, George	P	6-0	195	Penn State
10.	Vann, Norwood	TE	6-2	225	East Carolina
10.	Dooley, Joe	C	6-5	270	Ohio State
11.	Harper, Michael	RB	5-10	180	Southern California
11.	Love, Dwyane	RB	6-0	217	Houston
12.	Fisher, Rod	DB	5-9	186	Oklahoma State
12.	Bias, Moe	LB	6-1	220	Illinois

1984 SCHEDULE

September

3	DALLAS	6:00
9	CLEVELAND	1:00
16	at Pittsburgh	4:00
23	at Cincinnati	1:00
30	NEW YORK GIANTS	1:00

October

7	ATLANTA	1:00
14	at New Orleans	12:00
22	at Atlanta	9:00
28	SAN FRANCISCO	1:00

November

4	at St Louis	3:00
11	CHICAGO	1:00
18	at Green Bay (Milwaukee)	12:00
25	at Tampa Bay	1:00

December

2	NEW ORLEANS	1:00
9	HOUSTON	1:00
14	at San Francisco	6:00

VETERAN ROSTER

No.	Name	Pos.	Ht.	Wt.	NFL Year	College
31	Alexander, Robert	RB	6-0	185	3	West Virginia
52	Andrews, George	LB	6-3	221	6	Nebraska
62	Bain, Bill	T-G-C	6-4	285	9	USC
86	Barber, Mike	TE	6-3	237	8	Louisiana Tech.
96	Barnett, Doug	DE-C	6-3	250	3	Azusa Pacific
73	Bolinger, Russ	G	6-5	260	8	Long Beach State
50	Collins, Jim	LB	6-2	230	4	Syracuse
21	Cromwell, Nolan	S	6-1	200	8	Kansas
	Crutchfield, Dwayne	RB	6-0	235	3	Iowa State
70	DeJurnett, Charles	NT	6-4	260	8	San Jose State
88	Dennard, Preston	WR	6-1	183	7	New Mexico
29	Dickerson, Eric	RB	6-3	218	2	Southern Methodist
71	Doss, Reggie	DE	6-4	263	7	Hampton Institute
55	Ekern, Carl	LB	6-3	222	8	San Jose State
80	Ellard, Henry	WR	5-11	170	2	Fresno State
84	Farmer, George	WR	5-10	175	3	Southern
	Faulkner, Chris	TE	6-4	257	1	Florida
15	Ferragamo, Vince	QB	6-3	212	7	Nebraska
82	Grant, Otis	WR	6-3	197	2	Michigan State
	Green, Gary	CB	5-11	191	8	Baylor
44	Guman, Mike	FB	6-2	218	5	Penn State
60	Harrah, Dennis	G	6-5	255	10	Miami
26	Harris, Eric	CB	6-3	202	5	Memphis State
81	Hill, David	TE	6-2	228	9	Texas A & I
87	Hill, Drew	WR	5-9	170	6	Georgia Tech.
72	Hill, Kent	G	6-5	260	6	Georgia Tech.
47	Irvin, LeRoy	CB	5-11	184	5	Kansas
98	Jerue, Mark	LB	6-3	229	2	Washington
77	Jeter, Gary	DE	6-4	260	8	USC
20	Johnson, Johnnie	S	6-1	183	5	Texas
24	Jones, A.J.	RB	6-1	202	3	Texas
25	Jones, Gordon	WR	6-0	190	6	Pittsburgh
9	Kemp, Jeff	QB	6-0	201	4	Dartmouth
76	Kowalski, Gary	T	6-5	250	2	Boston College
1	Lansford, Mike	K	6-0	183	3	Washington
51	Lewis, David	LB	6-4	245	8	USC
83	McDonald, James	TE	6-5	218	2	USC
63	McDonald, Mike	C				
69	Meisner, Greg	NT	6-3	253	4	Pittsburgh
6	Misko, John	P	6-5	207	3	Oregon State
13	Nelson, Chuck	K	5-11	175	2	Washington
22	Newsome, Vince	S	6-1	179	2	Washington
58	Owens, Mel	LB	6-2	224	4	Michigan
75	Pankey, Irv	T	6-4	267	5	Penn State
30	Redden, Barry	RB	5-10	205	3	Richmond
64	Shearin, Joe	C	6-4	250	2	Texas
78	Slater, Jackie	T	6-4	271	9	Jackson State
56	Smith, Doug	C	6-3	253	7	Bowling Green
37	Sully, Ivory	S	6-0	201	6	Delaware
94	Wilcher, Mike	LB	6-3	235	2	North Carolina
66	Williams, Eric	LB	6-2	235	8	USC
28	Williams, Mike	CB	5-10	186	10	Louisiana State
85	Youngblood, Jack	DE	6-4	242	14	Florida

Vince Ferragamo

NEW ORLEANS SAINTS NFC West

Address 944 St. Charles Avenue, New Orleans, Louisiana 70130.
Stadium Louisiana Superdome, New Orleans.
Capacity 71,330 *Playing Surface* AstroTurf.
Team Colours Old Gold, Black and White.
Head Coach O.A. 'Bum' Phillips — fourth year.
Championships None.
History NFL 1967-69, NFC 1970—

Offense

A collection of young players, gathered around the 34-year-old center, John Hill, is crystallising into a fine unit. Guards Brad Edelman and Louis Oubre mount good protection for the running backs, who were without George Rogers for three early games. Equally, they gave up only 35 quarterback sacks and again, were protecting an immobile quarterback, Ken Stabler. The veteran 'Snake' Stabler must, one dares to suggest, be approaching the end of a career which has seen more than one cycle of the swinging pendulum. Furthermore, Dave Wilson has made slower progress than expected and, accordingly, coach 'Bum' Phillips traded with the Jets for Richard Todd. Coming off a disappointing season, Todd nonetheless has a good strong arm and could well unleash a fast set of wide receivers who are itching to probe the deep zones which hitherto have remained uncharted territory. Jeff Groth, a player under Phillips in his Oilers days, will be the primary target, closely followed by Eugene Goodlow and, at a greater distance, Lindsay Scott (although he could become another Mike Quick, the Philadelphia flier). All three players can be expected to improve on last season's average per reception, which in no case breached 12 yards. In addition, tight end Hoby Brenner is also likely to improve over 1983, in which he caught 41 passes for his most productive season. There are no problems with a rushing offense which centres around the mighty George Rogers,

ably assisted by Wayne Wilson who, during Rogers' absence through injury, tore off consecutive games of 108, 160 and 103 yards respectively. And even Wilson may have to share time with Hokie Gajan, whose 415 yards were gained at the average of 5·1 per carry.

Defense

Phillips has transformed the NFL's worst defense in 1980 into its second best of 1983. Led by an aggressive defensive line, they registered a club record 56 quarterback sacks which helped raise them to first against the pass, compared with a good eleventh against the rush. Left end Bruce Clark is a dominant force and attracts double coverage, allowing nose tackle Derland Moore and right end Jim Wilks to go on the rampage. Pro Bowler Rickey Jackson recorded 12 sacks, charging through from the right outside linebacker position, and though Whitney Paul is good by every measure, he could be pressurised by Rob Nairne and the returning veteran, Ken Bordelon. On the inside, Jim Kovach and Dennis Winston were prominent in a brawling defense which forced 39 turnovers (16 fumbles and 23 interceptions). The defensive secondary is yet another area of excellence. Right cornerback Johnnie Poe had a big season with seven interceptions, and though Dave Waymer at left cornerback remained empty-handed, he maintains limpet-like coverage. Strong safety Russell Gary is fast becoming one of the best, and free safety Frank Wattelet is a noted strong tackler, who is also prominent in special team play. Vernon Perry and Greg Stemrick, both former Houston players, provide experienced reserve depth.

Special Teams

The Danish-born Morten Andersen is a powerful kicker, with successes over 50 and 52 yards in one game against the Eagles. Punter Russell Erxleben maintains a 41·0-yard average but is not very well supported by a special team which allows an average of 10·1 yards per return. As a team effort, the Saints rated third equal in the NFC for kickoff returns but will need to improve on the 7·1-yard punt return average, which was better than only Philadelphia and the Giants in the NFC.

1984 DRAFT

Round	Name	Pos.	Ht.	Wt.	College
2.	Geathers, James	DE	6-7	280	Wichita State
3.	Hoage, Terry	DB	6-3	195	Georgia
3.	Anthony, Tyrone	RB	5-11	200	North Carolina
4.	Hilgenberg, Joel	C	6-3	245	Iowa
5.	Fields, Jitter	DB			Texas
6.	Thorp, Don	DT	6-3	255	Illinois
8.	Terrell, Clemon	RB	6-0	225	Southern Mississippi
9.	Hansen, Brian	P	6-2	200	Sioux Falls (S.D.)
10.	Gray, Paul	LB	6-2	230	Western Kentucky
11.	Bourgeau, Michel	DE	6-5	250	Boise State
12.	Nelson, Byron	T	6-6	269	Arizona

1984 SCHEDULE

September
2	ATLANTA	12:00
9	TAMPA BAY	12:00
16	at San Francisco	1:00
23	ST LOUIS	12:00
30	at Houston	3:00

October
7	at Chicago	12:00
14	LOS ANGELES RAMS	12:00
21	at Dallas	9:00
28	at Cleveland	1:00

November
4	GREEN BAY	12:00
11	at Atlanta	1:00
19	PITTSBURGH	8:00
25	SAN FRANCISCO	3:00

December
2	at Los Angeles Rams	1:00
9	CINCINNATI	12:00
15	at New York Giants	12:30

Bruce Clark

VETERAN ROSTER

No.	Name	Pos.	Ht.	Wt.	NFL Year	College
7	Andersen, Morten	K	6-2	190	3	Michigan State
47	Austin, Cliff	RB	6-0	190	2	Clemson
50	Bordelon, Ken	LB	6-4	226	8	Louisiana State
85	Brenner, Hoby	TE	6-4	240	4	USC
67	Brock, Stan	T	6-6	285	5	Colorado
75	Clark, Bruce	DE	6-3	250	3	Penn State
78	Clark, Kelvin	G	6-3	265	6	Nebraska
83	Duckett, Kenny	WR-KR	6-0	187	3	Wake Forest
63	Edelman, Brad	G	6-6	255	3	Missouri
99	Elliot, Tony	NT	6-2	247	3	North Texas State
14	Erxleben, Russell	P	6-4	219	5	Texas
46	Gajan, Hokie	RB	5-11	211	3	Lousiana State
20	Gary, Russell	S	5-11	195	4	Nebraska
88	Goodlow, Eugene	WR	6-2	190	2	Kansas State
72	Gray, Leon	T	6-3	258	12	Jackson State
86	Groth, Jeff	WR	5-10	172	6	Bowling Green
87	Hardy, Larry	TE	6-3	230	7	Jackson State
62	Hill, John	C	6-2	246	13	Lehigh
57	Jackson, Rickey	LB	6-2	230	4	Pittsburgh
34	Johnson, Bobby	S	5-11	189	2	Texas
60	Korte, Steve	G	6-2	270	2	Arkansas
52	Kovach, Jim	LB	6-2	225	6	Kentucky
64	Lafary, Dave	T	6-7	275	8	Purdue
93	Lewis, Gary	NT	6-3	260	2	Oklahoma State
98	Lewis, Reggie	DE	6-2	248	3	San Diego State
29	Lewis, Rodney	CB	5-11	190	3	Nebraska
59	Martin, Chris	LB	6-2	232	2	Auburn
84	Mauti, Rich	WR-PR	6-0	190	7	Penn State
19	Merkens, Guido	QB	6-1	195	7	Sam Houston State
74	Moore, Derland	NT	6-4	253	12	Oklahoma
55	Nairne, Rob	LB	6-4	227	8	Oregon State
66	Oubre, Louis	G	6-4	262	3	Oklahoma
51	Paul, Whitney	LB	6-3	220	9	Colorado
53	Pelleur, Scott	LB	6-2	215	4	Washington State
32	Perry, Vernon	S	6-2	210	6	Jackson State
76	Pietrzak, Jim	C	6-5	260	10	Eastern Michigan
25	Poe, Johnnie	CB	6-1	185	4	Missouri
58	Redd, Glenn	LB	6-1	225	3	Brigham Young
38	Rogers, George	RB	6-2	229	4	South Carolina
41	Rogers, Jimmy	RB	5-10	190	5	Oklahoma
80	Scott, Lindsay	WR	6-1	190	3	Georgia
16	Stabler, Ken	QB	6-3	210	15	Alabama
27	Stemrick, Greg	CB	5-11	185	10	Cincinnati
82	Tice, John	TE	6-5	242	4	Maryland
	Todd, Richard	QB	6-2	206	9	Alabama
73	Warren, Frank	DE	6-4	275	4	Auburn
49	Wattelet, Frank	S	6-0	185	4	Kansas
44	Waymer, Dave	CB	6-1	195	5	Notre Dame
94	Wilks, Jim	DE	6-5	252	4	San Diego State
18	Wilson, Dave	QB	6-3	210	3	Illinois
45	Wilson, Tim	FB	6-3	220	8	Maryland
30	Wilson, Wayne	RB	6-3	208	6	Shepherd
56	Winston, Dennis	LB	6-0	228	8	Arkansas
89	Young, Tyrone	WR	6-6	190	2	Florida

SAN FRANCISCO 49ers NFC West

Address 711, Nevada Street, Redwood City, California 94061.
Stadium Candlestick Park, San Francisco.
   Capacity 61,185 *Playing Surface* Grass.
Team Colours Forty Niner Gold and Scarlet.
Head Coach Bill Walsh — sixth year.
Championship Super Bowl 1981; Division 1970,'71,'72,'83.
History AAFC 1946-49, NFL 1950-69, NFC 1970—

Offense

The 49ers have a mature, reliable offensive line which is not without its class, in the form of Pro Bowler right guard Randy Cross. Left guard John Ayers excels in the subtle art of pass blocking (protection) and in this respect was the centre of a pattern which allowed only 33 quarterback sacks. The only question mark concerns the development of William 'Bubba' Paris, who certainly made progress after being injured for his rookie year, but has yet to convince a lot of experts that he 'punches his weight', all 300 lb of it. There are certainly no lingering doubts about quarterback Joe 'Big Sky' Montana who, in his fifth year, entered the list of all time leading passers, right at the top with a passer rating of 89·8. Having his best season so far with figures of 26 touchdowns and only 12 interceptions in a rating of 94·6, he was also prepared to take on the defenses, rushing for 284 yards. But of course, it is as an ice-cool, mobile passer that he earns his wages. He came within a whisker of eliminating the Redskins in the NFC Championship Game and no doubt regretted not having his favourite wide receiver, Dwight Clark, available when it mattered the most. Clark will be back to regain his starting spot, though his absence through injury gave Mike Wilson the opportunity to show off his moves. Wilson could push Freddie Solomon for the other starting position, with Renaldo Nehemiah on the sideline waiting for those circumstances which require speed of Olympic calibre. Tight end Russ Francis is a high class performer but has never quite regained the superb form of his days with New England, when he was considered by many to be the equal of the great Kellen Winslow. The arrival of Wendell Tyler and the instant maturity of rookie Roger Craig gave the 49ers a stunning one-two punch at running back, for the first time in many years. Craig's emergence enabled Bill Walsh to convert former running back Earl Cooper to the tight end position. Here, he caught fewer passes than in recent years but hauled in one for a career best 73-yard touchdown.

Defense

There was a tightening up on defense where the 49ers gave up the fourth fewest points in the NFL. Shifting into the 4-3 formation on obvious passing downs, to include defensive end Fred Dean, they registered 57 quarterback sacks (joint second in the NFL). Dean was hungry, logging 17½ for his best ever total as did Dwaine Board with his 13. Pete Kugler has gone to the USFL, leaving a hole at nose tackle which the 49ers hope to fill with either Manu Tuiasosopo or Louie Kelcher. Both Willie Harper and Bobby Leopold will be missed at linebacker but Frank LeMaster brings his veteran savvy from Philadelphia and just at the right time, the rookie, Riki Ellison, revealed unexpected maturity playing alongside Jack 'Hacksaw' Reynolds. The defensive secondary is not far short of the lot which wears Silver and Black, down in Los Angeles. Both Carlton Williamson and Ronnie Lott are shuddering tacklers and Eric Wright's corner is a no-go area. In 1983, Wright almost trebled his career interception total with seven, two of which he returned for touchdowns. In the same season, free safety Dwight Hicks returned both of his interceptions for touchdowns, covering 62 and 40 yards respectively.

Special Teams

Ray 'Mo-Hair' Wersching does everything well, kicking every PAT and missing only five out of 30 field goal attempts. On the other hand, punter Tom Orosz was not the solution and could be under pressure to keep his place. Dana McLemore returns both kicks and punts, making a speciality of the latter which included a 56-yard touchdown against Dallas.

1984 DRAFT

Round	Name	Pos.	Ht.	Wt.	College
1.	Shell, Todd	LB	6-4	210	Brigham Young
2.	Frank, John	TE	6-2	220	Ohio State
3.	McIntyre, Guy	G	6-2	265	Georgia
5.	Carter, Michael	DT	6-1	270	Southern Methodist
5.	Fuller, Jeff	LB	6-2	210	Texas A & M
9.	Miller, Lee	DB	6-0	180	Cal State — Fullerton
9.	Harmon, Derrick	RB	5-9	200	Cornell
10.	Moritz, Dave	WR			Iowa
11.	Pendleton, Kirk	WR	6-2	188	Brigham Young

1984 SCHEDULE

September

2	at Detroit	1:00
10	WASHINGTON	6:00
16	NEW ORLEANS	1:00
23	at Philadelphia	1:00
30	ATLANTA	1:00

October

8	at New York Giants	9:00
14	PITTSBURGH	1:00
21	at Houston	3:00
28	at Los Angeles Rams	1:00

November

4	CINCINNATI	1:00
11	at Cleveland	1:00
18	TAMPA BAY	1:00
25	at New Orleans	3:00

December

2	at Atlanta	1:00
8	MINNESOTA	1:00
14	LOS ANGELES RAMS	6:00

Ronnie Lott

VETERAN ROSTER

No.	Name	Pos.	Ht.	Wt.	NFL Year	College
68	Ayers, John	G	6-5	265	8	West Texas State
7	Benjamin, Guy	QB	6-3	210	7	Stanford
44	Blackmore, Richie	CB	5-10	174	6	Mississippi State
76	Board, Dwaine	DE	6-5	250	5	North Carolina A & T
57	Bunz, Dan	LB	6-4	225	6	Long Beach State
6	Cavanaugh, Matt	QB	6-2	212	7	Pittsburgh
87	Clark, Dwight	WR	6-4	210	6	Clemson
47	Collier, Tim	CB	6-0	176	9	East Texas State
89	Cooper, Earl	TE	6-2	227	5	Rice
33	Craig, Roger	RB	6-1	222	2	Nebraska
51	Cross, Randy	G	6-3	265	9	UCLA
74	Dean, Fred	DE	6-2	236	10	Lousiana Tech.
84	Durham, Darius	WR	6-2	195	2	San Diego State
50	Ellison, Riki Gray	LB	6-2	220	2	USC
71	Fahnhorst, Keith	T	6-6	273	11	Minnesota
54	Ferrari, Ron	LB	6-0	212	3	Illinois
81	Francis, Russ	TE	6-6	242	9	Oregon
24	Gervais, Rick	S	5-11	190	4	Stanford
75	Harty, John	DE	6-4	263	4	Iowa
22	Hicks, Dwight	S	6-1	189	6	Michigan
28	Holmoe, Tom	S	6-2	180	2	Brigham Young
	Kelcher, Louie	NT	6-5	310	10	Southern Methodist
66	Kennedy, Allan	T	6-7	275	3	Washington State
	LeMaster, Frank	LB	6-2	238	11	Kentucky
	Lindstrom, Bruce	NT				
42	Lott, Ronnie	CB	6-0	199	4	USC
53	McColl, Milt	LB	6-6	220	4	Stanford
43	McLemore, Dana	CB-PR	5-10	183	3	Hawaii
32	Monroe, Carl	RB	5-8	166	2	Utah
16	Montana, Joe	QB	6-2	200	6	Notre Dame
60	Montgomery, Blanchard	LB	6-2	236	2	UCLA
25	Moore, Jeff	RB	6-0	196	5	Jackson State
63	Moten, Gary	LB	6-1	210	2	Southern Methodist
83	Nehemiah, Renaldo	WR	6-1	177	3	Maryland
3	Orosz, Tom	P	6-1	204	4	Ohio State
77	Paris, Bubba	T	6-6	293	2	Michigan
65	Pillers, Lawrence	DE	6-4	250	9	Alcorn A & M
56	Quillan, Fred	C	6-5	266	7	Oregon
64	Reynolds, Jack	LB	6-1	232	15	Tennessee
30	Ring, Bill	FB	5-10	215	4	Brigham Young
61	Sapolu, Jesse	G-C	6-4	260	2	Hawaii
88	Solomon, Freddie	WR-PR	5-11	185	10	Tampa
72	Stover, Jeff	NT-DE	6-5	275	3	Oregon
79	Stuckey, Jim	DE	6-4	251	5	Clemson
	Tuiasosopo, Manu	NT	6-3	252	6	UCLA
58	Turner, Keena	LB	6-2	219	5	Purdue
26	Tyler, Wendell	RB	5-10	198	7	UCLA
14	Wersching, Ray	K	5-11	210	12	California
40	Williams, Vince	RB	6-0	231	3	Oregon
27	Williamson, Carlton	S	6-0	204	4	Pittsburgh
85	Wilson, Mike	WR	6-3	210	4	Washington State
21	Wright, Eric	CB	6-1	180	4	Missouri

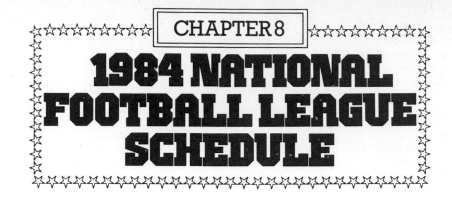

CHAPTER 8

1984 NATIONAL FOOTBALL LEAGUE SCHEDULE

(All times local)

Sunday, September 2 (First Weekend)	**Kickoff**
Atlanta at New Orleans	12:00
Cincinnati at Denver	2:00
Cleveland at Seattle	1:00
Kansas City at Pittsburgh	1:00
Los Angeles Raiders at Houston	3:00
Miami at Washington	1:00
New England at Buffalo	1:00
New York Jets at Indianapolis	4:00
Philadelphia at New York Giants	1:00
St. Louis at Green Bay	12:00
San Diego at Minnesota	12:00
San Francisco at Detroit	1:00
Tampa Bay at Chicago	12:00

Monday, September 3	
Dallas at Los Angeles Rams	6:00

Thursday, September 6 (Second Weekend)	
Pittsburgh at New York Jets	9:00

Sunday, September 9	
Buffalo at St. Louis	12:00
Cleveland at Los Angeles Rams	1:00
Dallas at New York Giants	1:00
Denver at Chicago	12:00
Detroit at Atlanta	1:00
Green Bay at Los Angeles Raiders	1:00
Indianapolis at Houston	3:00
Kansas City at Cincinnati	1:00
Minnesota at Philadelphia	1:00
New England at Miami	1:00
San Diego at Seattle	1:00
Tampa Bay at New Orleans	12:00

Monday, September 10	
Washington at San Francisco	6:00

Sunday, September 16 (Third Weekend)	
Atlanta at Minnesota	12:00
Chicago at Green Bay	12:00

Cincinnati at New York Jets	1:00
Denver at Cleveland	9:00
Detroit at Tampa Bay	4:00
Houston at San Diego	1:00
Los Angeles Raiders at Kansas City	12:00
Los Angeles Rams at Pittsburgh	4:00
New Orleans at San Francisco	1:00
New York Giants at Washington	4:00
Philadelphia at Dallas	3:00
St. Louis at Indianapolis	1:00
Seattle at New England	1:00

Monday, September 17	
Miami at Buffalo	9:00

Sunday, September 23 (Fourth Weekend)	
Chicago at Seattle	1:00
Green Bay at Dallas	3:00
Houston at Atlanta	1:00
Indianapolis at Miami	4:00
Kansas City at Denver	2:00
Los Angeles Rams at Cincinnati	1:00
Minnesota at Detroit	1:00
New York Jets at Buffalo	1:00
Pittsburgh at Cleveland	1:00
St. Louis at New Orleans	12:00
San Francisco at Philadelphia	1:00
Tampa Bay at New York Giants	4:00
Washington at New England	1:00

Monday, September 24	
San Diego at Los Angeles Raiders	6:00

Sunday, September 30 (Fifth Weekend)	
Atlanta at San Francisco	1:00
Buffalo at Indianapolis	1:00
Cleveland at Kansas City	12:00
Dallas at Chicago	12:00
Detroit at San Diego	1:00
Green Bay at Tampa Bay	4:00

Los Angeles Raiders at Denver	2:00
Miami at St. Louis	12:00
New England at New York Jets	1:00
New Orleans at Houston	3:00
New York Giants at Los Angeles Rams	1:00
Philadelphia at Washington	4:00
Seattle at Minnesota	12:00

Monday, October 1

Cincinnati at Pittsburgh	9:00

Sunday, October 7 (Sixth Weekend)

Atlanta at Los Angeles Rams	1:00
Denver at Detroit	1:00
Houston at Cincinnati	4:00
Miami at Pittsburgh	1:00
Minnesota at Tampa Bay	1:00
New England at Cleveland	1:00
New Orleans at Chicago	12:00
New York Jets at Kansas City	12:00
Philadelphia at Buffalo	1:00
St. Louis at Dallas	12:00
San Diego at Green Bay	3:00
Seattle at Los Angeles Raiders	1:00
Washington at Indianapolis	1:00

Monday, October 8

San Francisco at New York Giants	9:00

Sunday, October 14 (Seventh Weekend)

Buffalo at Seattle	1:00
Chicago at St. Louis	12:00
Cincinnati at New England	1:00
Dallas at Washington	4:00
Houston at Miami	1:00
Indianapolis at Philadelphia	1:00
Los Angeles Rams at New Orleans	12:00
Minnesota at Los Angeles Raiders	1:00
New York Giants at Atlanta	1:00
New York Jets at Cleveland	1:00
Pittsburgh at San Francisco	1:00
San Diego at Kansas City	12:00
Tampa Bay at Detroit	1:00

Monday, October 15

Green Bay at Denver	7:00

Sunday, October 21 (Eighth Weekend)

Chicago at Tampa Bay	1:00
Cleveland at Cincinnati	1:00
Denver at Buffalo	1:00
Detroit at Minnesota	12:00
Kansas City at New York Jets	4:00
Los Angeles Raiders at San Diego	1:00
Miami at New England	1:00
New Orleans at Dallas	9:00
New York Giants at Philadelphia	1:00
Pittsburgh at Indianapolis	1:00
San Francisco at Houston	3:00
Seattle vs. Green Bay at Milwaukee	12:00
Washington at St. Louis	12:00

Monday, October 22

Los Angeles Rams at Atlanta	9:00

Sunday, October 28 (Ninth Weekend)

Atlanta at Pittsburgh	4:00
Buffalo at Miami	4:00
Cincinnati at Houston	12:00
Denver at Los Angeles Raiders	1:00
Detroit at Green Bay	12:00
Indianapolis at Dallas	12:00
Minnesota at Chicago	12:00
New Orleans at Cleveland	1:00
New York Jets at New England	1:00
St. Louis at Philadelphia	1:00
San Francisco at Los Angeles Rams	1:00
Tampa Bay at Kansas City	12:00
Washington at New York Giants	4:00

Monday, October 29

Seattle at San Diego	6:00

Sunday, November 4 (Tenth Weekend)

Cincinnati at San Francisco	1:00
Cleveland at Buffalo	1:00
Green Bay at New Orleans	12:00
Houston at Pittsburgh	1:00
Kansas City at Seattle	1:00
Los Angeles Raiders at Chicago	12:00
Los Angeles Rams at St. Louis	3:00
Miami at New York Jets	4:00
New England at Denver	2:00
New York Giants at Dallas	12:00
Philadelphia at Detroit	1:00
San Diego at Indianapolis	1:00
Tampa Bay at Minnesota	12:00

Monday, November 5

Atlanta at Washington	9:00

Sunday, November 11 (Eleventh Weekend)

Buffalo at New England	1:00
Chicago at Los Angeles Rams	1:00
Dallas at St. Louis	12:00
Denver at San Diego	1:00
Detroit at Washington	1:00
Houston at Kansas City	12:00
Indianapolis at New York Jets	1:00
Minnesota vs. Green Bay at Milwaukee	12:00
New Orleans at Atlanta	1:00
New York Giants at Tampa Bay	4:00
Philadelphia at Miami	1:00
Pittsburgh at Cincinnati	1:00
San Francisco at Cleveland	1:00

Monday, November 12

Los Angeles Raiders at Seattle	6:00

Sunday, November 18 (Twelfth Weekend)

Cleveland at Atlanta	1:00
Dallas at Buffalo	1:00
Detroit at Chicago	12:00

Kansas City at Los Angeles Raiders	1:00
Los Angeles Rams vs. Green Bay at Milwaukee	12:00
Miami at San Diego	1:00
Minnesota at Denver	2:00
New England at Indianapolis	1:00
New York Jets at Houston	3:00
St. Louis at New York Giants	1:00
Seattle at Cincinnati	1:00
Tampa Bay at San Francisco	1:00
Washington at Philadelphia	1:00

Monday, November 19

Pittsburgh at New Orleans	8:00

Thursday, November 22 (Thirteenth Weekend)
(Thanksgiving Day)

Green Bay at Detroit	12:30
New England at Dallas	3:00

Sunday, November 25

Atlanta at Cincinnati	1:00
Buffalo at Washington	1:00
Chicago at Minnesota	3:00
Houston at Cleveland	1:00
Indianapolis at Los Angeles Raiders	1:00
Kansas City at New York Giants	1:00
Los Angeles Rams at Tampa Bay	1:00
Philadelphia at St. Louis	12:00
San Diego at Pittsburgh	1:00
San Francisco at New Orleans	3:00
Seattle at Denver	2:00

Monday, November 26

New York Jets at Miami	9:00

Thursday, November 29 (Fourteenth Weekend)

Washington at Minnesota	9:00

Sunday, December 2

Cincinnati at Cleveland	1:00
Dallas at Philadelphia	1:00
Denver at Kansas City	12:00
Detroit at Seattle	1:00
Indianapolis at Buffalo	1:00
Los Angeles Raiders at Miami	4:00
New Orleans at Los Angeles Rams	1:00
New York Giants at New York Jets	1:00
Pittsburgh at Houston	12:00

St. Louis at New England	1:00
San Francisco at Atlanta	1:00
Tampa Bay at Green Bay	12:00

Monday, December 3

Chicago at San Diego	6:00

Saturday, December 8 (Fifteenth Weekend)

Buffalo at New York Jets	12:30
Minnesota at San Francisco	1:00

Sunday, December 9

Atlanta at Tampa Bay	1:00
Cincinnati at New Orleans	12:00
Cleveland at Pittsburgh	1:00
Green Bay at Chicago	12:00
Houston at Los Angeles Rams	1:00
Miami at Indianapolis	1:00
New England at Philadelphia	1:00
New York Giants at St. Louis	12:00
San Diego at Denver	2:00
Seattle at Kansas City	12:00
Washington at Dallas	3:00

Monday, December 10

Los Angeles Raiders at Detroit	9:00

Friday, December 14 (Sixteenth Weekend)

Los Angeles Rams at San Francisco	6:00

Saturday, December 15

Denver at Seattle	1:00
New Orleans at New York Giants	12:30

Sunday, December 16

Buffalo at Cincinnati	1:00
Chicago at Detroit	1:00
Cleveland at Houston	12:00
Green Bay at Minnesota	12:00
Indianapolis at New England	1:00
Kansas City at San Diego	1:00
New York Jets at Tampa Bay	1:00
Philadelphia at Atlanta	4:00
Pittsburgh at Los Angeles Raiders	1:00
St. Louis at Washington	1:00

Monday, December 17

Dallas at Miami	9:00

Postseason

Sunday, December 23	AFC and NFC First Round Playoffs
Saturday, December 29	AFC and NFC Divisional Playoffs
Sunday, December 30	AFC and NFC Divisional Playoffs
Sunday, January 6	AFC and NFC Championship Games
Sunday, January 20	Super Bowl XIX at Stanford Stadium, Palo Alto, California
Sunday, January 27	AFC-NFC Pro Bowl, Honolulu, Hawaii